40p

The Naked Investor

Contents

This book grew originally out of my work for the *Investor's Guardian*, an excellent British publication which died an untimely death through no fault of its young, energetic and able staff – all of whom appear to have moved on to better and higher things. My attitude to matters of investment was also strongly influenced by my experience on the London *Observer* and, in particular, by my long friendship with John Davis of that newspaper. To him and to many other journalistic colleagues I owe a great debt: if I mention specifically John Thackray of New York, that is because of the unique window which he has opened on Wall Street in the years since I left there. As with my earlier books, Felicity Krish has been a vital help. The dedication, however, can only be made to the hero/victims of the events which this book primarily describes. As with those who suffered the military catastrophes of our century, the prime actors in these financial events were mainly anonymous. So I dedicate this book to

The Unknown Investor

Part I. The crisis of the equity

1. The Second Great Crash

For three decades, which spanned the most murderous and destructive war in history, the western world was haunted by another living nightmare: the fear that, just as the 1914–18 holocaust had been repeated on a more frightful scale after only twenty-one years, so the Great Crash of 1929, and the Greater Depression that followed, would be replayed by history.

Thirty-five years on from 1929, in the mid-sixties, the nightmare seemed only that – a bad dream, far removed from the reality of ever-expanding gross national products and of a mass capitalism that generated apparently everlasting growth. A $1000 bill invested in IBM, the paradigm of the new capitalism, at its beginnings, was worth some $6·7 million in 1968; and this was no Wall Street ramp, no golden calf reserved for plutocrats, but a share held by the new masses, not only as individuals, in their hundreds of thousands, but through pension funds and mutual funds and investment trusts. Safety in numbers was the name of this new economic game – a game in which everybody apparently won.

Ten years further on, in 1974, the statistics of Wall Street read like an inventory of Hiroshima property after the bomb. Midway through the previous year the fall of the Value Line index of 1500 stocks had reached 57·2 per cent in five years: or rather more than the *New York Times* index had collapsed in the dreaded autumn of 1929. Even that grisly statistic understated the real damage. Between 1968 and 1973 the value of the dollars in which stock prices are calculated had itself declined by 26·2 per cent. But that measured only the internal buying power of the United States currency, on which worse indignities had been inflicted in the markets of the world.

Between December 1968 and mid-1973 the price of gold (*en route* to a peak of nearly $200 in 1974) advanced from $35 an ounce to $120. This devastating devaluation of the dollar was unofficial (the

United States government, giving a passable imitation of King Canute, kept on pretending that it hadn't happened). But the result was real enough: where, in December 1968, the Dow Jones index would have cost a Swiss gnome 28·4 ounces of gold, by July 1973 the little fellow could have picked up the same bundle for a mere 7 ounces. The story was equally macabre in terms of the yen, the Swiss franc, the German mark; and more alarming still if the larger Value Line Index, rather than the Dow, is taken as the benchmark. In July 1973 an Arab sheikh or European plutocrat owning gold could have lapped up the cream of United States industry for an eighth of its 1968 cost.

The Europeans, however, would have been most unwise to count any chickens – or even any eggs. What had decimated Wall Street was about to destroy savings just as surely in Frankfurt, Tokyo, Paris, Milan and London. That July, London share prices were only a fifth down from their all-time peak. Within eighteen months the *Financial Times* index had collapsed to 146 – a quarter of the historic high reached in 1972, and a decline far more catastrophic in magnitude even than Wall Street's.

There were, as in 1929, powerful economic reasons for a collapse in values which had few parallels, either in extent or duration, in history. The Weimar Republic had it worse: with marks falling like hailstones, anybody with a stable currency in his pocket became rich overnight. For 'stable currency' read 'gold' and you have a reasonable description of the disasters of 1973 and 1974. The economic explanations included the endless United States balance of payments deficits, the consequent rise and globular swelling of the Eurodollar bubble, the consequent escalation of inflation, the consequent undermining of living standards and savings, and so on, and on – until the quadrupling of oil prices set its seal on the catastrophe.

All these global developments were crystal-clear: certainly no crystal ball was required to identify either the trends or their inevitable consequences. As a writer on these subjects, and editor of publications which were supposed to offer authoritative guidance, I at least spotted and reported much of what was happening – which makes it even less excusable that, as an investor, my record was no better, if no worse, than anybody else's. I never made a fortune to lose – this is no tale by one of those miracle men who made a million in two years, months or days and who seek to make another by telling (and embroidering) the tale. Like everybody else, I had my successes – and my failures. At the end of the day, like everybody else, I had (and have) stocks in my collection that I would far rather forget about (and therefore have forgotten about). To the extent that this book draws on my experience, it is the experience of an average investor who should have known better – and, with luck, has learnt better from the mistakes of the past. At least those errors did not include any periods of infatuation with the boom : an innate cautious (or yellow) streak meant that, more often than not, I ended up regretting my inability to believe in the latest wonder stock from which my friends had wondrously profited.

One in particular constantly urged me to buy the penny stocks, dreadful things with names apparently dreamt up in Wall Street boiler-rooms, that were briefly the rage in the early sixties. That man, after two or three years, quit Wall Street with none too small a fortune; I bought none of his suggestions. Yet in a peculiar sense I was right. The penny stocks he peddled *were* intrinsically worthless : the buying on which his fortune depended was a mindless response in a manipulated market – the seamy bottom side of the boom mentality which in the early sixties was gathering its eventually fatal momentum. The fate was implicit in the fact that the boom bore so little relation to the surrounding economic realities of the times.

Stock-markets could in fact have survived these massive onslaughts of economic events, without staging a second Great Crash, let alone actually outdoing the original, had it not been for all the previous grotesqueries. Like some Frankenstein's monster, the worldwide boom in equities, from Wall Street to Hong Kong, from Tokyo to Throgmorton Street, destroyed its creators. The investing public was the victim of the Biggest Con : the greatest confidence trick ever perpetrated, not only because the sting was in the thousands of millions but because so large an army of deceivers told the tale and took a slice of the action. Stockbrokers, tipsters, bankers, hot-shot salesmen, mandarins, economists, promoters, managers, journalists, politicians – the names were legion, and the con so powerful that many of the insiders accomplished the con-man's ultimate coup: they deceived themselves.

To grasp the nature of the deception, consider an advertisement published midway through the awful year of 1973 by the valiant American Stock Exchange, 'Amex'. In rough paraphrase it exhorted the customers to roll up for the greatest bunch of bargains ever seen, hundreds and hundreds of them. 'You dare not refuse this offer, which we sincerely hope (for your sakes) is unrepeatable. These delightful stocks number over 1000, and you can buy them, on average, at a price *half* as high as you could a year ago. And that's not all, folks! Why, these goodies haven't been so cheap since December 1966, all of half a dozen years ago.'

Amex was able to announce the out-of-season return of Santa Claus by virtue of standing disaster on its head. The mute and miserable facts were that, at the end of April, 504 Amex stocks were selling at less than 10 times earnings. The median of all the Amex offerings was only 10·39: the few selling at the once-holy ratios of 30, 40, 50, 60, 70 and more sat on the bottom of the Amex bar chart like little black huts next to the towering skyscrapers of unloved and unwanted stocks.

But you can't keep a good salesman down. 'Lower price/earnings ratios are frequently associated with greater values,' said the advertisement, more in hope than with conviction. Many of the bargains, indeed, were 'representing an exciting future. These are the younger companies which are answering the new needs of a changing society – companies offering new technologies...' The insolence was staggering: enough to take the breath away, especially from investors who had backed 'younger companies' like Viatron (the bombed-out computer terminals outfit) or Memorex (a once-big deal in magnetic tape, another busted flush of the period) or Litton Industries, the youthful granddaddy of all younger new technology companies. The fall of Litton's shares, like the shot which killed the archduke at Sarajevo, proved to be the opening salvo of Armageddon: once over $100, Litton bottomed out at a feeble $10.

Yet still in mid-1973 the voice of the huckster was heard in the land, promising not just growth, but growth through new technologies (although most members of Amex knew less of these than they did of the dark side of the moon); and growth, moreover, which would be translated by the alchemy of good old Amex into gold in the palm.

Plainly, Amex had not even a little toe, still less a leg, to stand on at the time when it made its sales pitch. But the harsher truth is that the vision of real gold was equally deceptive at the acme of the equity: the week when the Dow Jones index, after much huffing and puffing, finally went through 1000 – a magic number which, in the way of most magic, misfired.

In that spring of 1973, in the very week of the breakthrough, a British writer, C. Gordon Tether, pinpointed the truth in a perceptive article published in the *Financial Times*. He noted that, because of the dollar's fall in value, when the 1972 index reached the same level as the old high of 1966, 'this composite collection of US stocks was in reality fetching only three-quarters of its price six years back'. This couldn't be blamed, moreover, on any lack of the economic growth which Amex held so dear. The United States economy has performed indifferently compared to those of Germany, Japan and the other major ruins of the Second World War. But in 1972 the gross national product was still a fifth ahead of the 1966 level in real terms – so stocks had actually performed, in relation to the economy, in a wretched style. Tether calculated that the Dow would have to hit 1700 before United States investors could make up the lost ground, or rather lost money, of six tolerably fat economic years; and that calculation goes a long way towards explaining why the index thereafter hit a 1975 low of 632·04.

As the adage has it, you can fool some of the people all of the time, and all of the people some of the time, but not all of the people all of the time. Large numbers of investors began to see, or sense, the great deceit. They had been encouraged to regard equities as a defence against inflation. Now, as inflation mounted to rates unseen in the industrial West since Weimar, stocks proved to be less protection against the demon than pound notes or dollar bills stored under the mattress – let alone gold coins or ingots.

To protect the innocent (or the wary and wily) from inflation, money must be placed in a reliable store of value. But what was the value of an equity in the years before the Second Great Crash? It couldn't lie in the dividend, since yields in all popular cases were much lower than the interest paid on savings deposits. By a curious inversion of logic, in fact, the safest and bluest of chips, fit for widows, orphans and retired millionaires to place all their eggs in, often yielded among the lowest returns of all.

Nor could the value of an equity lie in the assets, since the market capitalization of big companies generally stood well above the valuation of all its assets – fixed assets, those merely passing through and intangible ones. At a capitalization of $11,715 million, Xerox, for instance, stood at the end of 1972 at 4·7 times its asset value. To take a more humdrum case, Du Pont then sold at twice the underlying worth of the business: its factories, technology, patents, machines, unsold chemicals, material stocks, net debtors, offices – the lot.

True, the replacement cost of the fixed assets (the ones that couldn't disappear out of the plant door) is much higher than the figures in the books. That is a point of pure academic abstraction, since nobody proposes to buy the business: such a Midas might conceivably calculate how much, say, Ford Motor's historic River Rouge plant would cost to build anew, as a measure of what he is prepared to pay for it second-hand, but from the investing public's viewpoint, the assets are locked in. The public's concern can be only with the earnings that the assets generate.

But this merely begs another question. What price earnings? Even as Wall Street's lights went out, some stocks still shone through the gloom as if, like the Holy Grail, they were illuminated by some special inner glory. Xerox in April 1973 was selling at 50 times earnings, Polaroid at 101 times, while the common stock of McDonalds, the king of fast-food chains, was priced at 76 times earnings; a fact which prompted a writer for *Business Week* into bemused but intelligent thought. He pointed out that 'if McDonalds doubles its earnings every six years (a highly unlikely prospect), an investor who buys shares today . . . is theoretically buying earnings out to the year 2005'. John Maynard Keynes observed that we're all dead in the long run, and a run this long was ridiculous. The value of high-priced shares, investors were advised, was not their present-day worth, but their future price. In other words it was not only sage but positively cheap to pay the sun and the stars for some Wall Street bauble in the 1960s, because it would be worth the moon as well in the 1970s (if not earlier).

A bargain deserves its name only if it sells for less than others are willing, now or in the reasonably near future, to pay. The stock punters of the sixties were persuaded that stocks, by contrast, were bargains because they were highly expensive – because others were prepared to over-pay for these scraps of paper, and always would be, even unto the end of time. So long as the earnings went on marching inexorably forward at an invigorating pace, the investing public would always price the shares at the same extra-terrestrial multiple of earnings – if not higher still.

The hucksters' line flew in the face of logic, history and even the rules of good huckstering: never give a sucker an even break, but never let him catch on, if you wish to keep his custom. That same

Amex advertisement pointed out that 267 of the stocks listed on
the exchange had paid consecutive dividends ranging from 10 to
125 years. This information was 'for investors who focus on dividends and yields' – as opposed, presumably, to those who focus
on pies in the sky, like new technology ventures. It's the latter
group who came to regard Wall Street with much the same
affection as H. R. Haldeman radiated towards John W. Dean III
during the Ervin hearings on Watergate; or as wiped-out offshore investors now cherish for Bernie Cornfeld and his imitators,
like the Gramco property fund twins, Barish and Navarro. Once
conned, thrice furious.

The offshore gangs can justifiably argue that they merely carried
on (or off) the good work of the onshore investment Mafia. The
IOS sales pitch and investment practice were built on the back of
Wall Street's mutual fund boom: IOS shared a common ethos, and
many uncommonly lucrative commissions, with the 'performance'
fund managers who most heavily plugged the high valuation of
high-growth earnings. The offshore implication, like that of Amex,
was that 'investors who focus on dividends and yields' were some
sub-species of the genus, a separate and no doubt fuddy-duddy
breed of coupon-clippers who could be kept content with solid, sto-
lid fare: old English sheepdogs, as opposed to greyhounds.

All investors, however, are in duty bound to focus on dividends
and yields because that, in blunt fact, is all their money is buying.
Yet for decades the investment community sedulously diverted the
customers' attention from this basic reality. As the bandwaggon
rolled on towards the Second Great Crash, the motivation behind
this campaign against traditional valuation became increasingly
powerful. If the customers ever came to care about yields again,
the levels of stock prices couldn't possibly be sustained; indeed the
prices *were* maintained only with much difficulty – witness those
pained efforts of the Dow Jones index to break 1000, like Sisyphus
shoving his rock uphill.

The individual investor, wiser than his deceivers, had slowly cot-
toned on. A massive transference of share ownership took place as
the pieces of paper moved over from people to institutions. From
1970 to 1974, according to the calculations of J.H.C. Leach, individuals in Britain alone offloaded the staggering sum of £6500 millions' worth of securities – and that *included* their holdings through
unit trusts. The average man is brighter than he believes when it

comes to the higher finance. Assemble many thousands, or even millions, of average men in a crowd, and they generally show a remarkably shrewd collective appreciation of the side on which their bread is buttered. These common investors had become progressively harder to sell on the equity dream even before the moment of truth arrived: when the irresistible force of a steep rise in interest rates met the highly movable object of a stock-market founded on indefensible multiples of earnings.

In the consequent débâcle, all manner of unheard-of and untoward events occurred. Switched-on, hepped-up groups of impeccable international reputation, like Massey-Ferguson, the tractor kings, and the B.F. Goodrich tyre and rubber empire, fell down the rabbit hole until they were selling at *less* than the working capital per share. An air-minded Anglo-Frenchman could have bought 51 per cent of the entire United States aerospace industry for less than the price-tag on developing the Concorde supersonic airliner. A door-to-door cosmetics firm, Avon Products, for the last moments of its years of stock-market glory, was capitalized at more than the whole United States steel industry.

These topsyturvy values, like those they replaced, could never last. But they were an inevitable over-reaction to the long years of heady indoctrination in the belief that, because stocks and shares had no intrinsic worth, they should sell at any value that an eager public, and a more avid investment community, cared to place upon them. A perfect illustration of the prevailing idiocy came from one pocket Nero, fiddling while his Rome burned in the summer of 1973. Xerox, he observed, 'looks attractive' at a price–earnings multiple of 50; the attraction lay in a projected earnings growth of 17 per cent annually. A multiple of 50 meant that if Xerox had paid out every cent of its earnings the investor would have pocketed $2 on every $100 of stock. If that projected 17 per cent growth had materialized (it didn't, of course) and had been equally fully reflected in dividends, the yield *after a full decade* would still have been under double figures, and if that was 'attractive' so was an investment in the South Sea Bubble.

The similarity between the second débâcle and the first (not to mention the South Sea Bubble) lay in the weight of money piling on top of inflated values. The difference lay in the fact that the 1929 investors, having borrowed the money which they plunged into stocks, were consequently forced to sell, and be wiped out, by the collapse. Thirty years on investors, for the most part, had invested their own savings. These were just as effectively decimated, but the pressure to sell was far less acute, and the degree of obliteration less absolute.

Many could afford to sit among their share certificates, like wartime Britons in the bombed-out ruins of their homes, and wait until Xerox was again able to look a dollar bill in the face. But they are unlikely to feel the same fine, careless rapture about equities ever again. Other allures have become enticing. As Wall Street's slump slid on and on, increasingly exotic items featured on North American shopping lists. It wasn't only gold: an active futures market in Mexican pesos started up in Chicago – and when people prefer pesos to Polaroids, the world has changed. Yet the quest in which the investors of the world united still has its compulsion. We may have been sidetracked. But the simple objective remains: to be able, like our grandfathers, to save, to guard our savings, and to augment our savings by placing them in other people's hands. The road to that destination starts from understanding what went so disastrously wrong; from uncovering exactly why the cult of the equity came near to ruining its well-meaning devotees; and from doing our best to ensure that, if it happens again, it won't happen to us.

2. The problem of savings

The cult of the common stock, or equity, was not invented by the high priests by whom it was ruined. It arose through the brute force of economic nature, and was as necessary an invention as Voltaire's God. Like the spread of supermarkets, or the proliferation of the car, or the onward and upward rush of packaged foods, the common stock responded to basic human needs. Like them, too, it was dependent on the multiplier of the gross national product.

The cult of the equity swelled to satisfy the demand created by an upsurge of savings with neither parallel nor precedent. In an age when the passing of thrift was customarily bemoaned by the conservative, and when hire-purchase debt mushroomed to heights that terrified the fiscally cautious, people collectively saved in colossal quantities. They were obeying the economic law that savings represent a relatively fixed proportion of incomes, and that this ratio tends to rise as incomes advance.

It followed that, as the average western man grew richer, so his savings piled up – not necessarily his private nest-egg, but all the various forms of collective savings as well: the pension fund, the insurance policy and so on. To give some idea of the mammoth sums involved, the institutions of poverty-stricken Britain at the end of 1974 held short-term assets totalling some £4000 million. Simply placing this Niagara of wealth was a giant problem in itself. Even given the insatiable appetite of the world's governments for money, there were limits to the potential growth of their borrowings, the national debts; equally, there are strict bounds to the amounts that can go into private-house finance, or into fixed-interest loans to industry. The stock-market provided a perfect solution to the dilemma.

Money pumped into equities went nowhere else. In theory an investor in stock-markets is financing industry; in practice he is merely exchanging one piece of paper (currency) for another (stock) – and in most cases the currency is not put to useful purpose, or to any purpose at all, by the company which issued the shares in the first place. There is thus no finite limit to the amount which equity markets can absorb – so long as the price of stocks and shares is free to rise.

At this point a benevolent circle, the very contravention of the vicious variety, begins to revolve. As the market moves ahead, spurred by the funds seeking investment, so the valuation of the market (the so-called capitalization of all the stocks in which it trades) becomes larger, thus expanding its apparent ability to absorb still more funds. Moreover the decision of investors and investing institutions to venture into equities is, by the same token, amply justified – the prices of stocks are rising, so they must have been brilliantly right to buy stocks.

The question of who invented the cult of the equity is not especially important: like bread, fire or wine, the invention sprang from nature as much as from natural genius. But one Briton, George Ross-Goobey, has been credited with playing much the same part in the British cult as St Paul did in the propagation of Christianity.

He was running the pension fund of Imperial Tobacco in the 1950s when he concluded that equities were too cheap in relation to gilt-edged government stock. In those far-off days gilts, because they were considered to be risk-free, yielded less in interest than equities, which were thought to be inherently risky. Right up to 1959, consols (the government investments of Victorian propriety) yielded 5 per cent when equities offered 7 per cent. But Ross-Goobey saw that dividends, and even dividend growth, could be relied upon in the post-Keynes era; and the heavy buying of equities by Ross-Goobey and his countless imitators soon eliminated the yield gap. Indeed they set to work with such a will that the gap went into reverse – equities in 1960 began to yield less than gilts, later much less. In 1972, when equities yielded 4 per cent, consols paid 11 per cent; and as late as August 1975 top-rated corporate bonds, at 8·9 per cent, gave twice as much yield as Wall Street stocks. This wasn't because the riskiness of common stocks had been removed by some suspension of the laws of business economics, some sudden conversion of managements into financial supermen; it was because fixed-interest stocks were fully and alarmingly exposed to the double villains of the New Economic Age – taxation and inflation.

Interest paid was subject to tax, often at frighteningly high rates, while the 'gilt-edged' government stock, far from being gilded, offered little or no protection against the persistent fall in the value of money. This mattered less in periods when interest rates stayed more or less stable. From 1933 to 1950 the British bank rate stayed at 2 per cent, believe it or not. By the later 1950s 7 per cent had been touched. A decade later 8 per cent was breached. But as the inflation problem grew more serious, interest rates began to oscillate in ever-widening circles. In 1973 the rate swung from $8\frac{1}{2}$ per cent to 13 per cent in a single year – and that movement was enough to lose a man one-third of his precious capital.

The equity gave apparent protection on both counts. In the first place the company didn't need to pay a dividend if the management and the stockholders didn't want it paid. The profits could be kept in the business, free of personal income tax, to be reinvested to produce still more profits. The price of the shares would rise to reflect this mounting profit – and the investor could pocket his proceeds as capital gains, taxed at the lower rate (and in Britain until the early 1960s not taxed at all).

As inflation rumbled on, profits would automatically be inflated, too, so the share price would rise in step with inflation on this count as well. Nor was that the only insurance: behind the price of the stock stood the assets, which plainly became worth more in current money with every fresh twist in the inflationary cycle. This argument was so plausible, on its bland face, that almost nobody recognized that it was the economic equivalent, intellectually speaking, of fool's gold. Ever since money took over from barter, men have searched for the ideal investment, which would combine maximum return with maximum security: the golden goose that lays the golden eggs, but with an axe-proof neck.

In the harsh reality of economics, alas, high security tends to go with low yield, and vice versa. Only some of the people were greedy enough to ignore this law, or to believe that it could be repealed for their special benefit. The majority were in all probability happy to settle for a cash depository that would preserve their capital in real terms and provide, over the long run, a reasonable return on the money, after tax.

Take a fairly simple case: you have $100 invested over twenty years, a period in which mild inflation (around 3 per cent a year) halves the value of your money. So you need a 100 per cent capital gain to preserve your capital. But wait: there is gains tax to pay.

Assume the old United States rate of 25 per cent (it is now 28·75 per cent) and that means you are throwing for a gain of 166·66 per cent (recurring). That's no more than 5 per cent compound, a long way short of Polaroid or Xerox standards, and the kind of aim a well-oiled management ought to take in a single stride. However, there is also the question of income. Say that the investor wants a real return of $3\frac{1}{2}$ per cent on $100. Left to compound over two decades, that interest would yield a lump sum at the close of $100. To make the sums simpler still, assume that the stock pays no cash dividends. (This is no fantasy: several companies, most notably Litton Industries, succeeded in getting away with this ultimate absurdity of the equity cult, paying 'stock dividends' in place of cash on the strength of the apparently irresistible rise of their share prices.) With a dividendless stock, the investor's $100 has to rise to $400 net to protect the original capital (remember that the value of money is halving) and to provide a $3\frac{1}{2}$ per cent net annual return, duly compounded.

After allowing for the tax on capital gains, that means a total rise over the two happy decades of 400 per cent, or something short of $8\frac{1}{2}$ per cent per annum compound. As a matter of hard historical fact, relatively few of the stocks proudly listed on the world's exchanges have managed this feat. And bear in mind that it is the *minimal* standard: the majority of stocks paid dividends, and the higher tax on the latter means that the gross return (dividends plus capital gain) would have had to average better still.

London is a painful example of what actually happened. The growth leagues published by *Management Today* show that, out of the two hundred largest companies listed on the Stock Exchange in April 1970, ninety – that's rather more than two in five – had made this none-too-demanding grade over the previous decade. A year later the proportion was down to below one in five. On Wall Street a year after that, *Fortune*'s five hundred showed just over a third of America's biggest corporations passing the test. All this was before the calamitous drop in stock-markets in 1973 and 1974. So the odds barely favoured the investor trying his luck at bettering the fixed-interest return, even at a modest rate of inflation.

But a faster fall in the value of dollar bills, pound notes or other paper currencies, and the cult of the equity is in serious trouble. At a 7 per cent inflation rate, the dividendless stock needs to double in only ten years to compensate for the erosion of capital; it requires a further 80 per cent gain to provide a compounded $3\frac{1}{2}$ per cent annual return. After tax, that adds up to 240 per cent, or an annual bonanza of 13 per cent – which is the kind of target that the hottest of hot-shot companies aimed at (and mostly missed) for annual growth in earnings per share (which by no means necessarily equates with growth in the share price). To sum up these sums, the worse inflation became, the *less* likely it was that equities could provide an acceptable defence against the gnawing away of the value of money.

Whether common stocks were a better anti-inflation defence than anything else depended greatly on the point from which you started. If you began with the great Ross-Goobey, when equities were yielding more than government securities, the game was fixed in your favour: simply because, as the yield on stocks first came down to that on these 'gilt-edged' offerings (the gilt being no more substantial than the vermouth in a really dry martini), and then went lower still, huge capital gains were bound to follow.

But they were once-for-all gains. Once the epochal adjustment had been made, equities were on their own, running for dear life to stay in the same place. If a common stock is yielding 2 per cent, for example, it must grow by 6 per cent year in year out, to keep abreast of a gross fixed-interest yield of 7 per cent. The race was no longer fixed: it went only to the very swift, of whom there were, by definition, very few.

The search for gold amid the surrounding dross was bound to lead to unbridled lust for weird and wonderful stocks. Perhaps the weirdest of these wonders was a computer services stock which differed from all its brethren by actually making a profit: the others, when they came to market, were all happily in loss, which made their price–earnings ratios infinite. When the prospectus for this superior offering was published on Wall Street, the investing institutions which had subscribed for the issue suffered sharp attacks of financial angina.

Because the company was showing some earnings (i.e. was actually profitable) they could assess how much they were paying for their new nest-egg; and the price–earnings ratio was in treble figures. They promptly dumped the stock; had it been a loss-maker, like the standard and presumably less successful entrants, the blue-chip investors would have been happy to hang on.

Since even sophisticated investors (as above) act in a remarkably irrational manner, any argument for investing in equities which is based on reason is bound to fail, sooner if not later. That truth applies to the ordinary, run-of-the-mill behaviour of the market, which by definition oscillates round the norm. But any hopeful soul who rests his policy on substantially beating the norm – and this, as noted, was essential to meet the modest aims with which the equity cult began – is moving into the realms of the higher unreason.

He is like a man pressing a button in the knowledge that, half the time, a moderately valuable red ball will pop out of the box. The rest of the time will be equally divided between the appearance of a money-losing black ball and a rich gold one; yet knowing this, the man consistently bets on the appearance of gold. The searcher after stock-market performance is like that man. Yet for every once that he comes up gold, he must receive two red and one money-losing black number. It doesn't make much sense: the average performance of stock-markets round the world (which is all the great majority of investors could hope to achieve) wasn't good enough to live up to the billing of the equity cult. But investors, and still more those who sold the latter their investments, were most unwilling to face this unwelcome fact. Instead they sought extraneous explanations.

In 1973, as the slide gathered momentum, they could blame all manner of outside mayhem: the world monetary crisis, the deepening shadow and stain of Nixon's Watergate and *Götterdämmerung*, and some scandals of rare juiciness even by Wall Street standards – such as the monstrous Equity Funding affair. Coming on top of massive thefts of stock certificates, this $100 million swindle, which involved the issue of phoney insurance policies – over sixty-four thousand of which didn't exist – and the certifying of imaginary deaths of fictitious people, can hardly have fortified wavering faith in an economy built on trusted pieces of paper. Nor did the Equity business help Wall Street to recover from its own loss of confidence following the rash of bankruptcies and near-bankruptcies among stockbroking firms: events which followed not only slavish, self-destructive obedience to the equity cult, but quite monstrous incompetence in the back offices which handle the paperwork of the greatest property-owning democracy in the world.

H. Ross Perot, one of the dabber hands at managing computer services, got sucked into the mess in Wall Street's top brokerage houses, starting with Francis I. Du Pont, through their heavy involvement as his prize Wall Street computer customers. Perot's $5 million initial investment proved to be one of the worst mistakes in business history. It coincided with the horrendous price drop in Perot's own Electronic Data Systems from $162 in March 1970 (making Perot a multi-millionaire) to $12 in October 1974. The Perot Comanches were forced to bow out of Wall Street, sadder and poorer rich men (down by $100 million on this count alone).

London was no more adept at handling the heavy traffic created by the inflation-hedge hucksters. The Second Great Crash stripped bare the pretensions of so many brokers that the Stock Exchange in 1974 had to cough up many millions in compensation to the unhappy customers of the failed brethren. Yet the brothers were mostly down, rather than out. When the London market rallied in January 1975, rising by almost two-thirds in no time at all, the professionals resurfaced in a flash; it was rather reminiscent of dormant animal life being suddenly wakened by the heat. But this phenomenon was different from earlier celebrations of the cult: the reaction against the past worship had been so severe that common stocks were now truly cheap – as opposed to the spurious cheapness of the past.

All the forces that made the equity a necessary inevitability in that past still exist: mainly the lack of any credible alternative for the investor who doesn't want his return fixed, and measured out only in modest quantities, from the very beginning.

The alternatives to equity investment are 1) the bed (the underneath thereof); 2) the super-bed, or interest-bearing deposits in banks and so on; 3) fixed-interest securities, such as government bonds and loan stocks; 4) property; 5) things – ranging from old and young masters to diamonds to old books via objects like Staffordshire portrait figures or Japanese *netsuke*; 6) commodities, including the prince thereof, which is gold. Either these alternatives lack the upward potential of the equity – the fact that you don't know where its rise, if any, will stop; or, if they have potential upwardness, they lack the sovereign virtue of liquidity, of easy translation into cash; or else they demand a degree of expertise that few investors can muster – even fewer than the number who know the difference between a high price-earnings ratio and a low one.

Adam Smith, the author of *The Money Game* and *Supermoney*, got badly burnt twice in hot cocoa, once directly, once at a remove – a Swiss bank in which he had invested harboured, unbeknown to itself, a genius who was foolishly set on cornering the world cocoa market. As for art, it shares the problem of difficult conversion into cash – the unlucky man might offer his heirloom at auction when there is a close season on Gainsborough – and it also demands both expertise and love. He who genuinely loves his Staffordshire Sir Robert Peel, his Francis Bacon screaming pope or his monochrome K'ang Hsi porcelain will sell it only in the direst emergency. That puts him in the same cautionary spot as the family quoted by the aforesaid Adam Smith, who rigidly adhered through two generations to a paternal injunction never to sell their shares in IBM; they consequently became very rich – but the poor things never actually had much money.

Having money is, after all, the object of the exercise. And the prime definition of a proper counter in that game is that it must be easy to purchase, easy to mind and easy to dispose of, both psychologically and physically. There is nothing more understandable, or more pathetic, than the state of mind which hangs on to a share year after year 'because it's done me so well'. People in this mental condition often fail completely to notice that the stock has long since ceased to do anything for them at all. Like genuinely dishonest con-men, the promoters of equities battened off such failure. Since such customers didn't know they were being fleeced, or at least being sold a false bill of goods, they were hardly likely to complain. Now the cat is out of the bag. But human nature is such that it may be relatively easy to stuff the animal back in again.

The idea of the common stock, freely traded between individuals on open exchanges, is still a marvellous invention. Its only basic defect is that the people who man, run and serve the exchanges make their livings, not out of the success of their customers, but out of the volume of the trade. They have a built-in incentive to oversell, and thus to overkill geese and golden eggs alike. Their intellectual apparatus, or rationalization, is part of their salesman's pitch: samples carried round in the attaché case, often nothing but gimcrack – as the next chapter will reveal.

3. Has investing changed?

During the days when performance was in flower, many and wondrous were the theories promulgated for making sure mints from markets. At one end of the spectrum, investors could put their all and their faith in computers, which supposedly brought to bear on investment problems the ability to out-calculate Einstein and Newton together, and combined this mathematical talent with more information about the stock-markets than a million analysts beavering away for a hundred years could assimilate. At the other extreme, the punter could pick the man rather than the machine, opting for some fabulous wizard of the market, like Manhattan's once-celebrated Chinese-American Gerald Tsai. He translated stunning success at Fidelity Capital Fund into the knock-out launch in 1966 of the Manhattan Fund with $247 million of other people's money; such men seemingly didn't need a system to set the welkin ringing – the mere touch of the Midas sufficed. In between, however, lurked any number of systems.

The customer could choose technical analysis, or chartism, in which the behaviour of the market was reduced to lines and patterns on graph paper. If that seemed too mechanistic, he could select several methods by which high-performing shares could in theory be picked out, like sixpences from a Christmas pudding, from the surrounding stodge; if that seemed too hazardous, then he could favour stocks with high asset backing, or high yields, or high cash flow per share. You name it, and it was on offer – and it always worked.

For the terrible truth is that in soaring markets all theories work, while in sinking markets, no theory succeeds – and no Midas touch produces gold either. Tsai's funds soared in boom years; in 1968, when the Midas did his shrewdest deed by sharply selling out for $30 million, Manhattan slumped as markets turned against Tsai's style. In markets of either variety, however, no expert will ever confess to the boom–bust truth, one which so grossly reduces his own claims to expertise. If investment is solely a matter of riding a galloping market and jumping off a recessionary one, then what distinguishes a silver-haired, sharp-witted partner in Lazard Frères or N. M. Rothschild from the face in the crowd? The main difference, actually, is that the partner sells his advice and opinions, while the crowd buys them.

Any test of the recommendations of the aces has usually shown that they are neither more nor less reliable than racehorse tipsters: that is, their success is no more than random – which happens to be the way in which, according to the highly respectable academic theory of the 'random walk', stock-markets do behave.

Stripped of its maths, the theory holds that share prices fluctuate in random fashion round a price which is the intrinsic or underlying value of the stock. This begs the big question of what intrinsic value can possibly mean in a price determined by market forces; but this large quibble is insignificant compared to the results of a test conducted by a computer at the Chicago Graduate School of Business. It computed, chosen at random, 56·5 million buying and selling transactions on the New York Stock Exchange. It wound up with a median rate of return of 9·8 per cent annually and a chance of achieving a profit which was not only better than three out of four, but far better than the results of following the non-random choice of the typical expert.

No better proof of this accusation exists than the experience of a group of Wall Street veterans who gather each year for 'a pre-Christmas luncheon and a Christmas list of favourite stocks'. The words are from *Newsweek*, which made its readers privy to the menu at the Christmas 1972 beanfeast. The point is not so much the 1973 tips (which ran to companies with worrying names like Etz Lavud, and of which more later) but the blithe way in which the veterans sailed ahead undeterred by the record of the previous festivities.

They had tipped twenty-three stocks, of which thirteen had fallen between lunches. Of the remaining ten, only eight managed to grow by more than the Dow Jones index. Now 1972 wasn't one of the horror-show years to come, in which the Dow Jones attempted to break new depth records. The market had actually risen by 13·6 per cent since the veterans had last tasted Christmas pudding. Had the convivial old-timers invested in all twenty-three stocks (they were probably too old-time, or not convivial enough, to back one another's judgement quite so wholeheartedly), the average gain would have been 7 per cent, or about half the rise recorded by the market as a whole.

The veterans would have lost half their money on two of the twenty-three, and made 50 per cent or more on only four. Counsel for the defence would no doubt begin by saying that these are about the right odds for an investor in search of what *Newsweek*'s Clem Morgello calls the 'big winners' – by which he means the company, often little known or temporarily out of favour, that promises to catch fire and race ahead in a short period of time by half or more. That kindly judgement only proves that the quest for big winners is a mug's game in the first place; and that these veterans, who are no different in this respect from any other Wall Street or London group you care to pick, are no better at the game than you would expect a mug to be.

Two winners out of twenty-three, or 8·7 per cent, are not the kind of odds, or the kind of form, that would attract any halfway sensible bettor. In fact it's doubtful whether the record of this Christmas gathering would have inspired much confidence in the type of person who buys Brooklyn Bridge.

Potential 'big winners' are better named 'maybe' stocks. To take the veterans' list as an illustration, *maybe* the Wankel engine was going to make it big (it did, briefly enough, and so in 1972 did Curtiss-Wright, which had a licence on the invention). *Maybe* Leasco, the empire built up from nothing by the Muhammad Ali of computer leasing, Saul Steinberg, would climb up off the canvas, on which it had been deposited by a number of untoward events, including the collapse of computer leasing (but Leasco stayed down, and so did the shares). The biggest *maybe* in the bunch was National Patent Development, which attracted the attention of the experts because it was deep into the soft contact lens caper. But the soft product ran into the red, and the shares, in a Wall Street term of peculiar beatitude, 'headed south'. They ended the year off 61·3 per cent, a fair way towards the Antarctic, after having been 95·6 per cent to the good at one point.

Here beginneth the second defence. With fireball or *maybe* shares, you must know when to head, not south, but homewards. The veterans pointed out that the average gain of their Christmas selection from lunchtime onwards to the 1972 highs was almost 62 per cent, compared to only 16·7 per cent for the Dow Jones index. But this defence, one beloved of stock-market tipsters, will never wash. It represents the purest mountain water of hindsight. The tipster is saying that *if* you had known when each stock was going to peak, you would have come out splendidly ahead of the game: and that is as hypothetical as an 'if' can get. It postulates perfect timing, which is difficult enough with one stock, let alone with twenty-three. It compares, moreover, the peaks of these selected stocks, all presumably reached at different dates in the year, with the level of a market index (which is arrived at by averaging the peaks, lows and in-betweens of a totally unselected group of stocks) on just one day in 1972.

To add one other maybe to the list, *maybe*, if the Dow-Jones constituent stocks had been measured from Christmas Eve to their respective individual peaks, a better gain than 60 per cent would have been achieved – and there are precious few fireballs, 'big winners' or hot stocks in the Dow-Jones.

To be fair to this group of aces, it is unfair to single them out for special attention. It is true that, asked to pick their favourite stocks for 1972, they produced so duff a list as to cast doubts on their expertise and that, confronted with this unhappy fact, they sought to conceal the truth with mathematical sophistry. But any group of investment experts, forced to defend their record against the evidence, would have engaged in much the same subterfuge; and any group, asked on Christmas Eve to name an individual stock which will cover itself and themselves with glory for the whole of the ensuing twelve months, is liable to come ingloriously unstuck. Failure is the name of this particular game: because the exercise flies in the face of the essence of markets, which is to fluctuate and to be illogical.

There is an old and valuable truth about fine wine: that there are no good wines, only good bottles. By the same token, there are no good buys in shares, only good sales. If you sell a share for more than you paid for it, the buy was good. If not, not. But the tipster operates on the comfortable thesis that there are no bad tips, only good ones. The bad ones he forgets about, on the general line that the good that men do (in the stock-market at least) lives after them, while the evil is interred with its own bones.

This is beautifully illustrated by the chartist. Studying his 'heads and shoulders', 'base areas', 'upside projections', 'reversal patterns', 'top areas' and other graphical joys, the chartist will advise that a certain stock is set to head from, say, 167 to 264. If it fails to do so, sliding perhaps to 130, the chartist is not the least bit abashed. The pattern, he will confidently report, has 'aborted'. In other words, the whole process is nothing whatsoever to do with him, God, nature or the stock itself. It has simply failed to conform to the mysterious law of which, although totally unable to establish its workings, the chartist is the sole and well-paid custodian.

Anybody who claims, like the Wall Street veterans, that a bad tip was really magnificent, because you could have sold at a profit, had you only known when to do so, cannot retire behind the excuse; he must produce evidence that he actually advised the customers to sell at the peak point. After the event is the easiest time to be wise.

Moreover, if you are dealing in fireballs, and counting only their gains to the peak level, you are cooking the books in another respect – any fireball that does explode may travel so fast and far that it outweighs the indifference of the rest of the pack. No less than a quarter of the 60 per cent gain which the Wall Street choices showed from their Christmas price to their respective peaks was owed to one stock: Curtiss-Wright, the Wankel wonder. It finished the year up 172 per cent. Without this one star performer the entire portfolio of hot tips would have shown a year-on-year gain of precisely nothing.

The cult of performance, however, forces the expert to choose hot stocks rather than cool performers. The public of the bubble period was woefully unimpressed by safe and solid selections, even though several uncomputerized exercises at choosing a portfolio with a pin produced results that were no worse than those which investment experts of various persuasions picked with an eye to unsafe, far-from-solid performance.

In one exercise carried out in 1973 two random selections of stocks were pitted against one another, in a stock-market replay of Aesop's race between the tortoise and the hare. The tortoise stocks were rich with asset value, high in dividend yield and deep in defensive qualities. The hares, in contrast, were all selling at the astronomic multiples of earnings which in the last days of the Big Bull Market designated a high-performance growth stock. The results were entirely predictable. While neither portfolio resisted the Second Great Crash, the tortoises were slower going down the slide than the hares, a third of which disappeared off the bottom altogether. The moral of this true fable is that every single hare had been vigorously backed by the investment experts; hence their soaring price–earnings ratios.

Indeed at a London dinner meeting similar to the Wall Street Christmas luncheon, in that the assembled pundits were asked to pick their favoured share, the tortoise and hare philosophies came into direct conflict. The tortoise was the once-dreary old sugar company, Tate & Lyle, best known for its implacable objections to being nationalized. The hare was Associated Dairies (Asda), a milk firm that had risen like a meteor from obscurity by its success in promoting American-style superstores in the nether reaches of England. The diners overwhelmingly rejected slow-and-steady sugar in favour of fast milk, convinced by a merchant banker's eloquent testimony to the brilliance and depth of Asda's management, and the dazzling scope of its growth potential. There was nothing wrong with this analysis (although investment experts are often glaringly mistaken about management, markets and men) – except that it totally misread the future of the shares. As the Great Crash (Mark II) bottomed out, the sugar company was selling at about the same price as on the day of the dinner. The superstore hare had fallen by two-thirds.

In bear markets, as a general rule, the 'defensive' stock does better than the aggressive one – just as, when the action roars away, the aggressors make the running. But few expert advisers ever observe this fundamental rule of markets, or any other of the ancient reliable rules of thumb which substitute experience for inspiration. Their customers were in an uncertain state of mind, anyway. They had perhaps grasped the rule that the higher the interest, the greater the risk of the investment; they were now being asked to accept that in the stock-market the reverse was true – that the high-yield stocks might actually be safer than the one with a virtually invisible dividend return on the purchase price. Many were unable to make this psychological transition – especially since the high-yield stocks either were 'dogs' (i.e. duds), or were valued as such, while the low-yield ones were 'high-fliers' and therefore obviously desirable.

This mental confusion achieved a neglect of first principles in investment, which had never actually changed but which were increasingly flouted as the boom sputtered on to its bust. As investors bought 'growth', past and projected, instead of the dividends which were the only reality, so their actions, and the reflections of those actions in share prices, became further and further removed from the bases of investment. This placed the expert himself in an invidious position. Even if he knew the basic truths of investment, even if he realized that something as fundamental as the relationship of bond yields to equity yields still had to rule at the end of the day, markets were being swayed in the meantime by other considerations entirely, such as the potential for soft contact lenses.

The 1973 list rattled up by the Wall Street lunchers, despite their disappointing performance the previous year, shows that the penny (unlike the dollar) had not dropped. They showed more interest that time round in large companies which had been heavily bombed, but (hopefully) were at least as intact as North Vietnam – like American Motors (a hardy perennial in such lists), Chrysler, Reynolds and Westinghouse. They also found a peculiarly delectable railway, the Providence and Worcester, whose total network of track is precisely forty-one miles. But the authentic flavour of their selection is better conveyed by stocks like Alpex Computer, which hadn't made a profit in its life, but which – there's that *maybe* again – maybe would some day. (Alpex has since disappeared off the face of the stock-market.) There was also Soundesign, which made hi-fi equipment and mini-computers in those familiar bulwarks of the United States economy, Japan and Taiwan. And (which is where those soft contact lenses come in again) good old National Patent Development (NPD) came up for the second time. Now it seemed, the lens problems had been sorted out, and a mouthwash and a dental chemical were thrown in for luck. It didn't do any good: NPD and Soundesign ended up in early 1975 in exactly the same place as in 1972, with prices that left plenty of change from a $10 bill.

The obvious question is what makes Wall Street's wise old birds, deep though they may be in the lore of convertible debentures, the mysteries of bond-washing, the infinite beauties of incremental earnings growth, think that they know anything about mouthwash, except where to use it?

Computers used to exert an uncanny fascination on men who at that time hadn't even mastered the electronic adding machine. Yet these same ignoramuses solemnly, year after year, put their mouths and sometimes their money into stocks solely on the strength of technologies about whose nature and market potential they were wholly ignorant. Not only that: they gave these wonders far higher ratings, and pronounced them better bargains by far (despite horri-fyingly high prices), than solid steady companies about which they often knew an unusual amount.

Under any investment regime, of course, it pays to find a company whose profits (genuine ones, that is) are going to rise much faster than the norm. If the company is a small one at the moment of dis-covery, so much the better: then the effects of heavy demand on a light supply of stock will have the same beneficial effect as the laws of economics will produce in any market. But it is essential that the commodity should be unrecognized, not known about and sought after by every money-grubber in that market. A high-growth stock at a high price is by definition not a bargain: a high-growth stock at a low price is that most precious of all stock-market beasts, the Anomaly, a quarry we shall be pursuing later in this study.

The Second Great Crash went so far, in fact, that the whole mar-ket became anomalous. At one point Rapidata, a computer service, found 500 corporations out of 1300 selling below book value. Now book value (as British investors found when companies like Burmah Oil, British Leyland and Jessel Securities bit the dust, leaving either not a wrack or not much more behind) is as may be. But Rapidata went on to unearth 220 of these companies which were selling below both book value *and* the value of their liquid assets. In other words, you could buy the company for and with its own cash – a ridiculous situation. Just as the boom had parted company with real values in the upwards direction, so the Crash (like 1929–32 before it) left reality behind in the opposite direction.

An anomaly, in this case a whole market, can be initially recog-nized by its cheapness; further investigation is needed to discover exactly why it is cheap. But few of the experts, gun-shy and shell-shocked as they must have become, were ready in 1974 to advocate a return to equity investment, any more than most of them had shown any inkling that the Second Coming of 1929 was about to strike.

Over the years of guessing wrong about the unguessable, pundits learn that they cannot afford to be without two hands – on the one hand this, on the other that. This Delphic device keeps their necks where they should be: not sticking out. But psychology, and the need to encourage the customers to buy, dictates that it is safer, hand-wise, to ride with the crowd when the market is rising. When it is falling, contrariwise, the two hands dictate that silence is the best policy. That leaves the average man with the mental difficulty of accepting that experts truly know no more about which stock will rise, and which fall, than he does; and that even those who understand the fundamentals of investment, and have correctly sailed with past tides, can still pick rotten apples with the same unerring facility as the rest of us.

The pension fund run by one of these all-time greats was reported, as the Second Great Crash bumped along the bottom, to have large stakes in an unhealthy number of burnt-out stocks, all overpriced pets of the bull phase. You can't win them all, but one way to lose them is to believe in the ever-victorious expert, some of whose far from triumphant works we are about to examine.

4. The tale of the two growth stocks

One of Britain's most successful investors, whose own company's stock used to sell at a price–earnings ratio of well over 40, was once confronted with the proposition that no stock is ever worth a 40 multiple. To this he retorted, with unimpeachable accuracy, that none was worth 30.

Anybody who followed stock-markets through the 1960s must regard this as a weird untruth. Many of the most eagerly sought counters in the period regularly boasted ratios in the 30s, even in the 40s and 50s; and any sceptic who queried the received idea that an IBM, or a Marks & Spencer, or a Polaroid, or a Tesco supermarket share had not been the best of buys throughout the period would have been downright disbelieved. But the sceptic is right, the received view (as usual) wrong. The sceptical truth first struck home when some figures for the magnificent Marks & Spencer, certainly one of the world's best-managed retail chains, confronted me with much the same effect as a 'Dear John' letter from a deserting fiancée. The increase in the company's share price from the middle quotation of 1963 to spring 1973 (still a relatively good time for London markets) was only 86 per cent, according to this figuring – plainly erroneous, or was it?

The number was perfectly correct: which meant that, after paying capital-gains tax, an investor would have realized less in the depreciated pound notes of 1973 than he had started with a decade back. Was this some freak of the end of the long boom? Checking back unearthed the fact that from 1963 to 1967 Marks was not a growth investment by any stretch even of a gin-sodden imagination. In 1968 there was a little leap forward of 27 per cent, but the shares bogged down again until 1971, when a 38 per cent hop would at last have enabled the 1963 buyer to double his money – at which point the shares promptly bogged down again.

Doubling in eight years equals 9 per cent annual compound

growth: worthy, but not wonderful. Moreover anybody who purchased the share at its peak in any of these eight years would have shown a loss at some point in the next year – ranging from a minimal 8 per cent to a full third in the worst year of all. Yet decade in, decade out, the firm as a firm truly performed – its sales almost trebled, its profits jumped by 212 per cent, its pre-tax margins (the vital statistic of a retail business) were maintained right across the years, which merits a toast in the company's St Michael Beaujolais any day: its earnings per share rose by 10 per cent per annum compound.

Plainly the malaise lay not in Marks but in the whole concept of the 'prime long-term growth situation', to quote one lyrical supporter of the Marks shares. It could be argued that Marks is an unfair choice: large even at the start of the comparison, with £184·9 million of sales, a very fair figure by United States, let alone British, standards; and, moreover, stuck in retailing (not the most dynamic of lines) and in Britain, the least dynamic of the industrialized economies.

A fairer test of prime long-term growth would surely be the Xerox Corporation. Back in 1964 its great invention of dry copying was off and running; but sales had reached only $281·55 million. The company plainly had plenty of dynamism ahead of it. This turned out to mean expansion of sales by 12·7 times, which makes the electricity of Marks and most other monuments to capitalism look decidedly static. Unlike the British firm, too, the corporation had the world as its oyster. Its management, after recovering from the shock of discovering that the invention lugged into its offices by Chester B. Carlsson, almost as a last resort, was a licence to print money, learnt its lessons fast enough to become one of the world's most renowned practitioners of the ever-lasting sell. By leasing out their copiers, binding the lessees to lucrative supply contracts and keeping up a smart pace of product innovation, men like Peter McColough earned their spurs and their multi-millions. How did all this virtue translate in stock-market terms?

On the long view, from 1964 to 1972 the share price failed to keep pace with the growth, not of sales (up 8½ times), but of profits (up 6¼ times). Taking the middle price of each year, the stock brought joy to its 1964 holders – but perhaps not enough joy, growing 4·3 times. The 1964 purchaser, what's more, did much better than his successors. Again, taking the middle price, the stock doubled in three years from 1964; it took five years to treble the 1964 starting price, and a full nine years to quadruple. That still sounds like mighty fine multiplication – but not when you consider that the starting price of these comparisons, $33·56, inevitably became a smaller and smaller percentage of the subsequent prices of the stock. Somebody who bought in at the middle price, exactly between the high and low points, of 1964 had to wait four years to double his money. The 1965 middle-price buyer had a two-year wait. The 1966 fellow had to hang on until 1971. The same time-lag affected buyers of the class of '67 – five years until 1972. The johnnies who came lately from 1968 onwards never managed the doubling at all – even though Xerox made some fine and fancy share prices until the rains came in 1974.

At the low of that year, anybody who had bought Xerox at its peak back in 1964 would have shown a gain of only 11·7 per cent. And even that was purely a paper rise, wiped out in real terms by the inflation of 1974 alone. Any subsequent peak purchaser, from 1965 onwards, would have lost large sums of money, in real, unreal or any other terms.

The friends of Xerox will complain that the artificially low price of 1974 cannot fairly be taken as a test. But unlike the residents on the Xerox ground floor of 1964, any later buyer of Xerox stock at the peak of any one year had to wait until 1972 to double his money. In other words there was no point whatsoever in having your funds locked away in Xerox, at any purchase price above $84, until 1971; and there wasn't actually much point in holding the stock at any entry price above $65, since you could have entered the lists at that level as late as 1970.

These are entirely theoretical exercises. Many investors could get in and out of Xerox, and did, at various times in the decade, maybe several times over, with luminous profits. What could not have been done, at any point after 1964, was to buy this wonder stock *regardless of price*, secure in the knowledge that it would fetch a handsomely higher price at any time you wished to sell in the next five years. Moreover it was clearly a false move ever to buy the stocks when the case for them was at its most glamorous and gushingly advocated – which is when the stocks were selling at their proudest price-earnings multiples. From 1964 to 1969 the multiple rose as high as 71, and never fell below 33. In the next five years, however, the multiple never got above 54, and slipped as low as 27 (in 1970) before the 12 times calamity of 1974.

Therein lies the explanation of the two linked mysteries, which are the disappointing performance of Xerox for many of the investors who jumped aboard in the 1960s, and the failure of the share price in that period to keep in step with the corporation's bounding growth, brilliant publicity and excellent endeavour. As the years went on, investors simply grew less and less willing to accord Xerox the highest accolades of 'prime long-term growth'. They were not reacting out of mere boredom. The figures for earnings per share reveal quite clearly that some anchor was tugging at the company.

In the three years 1964–6 the earnings per share jumped by 89 per cent. In the four years to 1969, growth was down to 66 per cent. In the next four years, to 1972, the figure slipped again, to 52 per cent. Finally, the three years 1972–4 saw a 32 per cent advance. That rate of progress was not much above a third of the pace set in those opening three years when briefly, Xerox chips were worth so much more than their weight in gold.

Behind the statistics, and behind all the mysteries of the market, lies the inevitability of arithmetic. An extra \$281·55 million of sales doubled the company from its 1964 base. The same increment in 1973, when competition had expanded (although none too formidably), but when markets were more thoroughly saturated, added less than 10 per cent to the volume. And \$280 million of new business, because of the saturation factor, was no easier to win than when the same increment doubled the company's sales.

Indeed the lessening of growth prospects in its own market was presumably one of the prime forces pushing Xerox into computers – and into the mammoth operating losses on the Scientific Data Systems buy (a \$900 million touch) which marred its once magnificent margins to a mean extent. We shall encounter this catastrophe in another context later. However, operating income as a percentage of operating revenues slipped fairly steadily from 46·2 in 1964 to 37·4 nine years on.

The conclusions are impregnable. This company, no worse and mostly much better than other sizeable corporations, is the perfect demonstration of the difficulty of living up to a growth stock's own growth record. The intoxicating price–earnings ratios once commanded by the stock made sense (and not much, even then) only if the company was able, not only to maintain, but to accelerate the pace of its growth.

The realities of business life dictate that, as the shark's size increases to whale dimensions, so it is increasingly unlikely to keep up its speed of movement. Thus the further into the future its sustained growth has been anticipated, the further its actual performance must diverge from the dreams, and the sooner the dreamers must be faced with the fact of divergence–at which point their dreams turn to ashes. The final break usually comes when some untoward incident, of the kind that comes to all companies and men, acts as trigger: if not the Scientific Data Systems fiasco, then a low punch from the anti-trust authorities. In its boom periods the wonder stock readily rides out these assaults of fate. In its vulnerable situation of promise perennially denied even by good performance, the wonder wilts, to be succeeded on stage by another paragon, which will repeat the history over again with all the inevitability of the tides.

The case of Xerox, however, may not convince the pure growth enthusiast. After all its performance *did* decline in relative terms over the years. What if it had proved an exception to the law of diminishing returns from increasing size? What if it had not been forced to carry the burden of comparison with its own super-charged early years? Wouldn't Xerox then have justified, if not its multiples of 70, at least the average rating of 40 or so?

Alas, the evidence of history fails to support this comforting theory either. The London market provides an example of a company whose real performance actually improved over the years, but whose market behaviour was as disappointing, and as disillusioning to growth theorists, as that of Xerox.

The anti-hero of this tale is the Beecham Group, which in the fiscal year 1964–5 was already a star company. Its architect, Leslie Lazell, had moved into a disorganized, disrupted business, that ran around like a decapitated chicken because its head actually had been cut off. An old ogre named Philip Hill, the banker who banged Beecham's together, had died, leaving behind some bright brand names and some notably less refulgent successors.

But Lazell had developed a management and marketing style at Maclean's, selling toothpaste, stomach powders and whatnot, which proved brilliantly apt for the whole Beecham's business (it also took in Brylcreem, the Lucozade glucose drink and a number of other proprietary money-spinners). Add to his genius in exploiting proprietary brands his bravery in invading the United States market, first with Maclean's (a wow), then with Silvikrin shampoo (a flop), next with Brylcreem (a palpable hit) and finally with a near-Xerox-style winner in synthetic penicillins, and you have in Lazell the best British professional manager of the postwar period. In 1964–5, despite a blotch on the escutcheon over some magnificent mismanagement on the foods side, the stock was reasonably well regarded – but only reasonably well.

In July 1965 the dividend yield was 5 per cent, which by the standards of the equity cult in full flower was near to handsome. By July 1968, however, the share was a very different kettle of prime white fish – the dividend yield was down to a Lilliputian 1·84 per cent, and the earnings multiple, which had been only (and the only is strictly relative) 18 three years before, had climbed to the relatively dizzy height of 30. Nor could you have said, if gifted with perfect foresight, that Beecham's was a bad buy at 30 times earnings. From the fiscal year then just completed until 1972, the earnings per share bounded up by 17 per cent a year. Had people who pounded into Beecham's at a multiple of 30 times earnings in 1968 known for cast-iron certain that they were buying a 17 per cent earnings growth, they would never – not even for a split second – have considered pounding right out again. Damned good show, they'd have said, lowering another pink gin. And they would have been absolutely wrong.

To see why, let's backtrack to 1964–5. From that point to 1971–2 Beecham's was a model not only of goodness but of consistency. Profits before tax more than trebled; earnings per share also trebled; true, the percentage return on capital declined over the period from 45 via a 49·7 peak to 40·8 – but at the latter point it was still marvellous by most industrial standards, British or United States. The lowest annual increase in earnings per share was 11 per cent in the third year of the series. The highest was 23 per cent in the sixth and penultimate year. Performance, in fact, tended to get better with time, mainly because of the last of Leslie Lazell's master-strokes – the profits that poured in from his decision to concentrate research on fermentation chemistry, which eventually produced his phenomenally rich family of synthetic penicillins.

In the four years from the 1965 fiscal year earnings per share had risen by 73 per cent; in the four years from 1968 the increase was 89 per cent. But (and this is the peculiar and critical point) the share price moved in a completely different way.

From 1964 the four-year high-to-high performance was a 207 per cent gain; from 1969 to 1972 the score was 41 per cent. There is no rational explanation for this, even with hindsight. It can't be argued that investors sensed that miracle-drug wonders were about to be worked, and jumped off the gravy train as soon as the good news came through into the profits. The strange behaviour of the share price hinged entirely on the matter of the status of the shares – which is where the story began, with Beecham's selling at a multiple of 30 in July 1968. Suppose that Beecham's had never sold above, or below, a multiple of 18 over the entire seven years. The share price would still have trebled over the period (because the earnings did), but it would have taken far longer for the peaks to be reached. For instance the 1968 high of 241·6p would have been delayed until 1971. This means that money placed on the Beecham's bet until 1968 was anticipating something like three years of further exceptional growth. Whether the bet was wise, therefore, depended on whether, three years on, punters would still think it worth their while to discount three whole years of future advance. They didn't. The nearest the multiple ever came to that lofty figure of 30 in any subsequent July (that being the month when Beecham's files its annual reports) was in 1971, when it hit 25. Even at a multiple of 18, this share had been well ahead of the market. But for most of the latter years in the period of its shining and accelerating business success the stock was anything up to twice as expensive as the average counter.

That explains the phenomenon of its falling rate of capital gain. The multiple consequently edged downwards until in mid-1973 the share was selling at barely above the pack – and that was before (but no doubt contributory to) the Great Crumple.

Over time, in summary, all stocks regress or progress towards the norm. Thus Xerox, thus Beecham's. Inherited intelligence does much the same thing; possibly this is merely the expression of some natural law. If the investor buys above the norm, on this evidence, it follows that the most important activity he can pursue thereafter is to look out for the first sign of regression – and get out. If he is buying below the norm, however, then sooner or later, all other things (like actually earning some profits) being equal, he can confidently expect an upward progression, irrespective of the market's general behaviour.

The law of prime long-term growth is therefore no law at all, having about the same relevance to reality as Adolf Hitler's theory about Aryan superman. 'Prime long-term growth' is an abstraction, one of the competitive and contradictory stock-market theories which are apt to send the contemplative soul into total withdrawal – a state characterized by observations like: 'I buy stocks because I think they are going to rise, and I sell them because I think it's time to do so, but I don't know why I do either.' Such simplicity, however, has been turned into complex fortunes, not least by one firm of London stockjobbers which never took a view of its wares at all: the partners moved the prices of stocks up and down simply on the basis of money on the table, closed their books every night, and went home to dream peacefully, not of the millions they were going to make, but of those they had actually realized.

Beecham's and Xerox were never worth more than one thing: not what people *would* pay for them in the future, but what they were willing to pay in the here and now. If they are paying a great deal today, in the sense that the shares are priced way above the market, then it is all the gold in Fort Knox (that's assuming there is any left) against a set of dental fillings that in the none too distant future they will find that other investors are only willing to pay all too little for exactly the same piece of desirable stock-exchange property.

Part II. The basic lies

5. The hedge against inflation

All investment is a would-be hedge against inflation. That is, no investor puts money anywhere more sophisticated than a piggy-bank, whether it be a wonder stock like those dissected in the previous chapter or a mere interest-bearing deposit, unless he believes that he will regain his capital intact and earn a palpable return thereon. The belief may be too fond – in fact some distressed investors stuff their all into mattresses under the remarkable illusion that dollar bills or pound notes or franc *billets* still keep their value. Nevertheless, that is the true name of the investment game: the preservation and enhancement of capital.

The theory of natural interest fleshes out this definition. According to this plausible hypothesis, there is a 'natural' rate of interest, as natural, indeed, as the fact that two parts of hydrogen to one of oxygen create water. This natural rate appears to oscillate round 3 per cent (the hypothesis is based simply on the observation that over the centuries people have generally been prepared to accept this rate on their money). Any interest above the 3 per cent water line therefore contains a useful element of protection against the declining value of money. It follows that the faster money is depreciating, the higher interest charges must be – otherwise the 'real' rate of interest (the face rate minus the rate of inflation) will fall below the 'natural' rate of 3 per cent.

Plainly, the more devastating the pace of the cost-of-living rise (which is the reciprocal, or reverse side, of the fall in the value of money), the harder it is for interest rates to stay in the race. With a 20 per cent escalation in living costs, investors should in crude theory demand a 23 per cent return.

But if industry has to pay 23 per cent on its borrowed funds, what prices must companies charge to keep profits ahead of their borrowing costs? In the severe reality of economic life, sky-high interest costs act as a potent curb on the profits of everybody (except bankers) and as a mighty irritant to anybody, such as a home buyer, who needs to borrow cash. Hence there is an artificial barrier to the efforts of money to find its own level in terms of price. The consequence is that in times of rapid inflation investors as likely as not receive a *negative* return: their interest receipts are less than the amount by which inflation erodes their capital.

This was plainly happening to beleaguered Britons in the mid-1970s. Adding injury to insult, as the price of money in early 1975 came down to 15 per cent, the rate of inflation rose to 20 per cent – thus effectively lopping a twentieth off any funds deposited at fixed interest *before* tax. Anybody paying the top rate on investment income – an all-but-confiscatory 98 per cent – was losing almost a fifth of his capital without so much as a by-your-leave.

By the same token, or rather by its reverse, borrowers of the aforesaid funds are *paying* a negative rate of interest: they will actually have to repay, in real terms, less than they received – even with heavy interest charges thrown in.

You would therefore expect, in such circumstances, a stampede to borrow worthy of the California gold rush and a great, indeed an overwhelming, reluctance to lend. The true-life world doesn't behave like that, for reasons to be explained. But it is true that, when interest turns negative, savers do initially turn against lending: they cast about for some other home for their money, be it gold coins, like the Krugerrand, or goods like a new quadrophonic sound system, or debatable investments, like wolfram or antique silver.

In the good old days of the equity cult, however, there was no need to pursue exotica. The panacea for everyman was the common stock, the ordinary share, which was the only investment medium to contain (like the wonder ingredient in petrol or toothpaste) built-in protection against inflation. This was basically promoted on the argument that earnings and dividends in industry were free to rise in response to economic forces, including the attacks of inflation, while fixed interest was just that – fixed at whatever rate prevailed at the time of purchase. You might not (almost certainly would not) be able to buy equities at a dividend yield which was the equivalent of the rate of inflation plus the natural rate of interest. But the capital-gains element as the stock advanced in value would more than offset the loss of income – and inflation plainly tended, or so people imagined, to make capital gains more likely.

In practice, events failed to work out so smoothly, even in the mind, let alone on the market. Turn the calendar on from the early 1960s, when the stock-market's faith in the efficacy of inflation was at its height, to the winter of 1972 when a Tory prime minister, Edward Heath, was wrestling in 10 Downing Street to achieve union co-operation in slowing down the cyclonic twists of the wage–price spiral. His predecessors had similarly wrestled with the union Satan. The two Harolds, Wilson and Macmillan, had won their days with the railwaymen by stressing, respectively, their parental ties with rail labour and (somewhat irrelevantly) the blood spilt at Pass-chendaele in the First World War. As Heath struggled in his turn, paradoxical repercussions took place back at Throgmorton Street, home of the London Stock Exchange. The market more or less obediently rose as the inflation talks made some worm-like progress, and fell down again as the worm encountered the next inevitable obstacle.

What was sauce for Edward Heath – a settlement that looked like checking the dread dragon of inflation – was apparently catmint for the market. On the other hand, if the talks collapsed in an orgy of wage claims, strike threats and price rises, the market would apparently collapse as well. Yet for adherents of the cult of equity, this could be construed only as extreme perversity.

Ever since the cult drove equity yields far below those on fixed-interest securities, the inflation argument for buying common stocks had waxed stronger by the year. Unlike (ugh!) government bonds or (almost as bad) savings deposits of various kinds, the shares were not only inflation-proof, so cultists argued, but doubly so. Profits would be inflated (as in practice they were) by exactly the same forces that pushed up the retail-price index; and also capital values (as house owners throughout the West discovered to their great delight) would often become inflated by even more than the general run of prices. The ordinary, common-or-garden shareholder thus had his income and price–earnings ratio protected on the one hand, and the asset base of his investment protected on the other.

On this argument, the London Stock Exchange was indulging in a fit of circular insanity. Whenever the chief trades-union spokes-man of the day, Vic Feather, uttered his soothing noises about wages in a voice full of molasses, shares rose. They should have fallen. Whenever more belligerent tribunes of the working man gave tongue, the market fell. It should have soared. Except that there is no connection between the behaviour of the market and the infla-

tion issue – or any other issue. Consider the New York Exchange
and its very similar gyrations over the war in Vietnam. At first sight
Wall Street's behaviour in 1972 made perfect sense. Peace talk set
the shares rising; disappointment dispatched them downwards. But
the war/peace issue had dogged Wall Street in one shape or another
ever since Potsdam. A decade earlier the question was whether or
not the cold war could be thawed: and there was once a massive
market sell-off based on fears that peace would devastate an
economy geared to a high level of defence spending.

That demonstration was followed, of course, by another collapse,
this time generated by wholly contradictory fears that a freezing spell
in the cold war would lead to hot exchanges of arms. In other words,
war scares and inflation operate just like the celebrated seventeenth-
century taxation device, Morton's Fork. You get caught either way:
damned if you do, damned if you don't.

The pattern of the stock-market, like that of any market, is truly
determined by the aggregate of a host of individual decisions, positive
and negative (the decision *not* to buy a share is no less significant
than a decision to buy). This market psychology always feeds off
itself: that is, the more people decide to sell, the greater the number
of pessimists, or bears, who join the unhappy throng. Some prevailing idea or preoccupation may well infect the air at the time (like
fears of inflation or hopes for peace in South-East Asia), and that
notion will undoubtedly affect some people. Even more certainly,
it will be seized upon by those whose job it is to read the entrails
of the market as an explanation of the latter's behaviour, *no matter
what that behaviour is.*

This analysis is thoroughly supported by the researches of Irwin
Friend and Marshall Blume of the Wharton School of Finance (USA).
Looking back over no less than four decades, they could find no evidence of any relation whatsoever between inflation and stock-market levels. There are times, true, when share prices rise as the cost
of living advances. But there are also times when the stock-market
inconveniently falls while retail prices advance at the gallop. Quoted
in *Business Week* in February 1975, Friend observed: 'The stock
market never has been an inflation hedge, and over the past eight
years, it has been an utter disaster.' He comes up with an explanation, which is that high inflation increases both uncertainty and risk,
which is bad for business. You could equally well argue that high
interest charges (which, as noted, invariably accompany high

inflation) not only raise the financial overheads of business, but by lifting the 'opportunity cost' level (that is, the value of an alternative investment) reduce the rate and number of new ventures.

There are other fundamentalist arguments. A Harvard man, John Lintner, maintains that there is good and bad inflation, from the market's point of view. In good, or early, inflation, companies are able to raise prices faster than they incur increased costs. Then, since one man's price rises are another man's higher costs, profit margins come under pressure. Still worse, they enter a third stage, in which phoney profits made on inventories play a bigger and bigger role in reported profits – but the companies must still pay taxes on these phantom gains.

In addition, depreciation charged on historical cost of plant and machinery becomes unrealistic as replacement prices soar, while needs for working capital are inflated, even though the physical volume of turnover may not have changed. So firms get strapped for cash, and their profits suffer accordingly as the managements try to raise the funds at a time of high interest charges.

These explanations are clever and sound, but somewhat beside the point. In the Great Crumple it made no difference whether profits went on rising, or whether or not borrowings increased. The shares still got clobbered. Nor was this because the X-ray sensitivity of the stock-market's collective unconscious had pierced through the veil of phoney profits to the uncomfortable reality beneath. The truth of the matter is that, during the cult years, profits had always contained large fictitious elements; but the most transparently misleading element of all had been sedulously ignored on all sides. This was the fact that £1 million or $1 million of profit reported in 1973 was not the same amount, by any manner of means, as the same sum reported in 1963. Nor was either million worth the same amount as the same digits reported in 1953. Equities failed to provide a hedge against inflation, in other words, because earnings were eroded, like all other money flows or cash hoards, by the declining purchasing power of currency. Anybody who bought equities to protect the real value of his capital must have presumed that the value of the earnings or the assets he was *currently* buying (as opposed to those that would be added later) would be at least maintained in real terms. But the boards of directors dutifully reported the shining achievements of every year in the unreal terms of depreciating money.

To take a case in point, no stock had a more devoted following of inflation-hedgers than International Business Machines – and few managements hedged more effectively. From 1968 to 1973 profits after tax ostensibly rose by 81 per cent, and earnings per share by three-quarters. But in that period United States prices were escalating by 4·8 per cent annually. The dollar of 1973 was worth 78·2 cents in the money of good old 1968. In those five years IBM had in truth grown by only half as much as appeared in the books – which means that the compound rate of growth had fallen (such being the malign magic of geometric progression in reverse) by *more* than half to a rather ordinary figure of around $6\frac{1}{2}$ per cent annually. This fall from grace might have given the most ardent equity cultist pause for thought. But remember that IBM was a high altar of the cult, far ahead of the typical shrine. In most other examples there was no real growth in earnings worth discussing, in which case it was difficult to argue that the underlying assets (since they had produced no increase in real values) had appreciated to any real extent.

Investors in a company which exactly kept pace with inflation (if stock prices had reflected exactly the movement of assets and earnings) would have got back exactly what they had put in: no more, no less. Their return would thus have been confined to their dividends – which for supposed growth stocks were very much lower than the yields available on fixed interest. Even that might have been tolerable, assuming that the gap in yields was less than the erosion in the capital value of the fixed-interest investment. On the one hand, say, you put $100 into a bond and get back the post-inflation equivalent of $80 (that's a fifth lopped off) plus $10 of interest. That $90 is a conspicuously worse deal than placing $100 in equities, and getting back $100 plus $5 of dividends (and that's without taking differential rates of tax as between dividends and capital gains into account). But all too many stocks recorded *negative* growth – that is, their earnings failed to rise by as much as retail prices, either over the whole postwar period, or over selected periods (and it is only a selected period, that between the purchase and sale of a share, that interests the investor).

Thus the earnings of the Ford Motor Company were no higher in 1968, in inflated money terms, than in 1956. The increase in their money value, again, was negligible in 1971. Even after a strong surge, the Ford profits in 1973 were only 30 per cent higher than eight years before – which was hardly the kind of behaviour to which Henry Ford I was accustomed.

The reality of profits becomes even dimmer if allowance is made for the various gimmicks, devices and deceits which corporate leaders adopted for the purpose of making their inflation-boosted profits seem higher still. Cynics have not missed the significance of industry's upsurge of interest in 'inflation accounting', which seeks to *reduce* reported profits by removing inflationary elements, at precisely the time when the stock-market ceased to have any interest in earnings per share – good, bad, indifferent or superb.

When earnings ceased to count, in market terms, managements grew more interested in money inside, as opposed to outside, the business. They promptly turned to ways, which had always been open to them in the glorious, cultist past, of reducing their taxation. The most remarkable illustration of this belated conversion was the big 1973 switch from FIFO (first-in-first-out) to LIFO (last-in-first-out). In 1955 only one American major company in three valued its inventory on a last-in-first-out basis. By 1972 the proportion was lower still: only a quarter of the major companies used this method. The technicalities will be examined more closely when we come to study the cult of earnings in chapter 24. But because LIFO values the cost of stocks used in sales at higher prices, profits decline in inflationary periods, which means in turn, other things being equal, that the tax bill will fall.

As the cash squeeze tightened in 1973, companies like Du Pont and Firestone proceeded to spot the error of their long-established ways. By moving over to LIFO, Du Pont (which actually enjoyed a reputation for conservative accounting beforehand) slashed its first half-year earnings per share by a mighty 19 per cent. Gains in cash flow, because of the lower tax bill, were also mighty, however – the Firestone tyre firm, for instance, improved its cash flow by a projected $46 million in 1974 by a similar change. Now did these giants of United States capitalism previously stick with FIFO (some had even switched to it) because they were unfortunately ignorant of LIFO's advantages? Or were they less interested in cash flow than in showing high earnings, on which the value of their shares and their stock options could be based? The least cynical of men can pick the right answer.

No doubt much the same factors explained the sudden uprising of interest in new-fangled ways of accounting that would, by taking account of inflation in more subtle ways than LIFO, serve the same purpose of reducing profits and taxes—which would at least be useful arguments to persuade politicians that business was not, whatever the appearances, turning a decent (as opposed to an honest) penny.

So successfully did the Confederation of British Industry press this line in late 1974 that the pink-blooded Socialist government of the day forked out £3000 million of tax relief. The same industrialists, without pausing for breath, were simultaneously pouring scorn on the stock-market for its insistence on valuing their shares at rock-bottom prices.

But if it were true that, on proper inflation-accounting principles, British business was earning little or no money, British investors could not be blamed for shunning the Stock Exchange like a plague spot. Nor had managements in earlier times rushed to warn shareholders that profits were not as large and lovable as they seemed. In fact Philips Electrical, the manufacturing pride of Holland, was considered to be a Netherlandish eccentric for its insistence on valuing stock at replacement cost and calculating depreciation on the same basis. The technical arguments which rage over this method and its rivals, however, are both abstruse and irrelevant. They ignore the fact that all accounting, inflation or conventional, in any case rests on convenient fictions.

Depreciation itself is nothing more than a method of avoiding tax. Nobody pretends that the depreciation money is actually set aside in a little tin box exclusively for the replacement of beat-up machinery. Nobody pretends, either, that the standard formulae for depreciation bear any relation to the actual life of individual plant. It's just an accepted convention designed to allow, in a rough and ready manner, enough untaxed money to accumulate for the replenishment of capital. If the depreciation percentage were charged on replacement cost, the untaxed funds would be much greater—even though there is no logical case for giving tax relief on a hypothetical value. It's the new machine which is going to cost more, not the old.

By the same token, any scheme which postulates that stocks which have doubled, trebled or quadrupled in value since purchase have actually not augmented the company's wealth at all is taking the fictions of accountancy into the realms of dreamland. And bad-dream land is where equity investors, contemplating the evaporation of profits which were once there, along with the disappearance of earnings whose infallible appreciation in step with inflation was supposed to justify the possession of equities, must think they are.

A 19 per cent fall in earnings like Du Pont's is not, after all, much of a hedge against inflation, or against anything else. Inflation *per se* never had any connection with the case for equities. It was merely one of the sales pitches; it turned out to be the most disastrous, and it is an argument which may safely be ignored in future investment policy. What investors won on the inflationary swings, which was much less than it seemed, was wiped out on the inflationary roundabouts. Far from resisting the pressures of inflation, the securities industry, or the peddlers of common stocks, as we are about to see, gave the garotte its final twist.

6. Our word is our bond

'Our word is our bond' *(dictum verbum pactum)*: so runs the noble motto of the London Stock Exchange, and so it is. Ring up your nearest and dearest stockbroker, request him to buy or sell a security, and you truly can trust him (more or less) to obtain the best price going, and to carry out your instructions to the letter (or thereabouts). It is a small daily miracle of commerce, no more than typical of the way in which the City of London hopes to go about its business.

The system has its breakdowns, of course, especially if the client's word is less binding than the City's. The fine old bullion firm of Johnson Matthey innocently took imposing buying orders for silver from a less innocent gentleman domiciled in Switzerland, and found itself holding an almost fatally expensive baby when the customer, his gamble having misfired, declined to take delivery. But in stock-markets and commodity-markets alike, public and purveyors in both hemispheres have gone about their business secure in the faith that pieces of paper mean what is printed, typed or scribbled on them, and that the promises on promissory notes of all varieties will be duly kept. The wicked exceptions have mostly proved a rule which is the indispensable foundation of commercial and, above all, financial life. The odd unveiled stockbroker has been discovered using clients' stocks as collateral for his own, generally inept, borrowing, which is criminal as well as dishonourable. Peccadilloes and peculations can occur as easily in brokerage houses and banking parlours as in any other localities through which tempting streams of money flow. But most of the blows which fate visited on brokers' clients were the result of sloppiness rather than fraud.

Unable to cope with the mountains of paperwork which the Great Bubble created, Wall Street fell so far behind the transactions which its publicity had avidly encouraged that a new style of business disaster appeared. Overworked back offices stretched thin management resources beyond the snapping point. The amazing grace is that only $500 million of securities were mislaid as the worst-snarled brokerage houses stumbled towards bankruptcy. Still, the back-office Golgotha should have served to remind customers that leaving share certificates with a broker is not quite the same secure step as depositing cash in the bank. The conditioning of investors by the possession and relative security of bank accounts goes far towards explaining the readiness of the investing public to leave its wealth in the care of persons unknown. And that, like trust in pieces of paper, is another structural foundation of the financial world.

After the seismic shocks of slamming bank doors in the First Great Crash, decades have indeed passed with no more than minor (or apparently minor) flurries in the banking system. Governments have grasped the central notion that the depositor is sacred. So long as he knows that, come what may, his funds will be forthcoming, the depositor won't join a stampede for cash – and a run on the banks of thirties' dimensions will be impossible.

Even gross failures like that of the Franklin National on Long Island have been absorbed in the interests of the sacred depositor. When the Franklin was brought down by its own over-aggressive management, culminating in foreign-exchange losses on a monumental scale, its peers and superiors in the world of the United States banker co-operated in the clear-up with evident reluctance. But the central bankers of the Federal Reserve were still able to ensure that the depositors were not bilked.

Unfortunately, the apparent safety of the banks has helped to lull investors into a false sense of security about all variations of parting with cash in exchange for less-guaranteed paper. The very act of soliciting money, paradoxically, seemed to confer a measure of respectability, just as asking bankers for an enormous loan automatically and perversely stamps the would-be borrower as a man of substance.

Suspicious financial journalists find it perennially hard to convince the public not to place funds with dreadful little outfits whose high interest rates alone are the red flag of danger. Beyond-the-fringe operators need make no special effort to attract deposits which, on the evidence of the recent past, will eventually be lost without trace. The treasurers of great corporations took precisely this risk, depositing huge sums with banks of small reputation, for precisely the same reason – a tempting offer of high interest – in the London of the early seventies. The wages of their greed, too, were loss. Nor did many investors lower down the scale understand that some monetary homes-from-home, while of adequate respectability, offered less security than the Establishment banks. This applied to homes of long-term investment as well as short-term. At least the banks would always give the customers their money back: a dollar for a dollar, a pound for a pound. Not so the insurance companies – as British policy-holders learnt with acute pain in the aftermath of the Great Crumple. This shattering event persuaded some life-assurance houses to reduce the surrender value of their policies. Thus some worthy citizen who had paid £42 of premiums to one company over three years was politely and unilaterally informed that, should he now wish to abandon the enterprise, the insurers would henceforward return precisely £6. Until this remarkable change, the same customer would have received a scarcely more handsome return: just £16 of his £42 would have come home.

The honest fellows made much play of the fact that this reduction was the first cut in surrender values for forty years. That sounded almost reassuring, until 40 was subtracted from 1975. The subtraction took the customer back to 1935, deep in the middle of the Depression. The insurers, having then reduced their surrender payments to take account of the worldwide slump in investments, were now congratulating themselves on making no more savage attacks on their policy-holders' purses in four decades of largely lucrative stock-markets.

But the men who sell insurance with such well-known assurance have always been careful to hedge round their promises with cautions. Since no customers were given any guarantee about surrender values of any size, they could hardly complain when those values were reduced, now could they? (Plainly a large number of the insured had mighty cause for complaint: policy surrenders in 1973 totalled £283 million, which wasn't far off the £327 million paid out on maturing policies.)

As for the other variable element of British life policies, the bonuses paid on the type of investment known as 'with profits', the insurers were always most careful to remind policy-holders that the bonus payments made in the past might not be repeated in the future. Few investors took much notice of the warnings. Few, anyway, even understood the working of the bonus system, which is approximately as clear as the Book of Revelation.

The low surrender values and uncertain yields of the insurance policy helped to open the door to practitioners who offered the same goods in a different, neater package. The unit trust or mutual fund is only an extension of the investment idea from which the insurance industry has made untold thousands of millions down the years. In both cases the fund managers place money belonging to the public in investments of the manager's own choice, charging the public not only for the managerial services, but for the richly nourishing commissions paid to the salesmen who rope in the customers. In the trust case, however, the investor has a substantial advantage. He can take out his money (or what's left after paying the above, often extortionate, charges) at any moment of his choice. He can also learn to the last decimal point what his investment is worth at any time. When enterprising operators in Britain cutely linked unit-trust offerings with life-insurance cover, the drawbacks of traditional insurance were still more nakedly exposed. Alas, the operators couldn't leave well and wealthy enough alone. They, too, veiled their promises in warnings. But their advertisements belied the caution. Graphs of the past performance of their precious funds showed lines shooting up as near to the vertical as geometric decency would allow. Often the simple trick of compressing the scale of the graph was pressed into service. Claims were couched in most incautious ways. '£50 or more to invest?' asked one advertisement. 'WORK your money – earn over 12% p.a. gross for as long as *you* like.'

The units concerned, as the *Observer* pointed out, were being offered at 13p, almost *half* the price at which they had been launched into the world over a decade ago. Somewhere in the small print investors were reminded that 'income can go up as well as down', which contrasted oddly with the promise of an everlasting 12 per cent. Yet this particular piece of persiflage was almost modest compared to the enthusiasm with which salesmen gilded lilies (and weeds) in the boom years.

At their best, or worst, the trusted trustmen had no scruples about dodges like cunningly selective choices of starting date. You couldn't blame an investor – even one of above-average perception – for supposing that an advertisement stating that 142 per cent growth had been achieved in seven years was factually correct, or even for succumbing to the implied promise that 142 per cent would be his, too, for the asking in the next seven years. In the first instance research was needed to establish whether or not the 142 per cent growth curve's bottom end had been conveniently located in the depths of a bear-market patch. In the second instance, the investor's own desire for 142 per cent of new wealth outweighed the knowledge that birds in the bush don't always stay there.

Among the more skilled bird-in-the-bush practitioners was Investors Overseas Services. The Dover Plan run by its British offshoot was subject to bracketing crossfire from local journalists, who objected, among other things, to its claims of past performance. As it happened, this was a legitimate section of the IOS operation, closely scrutinized by the Board of Trade, but as prone as the rest of the hard-selling IOS stormtroops to exaggerate past performance regularly, and as regularly to present the exaggerated past as a sure guide to the paradisaical future.

When actual performance became so poor that the illusion could no longer be worked, IOS turned to phantom figures – such as the notorious valuation of Alaskan land holdings at many times the purchase price on the strength of the sale of a fraction of those holdings to an intimately interested third party. This was only an advanced and conspicuous form of a species of share-pushing which followed inevitably from the axiom that the performance is the promise.

Other high performers and lofty promisers went in for eccentricities like 'letter stock', whose prime advantage lay in escaping the scrutiny of the Securities and Exchange Commission. Still others fell for stories taller than the Empire State Building – like the British fund operator who placed excessive loads of his investors' loot into a palpably non-existent Californian gold mine. The name of this fund was appropriately Surinvest: appropriately because the selling pitch of the funds always lay in surety, in the promise that you could be safe, secure, sure – and rich.

The requirement for fast bucks, however, obviated the possibility of security. The situation is illustrated in reverse by an absolutely secure investment – the mortgate-based activities of building societies in Britain or savings and loan outfits in the United States. The money placed by building-society investors is lent on solely for the purchase of homes by citizens whose financial worthiness is attested before the loan is made. The society is doubly secure: secured by the financial standing of the borrower, and protected by its mortgage on the property itself. Compared to these standards, any unit trust or mutual fund, since it had no base in real values, was insecurity itself. That description applied equally to the mutual property investments which staged the last and briefest swelling of the Big Bubble. Performance in equity markets had become progressively more difficult to achieve. But commercial property was seemingly advancing without let or hindrance. (Literally without let: many buildings were sold more than once, each time at a luscious profit, before they had ever found tenants.)

A variety of hucksters, ranging from sober and sedate City of London institutions to dubious Latins and denizens of the Bronx, sold stakes in property on the mutual principle. Any such fund owned choice properties all over Manhattan, or London, or England, or the globe, and the investors, so complete was their conditioning, took the operators' word for it when the latter alleged that such-and-such a skyscraper was worth $40 million, having been bought for a mere $25 million.

Each share in the fund represented a share in the hypothetical values of the properties. The greater the pressure on the fund to sell, however, the more hypothetical the value became. Not only were investors trusting that past appreciation in property values would continue unabated, they were trusting that the promoters would value these baubles conservatively, and (most important of all) that their fellow-investors would never force a sale of the assets by demanding more of their cash than the fund could conveniently repay.

The collapse of offshore operations like Gramco and the Real Estate Fund of America was inevitable in the wake of the IOS crash, as other offshore investors scrambled to get back to the safety of land. The true betrayal, however, did not lie in the fraudulence which was endemic, even inherent, in the offshore operations: after all, even building societies in Britain and savings and loans in the States had known their occasional illicit thrills. The betrayers were rather those, onshore as well as off, upright as well as crooked, who persisted in assuring the public, directly and indirectly, that investors could simultaneously enjoy great safety and high profit.

One reason why trust which was generally deserved by the respectable was extended so easily to the disreputable was that the latter, to a significant extent, were in cahoots with the former. Every one of the fraudulent or quasi-fraudulent operations had trustees and bankers of impeccable pedigree, bearing and repute. The list of backers for the public offering of IOS stock reads like a Debrett of the investment-banking world. (No doubt their presence on that roll of honour has already been expunged from the race memory.)

Those members of the public who were reassured by the names of prestigious trustees almost certainly failed to understand that at best the name guaranteed solely that their money would be placed in investments after no more than a reasonable delay, and that those investments actually existed. It by no means followed that the investments were either sage or sound – and the trustees had no fiduciary responsibility to assure themselves or anybody else that the money was being administered as scrupulously as (most of them) they invested the funds entrusted to their own loving care.

In much the same way, every balance sheet of a failed fund or busted company had been approved by some thoroughly distinguished firm of auditors. But their endorsement (as its weasel wording sometimes made deliberately unclear) extended only to confirming that the books were in accordance with the directors' statements, and that they did not conflict with reality – that reality being a most elastic concept. As the Great Crumple rumbled on, several firms of auditors in the United States were on the receiving end of lawsuits from shareholder plaintiffs arguing that in the cases concerned elasticity had been overdone. But in Britain, where corporate crashes were at least as numerous, every single auditor stayed safe behind the smokescreen of words and conventions which afforded them fees without undue responsibility.

The accountants could, it is true, point the finger at other establishments whose supervision was lax to the point of looseness. The best-established financial institution of all, the Bank of England, was fundamentally responsible for the burnt fingers of those treasurers who, as mentioned above, fell for the high interest rates offered by fringe or secondary banks. The Bank had encouraged the flourishing of the fringe into a banking boom that showered funds into all manner of banking bubbles, mostly in property.

With uncanny skill, the Crown Agents, an Establishment outfit which administers funds belonging to overseas governments and institutions, managed to back seemingly all the duff investments given the green light by the Bank. That fiasco cost the British taxpayer £85 million, just for starters, when an embarrassed government was forced to send out the lifeboats. Her Majesty's government's failure to supervise investments made under the very name of the Crown was perhaps the most staggering example of the extent to which standards of ordinary prudence, let alone probity, had dwindled as the Bubble swelled.

In the United States the supervising authorities must take their share of the odium. In the insurance industry not only Equity Funding but Standard Life Corporation might as well not have been supervised at all for the good that supervision did. By the time the Securities and Exchange Commission, the FBI and the United States attorneys got to the Standard offices, evidence had piled up (according to *Business Week*) of 'twiced-pledged collateral, computer fraud, executive self-dealing, forgeries, embezzlement, and stock manipulation'. A couple of thousand millions' worth of insurance policies were at stake in the Standard case. It emphasizes that, comforted by the excuse that no policing system can ever be perfect, the cops of the investment world rely greatly on the presumed integrity of its inhabitants: which is where we, and the investor, came in at the start of this chapter.

In the focal area of the Second Great Crash, the stock-market, the connection between integrity and protection is at its most imperfect. The exchanges are merely markets, where the law of *caveat emptor* applies with full rigour. The main exception is that if the failure of a member firm jeopardizes the holdings of its unhappy clients, the other members of the Exchange will collectively come to the rescue. (A principle that was strained to the point of cracking, if not beyond, by Wall Street's set of distinguished bankruptcies – the rescuers were in some cases in positions nearly as parlous as the rescued.)

Not surprisingly, the exchanges are less than fond of those who emphasize that *caveat emptor* is the central doctrine of their affairs. The London Stock Exchange worked itself into a rare lather when a BBC programme failed to present the market and its members in the all-wise, all-knowing and omni-competent light which they would have preferred. The Stock Exchange protested far too much. Stock-markets exist to enable people to trade their ownership interests – a perfectly desirable purpose, but that is all there is to the matter. The exchanges rarely fuel the engine of industry, as they like to pretend, by providing funds. At odd times, when interest rates are high and institutional funds are abundant, the stock-market serves to top up the equity funds of companies which are over-borrowed or otherwise strapped for cash. But Japan and West Germany manage to survive without any great use of the same facility. At most times, compared to the largesse distributed (at a price) by the banks, by governments (hardly ever for any price at all) and by shareholders in retained cash flow (at no price in any circumstances), the stock-market's money is a mere bucket in the ocean.

Like any commodity-market, stock exchanges create froth, speculation, false glamour, stupidities, phoney fortunes, opportunities for wrong-doing and being wrong-done and so on. But in the years of the Big Bubble, while protesting their virtue and utility, and even while imposing tighter rules on their members and on quoted companies (the London Exchange was well in advance of the government in demanding more information from firms), the exchanges were allowing murderous excesses to develop.

Old-fashioned *demi-monde* operations continued to flourish: this half-world included 'boiler-shops', which built up heads of steam under shares in which the stokers had a strong pecuniary interest, and the equally aptly named 'shell companies'. The technique here was to inject valuable assets into previously worthless stock-market counters. The device provided some of the fastest action around, although its only usefulness was to the sharp mechanics who grew to super-charged riches as a result. The grand old game of insider trading also exuberated into new ploys. In London an artisan with an effectively controlling interest in company A could bid for company B, in which his interest was no less effective. He thus not only knew when the bid was coming, but could actually fix the terms – and hence his profit.

With pranks like that in progress, and with share registers thick with nominee holdings that shrouded the true owner's identity as efficiently as numbered accounts in a Swiss bank, London's Stock Exchange powers-that-were could hardly lay claims to unsullied virtue. In truth the stock-market, on both sides of the Atlantic, played a pivotal role in the uprising of the fringe: a surge which, like the proliferation of some deadly fungus, proved poisonous to the whole system.

The rewards which accrued to the fringe were in themselves signs that something was rotten. At Triumph Investment Trust, a wonder bank which gurgled down the drain in 1974, the chairman was paid £59,000 in 1972 for achieving £67 million of turnover and £4·4 million of profit. Going rates at the time for an international manufacturing giant with over *nine* times the sales and profits were £43,341 for the top man. Two directors of the fringe bank, moreover, were paid twice as much as the chairman of Courtaulds, the textile empire whose pension fund, by a timely injection of cash a few years back, had started the fringe financiers on the road to Triumph and to failure.

Not only did the solid and respectable sit by while the fringe paid itself super-colossal salaries and other benefits, the Establishment went on nodding as the fringe augmented its income with every machination for making capital gains that ingenuity and ready access to other people's money could provide. Worse still, inordinate amounts of respectable money were funnelled into these undiscriminating receptacles. Almost to a man, London's fringe bankers borrowed short and lent long – the classic route to banking failure, because, if the loans are called in, the banker, having committed the money so far ahead, cannot realize enough cash to repay his depositors. Old-line bankers, who learnt the short and long rule along with their mothers' milk, connived at the destruction of the fringe by registering no protest at its excesses – and ended up, at the behest of the red-faced Bank of England, by footing a £1000 million bill as they were compelled to safeguard the sacred depositors of the fringe.

The most bizarre twist in the fringe's collapse lay in its attempt to exploit what, as noted above, is the insurance industry's most heinous breach of the investor's trust – the lack of guarantees. An invention called the guaranteed-income bond promised the investor a return which, in the light of interest rates at the time of their issue, looked safer than houses. But when interest rates unexpectedly rose higher still, the bond-holders (again exemplifying the rule that ordinary investors are a good deal smarter than the sharks suppose) began to switch in search of higher yields. The bond companies were consequently forced to realize investments at a loss in order to repay the departing holders. The parent companies of these foolish virgins in turn had to fill the gaping hole left by the forced sales – and as millions disappeared into these infinite depths, company after company followed in the same general direction.

Pity the poor investor in a world where the word 'guaranteed' turned out to be more dangerous than its opposite. Many of the unlucky ones who sought this particular refuge from inadequate returns in the established investment media were in effect robbed, and there was no one on whom they could vent their wrath. It was a crime of which everybody was innocent, but of which all were guilty: guilty of the offence of encouraging an acceptance of trust which wasn't worth the paper on which it *wasn't* written. Those who suffered, moreover, did not share the sin of avarice which afflicted the authors of the suffering. These victims wanted only a reasonable return on their money. For those who wanted more – who sought growth as well as the normal, age-old objectives of investment – still greater torments lay in store.

7. The growth deception

Since time immemorial investors have been interested in growth. They have viewed investment almost as a horticultural process: the money is planted in the earth and bears fruit in due season. Growth in the true farmer's sense of making two blades of corn sprout where one grew before is an easy enough concept to understand. But growth in the stock-market sense is undoubtedly a more complicated matter. For a start, is the investor possessed by growth of the company or of his own money invested therein? To the straightforward, honest soul, it might seem that the two would invariably go hand-in-hand. But as we saw in chapter 4, there are several and savage exceptions to this rule. Even if it were true that great corporate growth unfailingly produced territorial advances in the company's stock, a big question would go begging: what does great growth, or any growth at all, mean for the corporation?

Dynamism in a company can be demonstrated in several different dimensions, not necessarily all at the same time. Assets can pile up; sales can multiply a thousandfold; profits can soar in gross total; or, divided by the number of shares in issue, profits can rise in terms of earnings per share; the number of employees can be aggrandized; the return on capital or on sales can be pushed, pulled or kicked upwards. All or any of these figures can be presented as a prize achievement, a mark of corporate splendour and progress. Yet plainly the goodness of a 200 per cent growth rate on any of these dimensions can vary according to cases – vary so much, indeed, that what is good in case 1 is downright disgraceful in case 2. This truth can be seen in all its nakedness in the tale of a company which in the Britain of the sixties was widely acclaimed as an example to all corporate sluggards – the paper-based giant, Reed International.

Its dynamic reputation reflected in part the evident dynamism of its boss, Sir Don Ryder, who as a result of his reputation, and for his pains, was tapped and ennobled by Harold Wilson's Labour government as the saviour of unregenerated British industry. In the cooling heat of the boom years, the future Lord Ryder advised his shareholders, in words that were echoed by contemporaries from San Diego to Stavanger: 'Growth is one of our main corporate objectives, and I do not think Reed can be chided for lack of it.' As a matter of accuracy, Reed could rather easily be chided on that very score, depending (again) on what you mean by growth. The resident human dynamo can't have been thinking of earnings per share, which at the time in question (1972) were only a midge-bite higher than in 1969–70, when a pound note had been a distinctly more valuable piece of engraved paper. Compared with five years still further back, alas, Reed was actually 18·4 per cent down on this particular sterling statistic.

After several years of hard and dedicated slogging, Reed had, it is true, carried its pre-tax profits 55 per cent above the 1966 figure. But the value of money had dropped by 28 per cent in the intervening period – and that rise in profit by just over one half looks even less impressive compared to the increase in sales, which had fully doubled: 136 per cent, higher, no less. There, in the turnover figures, lay the indisputable growth, along with that of capital employed, pushed up by 81 per cent over the same heady period.

In 1970, however, Reed, like some business Oedipus, had married its own corporate mother. The International Publishing Corporation, the Jocasta of this real-life drama, and then the largest holder of Reed shares, boasted £167 million of sales and liked to describe itself as the largest publishing group in Europe. In the past Mother had proved perfectly capable of earning great profits: equal to fully half Reed's total, for instance, in the financial year which excited Ryder's prose poem to growth.

Growth by acquisition is growth of a kind, without doubt. But (to get back on the farm) is the farmer who makes two ears of corn sprout instead of one truly worth no more than the man who doubles up purely by buying the farm next door? The problem can be posed in corporate as well as agrarian terms. Which of the following two companies deserves the growth prize? Company A, with no acquisitions of much significance, increases its sales in four years by a quarter, its capital employed by 11 per cent, but its profits by a truly remarkable 371 per cent. Company B, on the other hand, boosts its sales by 412 per cent, its capital by 385 per cent, and its profits by 255 per cent: in other words, both profit margins and return on capital decline. Surely any holding-company chairman, any controlling investor, any common man or woman with a mite in the business, would value company A's growth performance and its management far above company B?

The mysterious A and B happen to be one and the same firm, both before and into its acquisitive phase: Britain's General Electric Company, on the way to becoming a multi-million-pound Euro-giant. The stock-market, as events turned out, made the appropriate judgement on A and B. In summer 1972 GEC shares lay lower than in 1968, before the somnolent giant Associated Electrical Industries was swallowed up and before the not quite so dozy English Electric was driven into the fold. A modest £1000 inheritance deposited into GEC at the peak in 1964 would have been worth £3702 at one point four years later. Left alone, the nest-egg would thereafter have dwindled mildly in cash terms and quite severely in purchasing power. In contrast, anybody who had arrived on GEC's ground floor would have seen £1000 climb to £16,000 in a few enchanting years as the group was hauled from near-bankruptcy into riches.

That 16 times capital appreciation is one real and wholly delight-ful form of growth – even though it is not a direct measure of management. That is the nub. There are evidently two kinds of expansion: shareholders' growth, shown by our GEC example in its company A phase; and managers' growth, as in the company B period – which is also the kind which Lord Ryder, to revert to his case, can't be chided for lacking at Reed.

Type A growth is characterized by super-charged increase in the returns from available assets; type B growth by an expansion in the assets themselves. Real growth in management is concerned with the relationship between these two types: about how to use the new resources created by organic growth to purchase new assets (through amalgamation or otherwise); about how far to finance type B growth by raising more money, through borrowings or issues of new shares (as, in effect, happens in most takeovers – the company is employing its shares instead of cash); about the optimum balance between the two types of growth; about how much type B expansion can be undertaken without weakening, by dilution of management effort and of the earnings themselves, the essential type A base.

These are all areas in which wrong decisions can easily be taken. From such false ideas wrong deeds automatically follow, whereupon the stock-market collectively refuses to turn thumbs up, or (worse still) turns them decisively down. It follows that the investor is wildly uninterested in managers' growth for its own sake. Consequently all the effort expended by stock-market experts upon fundamental analysis, replete with five-year forecasts of everything from cash flow and capital expenditure to earnings per share and dividend payout, is largely beside the point.

All these figures, anyway, will be calculated in depreciating currencies, unless world economic affairs begin to deviate substantially from their postwar norms. Thus the birds in the bush will be worth considerably less in terms of purchasing power than the one in the hand, even if the management promises are not belied by events. The shareholder is, in fact, interested in only one corporate statistic: the real, non-inflationary increase in the value of his piece of paper between the moment of purchase and the hour when he either values the holding or (a still more categorical act) disposes of the same. At least that is the theory of the investor's true interest. The practice is more than somewhat different, because the investor has the charming but unhelpful habit of forgetting or ignoring what he really paid, or what he could actually receive on disposal. Theory holds that the investor is always alert to the fate of his capital at the hands of others. Experience shows that the majority of shareholders often exhibit total indifference to the maltreatment of their money at the hands of bumbling and fumbling men.

The shock suffered by investors in Consolidated Edison, when that supposedly rock-solid security failed to pay a dividend, was all the greater because of their previous failure to take note of the mounting evidence that all was not well in the conduct of the great utility's affairs. Nothing short of such a cataclysm will shake the faith of the investor committed to a national institution. If you hold Du Pont stock and have seen no increase in your quarterly dividend from 1966, when it touches an annual figure of $6, to 1974, when it is still only $5·50, you still almost certainly never cease for a minute to feel the deepest sense of loyalty and gratitude to the providers of this diminishing lucre.

Reality is often a painful subject for human beings, and since investment (or the disposal of money) is among the most sensitive of human processes, its practitioners are often addicted, if not to flights of fancy, at least to flights from uncomfortable truths. Thus, in one imbroglio of the tangled seventies, a writer declared trenchantly that one thing that must 'have impressed itself on shareholders' minds is the share price... those who were in during the early years did wonderfully well, but the price has never reached more than half its 1969 peak'. The aforesaid shareholders promptly proved him wrong by flocking as one man to the side of the management in and under question.

With respect, as British politicians always say when they want to be revoltingly rude to their opponents, it's doubtful whether many of the individual shareholders had anything impressed on their minds by the behaviour of the share price. Most probably felt a) that the company's growth (which was indisputable) had continued to serve them well, despite the calamities since 1969; and b) that, even if it were true that the wonders had ceased since then, the miracles of the future would be equally electrifying, thanks to the management genius which had served them so wonderfully well in the now remote past.

The reason for such illogical attachments to anti-growth investments (as the above exhibit must have been for most investors at the time of the quotation) is self-evident. Any other stance would have forced the holders to recognize that, if they had held the shares before 1969, they should have sold them in that year, while if they had bought the objects later, at any price above the dismal levels plumbed during the imbroglio, they should not have done so. The man or woman stuck in a 'growth' investment which has grown in reverse is being asked to confess that he has been a fool – and, which is much worse, a fool with his or her money.

Money evokes deep and potent psychological associations, which for all anyone knows (there are many too many speculations on the point) may stem back to early memories of being breast-fed, or not being breast-fed. What is certain, however, is that the subject easily provokes an emotionally derived confusion in the minds of otherwise well-balanced and incisively intelligent people. Sensibility rather than sense rules in these matters, and it is an affront to the sensibility to admit to a mistake about money.

The big talk about growth is only a euphemism about money, and the word 'growth' can also serve very conveniently to screen the investor from his monetary mishaps. The growth deception works in several ways. It explains, for example, the paradox of the inflated portfolio: a manifestation which is common during any period of riotous stock rises, such as the more globular years of the Big Bubble. In those swollen days, almost any investor asked about his results was liable to trot out a gorgeous litany of capital gains. When added together, however, the golden gains almost invariably totted up to a more modest tally than the string of triumphs led either listener or speaker to believe. Like a mother's ear tuned to screen out all sounds save her baby's cries, the investor's memory blanks out his failures and records only his triumphs. This knack, along with a tendency to forget about small but expensive matters like dealing costs, is the key to the paradox.

But a more profound riddle lies behind these lesser deceptions. This resides in the clear fact that investment triumphs for the growth-minded investor so often have nothing to do with the pursuit of growth in the corporate sense. For every investor who owes his capital appreciation to the identification of a long-term growth trend in one of the standard corporate measures discussed earlier – profits, earnings per share, sales or whatever – there are many more who have profited from chance bonanzas, sometimes even of a *non-growth* variety.

This possibly puzzling observation can be illustrated by the case of a private investor who works in a university department of economics. Let us call him Mr Pareto, after the never-to-be-forgotten Italian economist who discovered the law of the significant few and the irrelevant many (which lays down roughly that 20 per cent of everything that any of us do yields 80 per cent of all the benefits we derive). Our Mr Pareto reckoned that he was 'in a better position than the average investor to interpret economic information', and he had in fact achieved a 50 per cent capital gain in not much more than five months – at a time when a 5 per cent uplift might have been considered exceptional.

Of what did this informed portfolio consist? There were three investments that may be styled deadbeat, in the sense that they had brought home no bacon at all. One fair gainer was up 22·4 per cent. A parcel of gold shares had appreciated by 65 per cent. And a single industrial purchase had soared away from base by 237 per cent, no less. On the face of it, Mr Pareto had shown excellent judgement in at least one respect – gold stocks were among the outstanding investments of this particular epoch. Anybody who fancied Western Deep Levels in 1963, for example, could have picked them up for under £2. In 1973 the same shares were worth over five times as much, at £11, before proceeding to the greater glory still of over £22 in the following year. Compare this to the 1963–73 gain of

165 per cent on International Business Machines (and that is with dividends and every other IBM *douceur* thrown in), and gold shares win hands, feet and elbows down.

But goldmining shares do not square in any particular with orthodox growth theory. They might or might not report higher earnings. The specimen above all but quadrupled its net profits between 1964 and 1969; yet in 1970 the share price averaged only around twice the 1964 level. The bonanza of the seventies coincided with an increase in earnings of just about a third. The shares more than trebled in the same period in response, not to the corporate performance, but in orchestrated sympathy with the prospects for a rise in the gold price.

The case for these equities lay in the strong probability that the finance ministers and central bankers of the western world would so mismanage international money as to cause a flight from depreciating paper currency into solid yellow metal. For those who (like both United States and British citizens at the material time) lacked legal access to gold itself, mining shares were the sole feasible substitute. But the indirect route into gold was the only attraction of the companies, which otherwise lacked any of the habitual characteristics of the cultist equity: no marketing, no hot-shot management, no dynamic strategies – just holes in the right parts of the earth.

Our economist investor, or Mr Pareto, can certainly claim professional credit for spotting that the under-valuation of gold was sure to lead to an upturn in gold shares. But setting aside the gold, turn for closer examination to the Pareto jewel – the industrial share which gained 3.4 times. This was a once-noted furniture manufacturer which, by dint of some epic mismanagement, had almost totally denuded itself of earnings some time before. A brand-new management team thereupon arrived on the scene, breathing fire, slaughter and noble resolutions. Within a couple of years the shares (on which the newcomers held healthy options) more than doubled. Flushed with this success, the new men thereupon proceeded to lose the best part of a cool million in the next two years, and the shares slid gracefully down to just above vanishing point. (As for the new management team, it disappeared without trace.) From this abysmal level, the shares staged the spectacular recovery from which Mr Pareto had benefited so magnificently. From any group of shares which have sunk to a few pence or cents, a few will rebound phenomenally. The snag is that, for every sparrow that becomes an eagle, several others become sparrow pie – and all the learning of all the books in all the libraries of all the economists cannot tell which sparrow will be which.

Just like gold shares, so-called recovery stocks, in which several individuals have achieved some of their most prized market coups, fail to fit the general profile of corporate or economic growth. But then, most growth companies don't fit the profile either. All the standard measures of managers' growth have one disadvantage or another from the shareholder's point of view. Expansion in sales is unlikely to be of any use unless accompanied by enlargement of net income. The same goes, emphatically, for any increases in assets or capital employed: not worth having, unless they go hand-in-hand with a genuine advance in net income. The latter augmentation, in turn, is of little avail, so any analyst would argue, unless accompanied by growth in earnings per share. An increase on the latter count, moreover, benefits nobody unless translated into a rise in the share price. A rise in the stock, to complete the round, is no good to man or beast, millionaire or collector of widows' mites, unless sustained long enough for the beneficiary to take his profit.

Finally, all these measures save the very last can be fiddled. Rises in net income or in earnings per share, in particular, are in the lap, not of the gods, but of the directors and their friendly auditors. That being so, the nature of real, true or genuine growth is shrouded in a fog reminiscent of the miasmas of Victorian London.

At the beginning of the seventies, when the Great Crumple was only a growing cloud on the horizon, my own magazine, *Management Today*, attempted an exercise which sought to clear away these mists. We looked at the biggest companies near to hand and tried to discern which had shown authentic as opposed to illusory growth. The exercise itself showed up many of the pitfalls which attend any effort to introduce scientific objectivity into these matters.

For an initial loophole, in comparing companies over any long period (1960–9 was taken), a grotesquely unfair advantage is given to firms which had a rotten year as the first of the series and prospered mightily in the last. The same difficulty applies in reverse – where the first year was magnificent and the last horrible, the afflicted company will suffer badly in any comparisons. In practice, such injustices are the exceptions rather than the rule. In most cases no company underwent manifest ill-treatment when tested by our definition of real growth: that the company should have increased its pre-tax profits by 176 per cent over the period – that is, doubling in real terms, after allowing for inflation. The return on shareholders' equity (meaning net income as a percentage of the capital which belonged to the investors) also had to be at least maintained from first to last. Growth, moreover, had to be reasonably consistent – that is, profits were allowed to fall or stagnate for only two years out of the nine under scrutiny. By no stretch of the imagination are these demanding criteria. But two-thirds of the companies examined had failed to double their profits in real terms, and 14 per cent weren't even earning as much in 1969 as they had done nine years before. Only sixteen firms, a 28 per cent handful of the companies surveyed, had passed the tests of consistency and profitability as well. Application of similar criteria produces similar results in any capitalist economy. In unreal terms, there is growth abundant from which to choose. In the real terms of constant money and continuous expansion, growth exemplars are few and depressingly far between, which points to an inescapable conclusion.

Investors in the sixties and early seventies were no wiser than the Lewis Carroll crew who engaged in the Hunting of the Snark. It wasn't their fault – we were all misled by the temper of the times. But we didn't in truth know what we were looking for, were led by people who knew just as little, and were likely to become sidetracked by extraneous considerations. Like the Snark-hunters, we followed the ringing of the Bellman's bell: it tolled for us.

The real growth, in shareholders' terms, did not lie in intelligent investment in properly identified corporate situations. It resided in successful speculation. Mr Pareto, the economist mentioned above, with his red-hot recovery stock and his gold stocks, was in with a better chance, not by virtue of his greater economic lore, but because he cared only for growth in his privy purse. This placed him in sharp and ultimately profitable contrast to the non-speculator who sought a steady, strongly upward growth trend in a company – but never properly identified the growth which he sought, and in any event stood to gain no personal advantage from the find.

It can't be repeated too often that the only growth which is meaningful to the investor – and this is the crux of the disillusion which caused the postwar equity boom to bust – is the increase in value between the purchase and disposal of the investment, or (which generally comes to the same thing) the rise in the investor's income from that investment over the period for which it is held. Even where there is real growth, it does not follow, as we have seen and shall see again, that the share price will reflect that reality faithfully or even to any degree whatsoever. Where the growth is unreal, reality will catch up in the only place it can, and in the place which hurts the investor most: the price of the stock

The investor hunting for growth is then even more closely akin to the pursuers of the Snark, who were warned of the dangers if their quarry turned out to be a Boojum. It did. And the finder 'softly and silently vanished away' – just like the capital of too many earnest and misdirected seekers after growth.

8. The built-in equity drag

Among the many services of *Fortune* magazine to the American corporate weal has been the annual publication of its roll of honour. This is the *Fortune* five hundred, a list of the magnificent and the mighty in United States industry, ranked by their sales and categorized by sundry other dimensions, ranging (in 1974) from General Motors of Detroit, with $35,798,289,000 of sales, to Avery Products of San Marino, California, whose $242,711,000 of turnover would have fitted into GM's pocket 147 times. A few years ago, however, *Fortune* added a column to its listings which undid much of its previous corporate benefaction. The offending tabulation was called 'total return to investors'. The concept, which had been employed by the counterpart British magazine, *Management Today*, since 1966, was to assess company growth by the gross return before tax to an investor, as measured by the capital gains and dividends received over the period.

The British exercise has demonstrated year after year that even in euphoric periods on the stock-market only a minority of big companies reward their shareholders with rates of return that justify the risks of equity investment. In bad years for stocks, the majority of equity investors have only pitiful yields to contemplate. But the *Fortune* reckoning was worse than pitiful in 1974: it was disastrous.

Among the top fifty of the corporate élite, the social register of big business, ten members in good standing had produced a negative return over the period from 1963. Their dividends over the years had failed to compensate for the drop, compared to ten years before, in their share prices. And this, remember, was in money terms, not in the more realistic language of post-inflation currency. Another eleven of the inner circle had failed to make the grade of a $3\frac{1}{2}$ per cent annual growth, which is just enough to double the investor's money after twenty years. Only a dozen members of the Hall of Sales Fame had achieved double-digit results for the stockholders since 1963. They were led by Atlantic Richfield, an oil company which had shot out out of nowhere to achieve a 17·52 per cent return. The venerable Eastman Kodak, the company largely ignored while all eyes were on Polaroid, had achieved 17·13 per cent to come in second.

Even a double-digit yield takes at least seven years to double a man's money. So four-fifths of the greatest of the great had failed an elementary test of investment. Sorriest of all, the crowned head of the industrial kingdom, General Motors, had returned to its stockholders, before tax and in depreciating currency, an annual figure of 0·3 per cent over the decade. At that rate an investor of 1963 in Detroit's finest would have been forced to wait until the year 2222 to double his dollars: and what will the dollar be worth then?

The issue is whether this extraordinary fact proves anything except that Wall Street, as everybody knows, staged a Second Great Crash. There is, as it happens, more to General Motors than meets the eye. Take any year in the seventies, and the decade's return from an investment in GM, while quite respectable, was never anything to drag investors away from savings bonds in a hurry. Was there some underlying force, heaving away in the waters of the market like the monster in Loch Ness, whose movements explain the phenomenon of 1974's Infinitesimal Total Return?

The answer is best approached through a parable. Imagine that you had advanced a needy friend a parcel of cash to develop his business: the manufacture and marketing of electronic crystal balls. He can't pay much in the way of interest right now, because the room for expansion in the shed at the bottom of his garden is limited. But he holds out the prospect of a gratifying rise with each upward step in his progress. As he advances first to his garage, then to a loft down the road, finally to an old rubber pants factory, and so on ever upwards, you will receive more and more – until eventually the yield on your original parcel of cash will top the highest interest rate that ever swam before the eyes of Arthur Burns and his boys at the Federal Reserve Board. Not a bad bargain, you might think, reclining in your garden chair and hearing the comforting noises of hard labour from the busy garage next door. There is, of course, a snake in your Eden. The dividends, as they rise, will attract increasing attention from the officials appointed by the State to deprive the well-meaning citizen of a goodly percentage of his take, whether the income be earned or unearned. But your crystal-gazing friend has thought of that, too.

His deal offers the prospect of capital gains, taxed at a lower rate, to offset the annoying depredations of the Revenue. He promises to repay the money at the same dividend yield as that at which you started. From that oath, you can derive some most alluring arithmetic. The starting yield was 2 per cent. If the friend's projections prove correct (and he is, after all, in the business of making crystal balls), the profits will increase by 20 per cent annually. This means that in approximately three and a half years your yield could be 4 per cent, and the price of buying you out will be double the original loan. Another forty-two months takes you to the seven-year pay-off. The yield will be 8 per cent, and the value four times that of the initial investment. Despite the doublings, the yield will still be far from dramatic, even by the standards of less usurious eras than the mid-seventies: an 8 per cent return before tax is strictly run-of-the-mill. But it's obviously worth putting up with meagre interest, especially *taxable* meagre interest, because of the earthly delight of the multiplier effect: every percentage point of extra interest being instantly translated into a 50 per cent rise in capital value.

All goes well in this parable: up to a point. The profits, certified by the friendly accountant who lives next door but one, rise by the promised 20 per cent with a regularity which speaks well of the product. But in the small print of the agreement you discover that your friend, while bound to raise the dividend, is under no obligation to match its growth to that of the profits. He doesn't want to lose your goodwill. He might need some more of your money one day. In any event, he has read about the suburban neighbour in Britain who, irritated by the family next door, filled its members with a supply of 22 bullets. So he keeps the dividend rising quite briskly – only, year after year it falls behind the growth in profits, until the compound rate of increase comes, not to 20 per cent, but 7 per cent.

You now face the unpleasant conclusion, which the accountant, who has a chunk of the same security, is only too unhappy to confirm, that instead of quadrupling your money in seven years, you will only double it in a decade. What seemed like a marvellous investment is no more than a dull drag – and you make one eternal vow: never again to place any of your hard-earned savings in such deceitful ventures.

A fanciful tale, this may seem, but it is stark reality. The whole account is an abstraction from real life, a rendering which encapsulates the concrete reason why the median return on *Fortune*'s five hundred fell from 10·12 per cent for the 1962–72 decade to almost half – 5·22 per cent – for the ten years 1963–73. Moving back across the Atlantic, it is a story whose progress can be picked up by the appearance in the *Sunday Times Business News* in the summer of 1973 of a list of 'consistent growth stocks out of favour'.

There were seventeen of these pearls. One of their most marked consistencies was that in all cases growth in dividends had lagged far behind the rise in earnings per share. In this respect they were in no way different from the investment in our parable. Over at staid old Arthur Guinness, which has kept the citizenry of Dublin supplied with excellent stout for many a long year, a 13·7 per cent rise in earnings stood against a 4·7 per cent advance in dividends. That was only par for the course. At a chain of garages injected with unlikely horse-power by a Harvard Business School graduate, Lex Services Group, the dividend growth was 19·4 per cent – an outstanding figure, except in comparison to the 52·8 per cent gain in earnings. Thus fact continued to imitate fiction.

The minimum figure qualifying these stocks for the 'consistent growth' label was 12·2 per cent annually. Of the seventeen, only three had achieved this rate of progress in dividends. In all cases, however, the stocks had been bought on infinitesimal yields in the expectation that the future increase, even if it only took the yield up into the minimal area, would be faithfully translated into capital gain by the magic multiplier.

The drawback is dual. In the first place, the multiplier may not be a constant, even though it was in our parable. The borrower in the story agreed that he would always buy back the security on the same basis of valuation. The market makes no such promise. You may always find a lower multiplier than you yourself paid being applied. It will be applied, what's more, to a lower dividend than you would have received had the profit growth been placed where your dividend cheque comes out.

This dual risk must exist even at times when interest rates are relatively stable. But when interest rates begin to embark on wider and wider, faster and faster swings, like an Olympic hammer-thrower limbering up, the risks become financially suicidal. The upward oscillations of interest rates in the early seventies, as governments sought to slay the inflationary dragon which they had created, turned the built-in equity drag into a free fall. Nor was there any parachute waiting to open.

When interest rates head for the hills, equity markets are bound to be depressed. This is partly because higher interest rates spell tight money, and tight money means that there is less loose cash lying around with which to invest in stock-markets; partly because the two conditions (usury and tightness) usually spell an economic crisis, which hardly encourages investors; partly because high interest charges make profits and dividends harder to earn (especially at the aforementioned time of economic crisis); partly because if a stock looks worth buying on a $2\frac{1}{2}$ per cent yield when fixed-interest rates are 5 per cent, it will look considerably less attractive when the fixed-interest figure doubles.

There is no terrestrial reason why investors should accept a yield of less than 5 per cent on an equity when a fixed return of 10 per cent is waiting in the wings. But that rise from $2\frac{1}{2}$ per cent to 5 per cent in the acceptable yield of the equity means that it will *halve* in value. It follows that the higher-yielding the equity (high-yielding, that is, in relation to fixed-interest rates), the less vulnerable it is to sharp upward movements in the price of money. The corollary of this statement, alas, has unsavoury consequences for the low-yielding growth stock.

In the circumstances detailed above, which recur with utter reliability every time the business cycle moves round to the appropriate position, the low-yielder is liable to be worst affected on two counts: first, the concept or cult of growth itself suffers a cyclical knock as various shooting stars of the past plunge into the sea; second, shares offering minimal yields must fare worse than those whose dividends are worth taking home to the bank, because of the impact of the forces fictionalized in our parable.

To take those 'consistent growth stocks out of favour' again, their norm for dividend growth had been around 7 per cent over the years. That rate of expansion still leaves a 1·5 or 2 per cent dividend looking skinny (at 3 or 4 per cent) after ten years of energetic and successful corporate enterprise. The never-in-favour inconsistent no-growth stock with a 10 per cent yield will also subside somewhat when interest rates surge to double figures. But it won't collapse to the same extent as the one-time people's pet whose low initial yield, as recorded just above, has climbed only to the foothills.

The increasingly wayward behaviour of interest rates was no accident which befell mankind from the mid-sixties onwards. Basic causes were present that the alert investor might have spotted personally, or that at least should have been pointed out to the multitude by those who claimed to be the expert few. The tendency of the experts during the Big Bubble was the same as that of the amateurs: to recognize that stock-markets bore some relation to the movement of national and world economies, but to assume that the relationship was mainly similar to that of barometers and the weather. That is, when business was good, the market (usually getting to the starting line before the economy) boomed ahead; when business turned bad, the market usually led and pointed the way downwards. The financial relationship between different investments whose only common denominator was a rate of return received strangely less attention. Seemingly wise old stock-market philosophers would prate about coming rallies, oblivious of the fact that interest rates were rising. The other way round, greybeards would cluck their tongues about the apparently irreversible depression of the market, when declining interest rates made it certain that equity prices would recover.

The most convincing, even epochal, proof of this simple formula came in early 1975 on the London stock-market. It had sunk so low on New Year's Day that it was conceivable to imagine an index figure, on the *Financial Times* computation, of under 100. Despite the fact that the economic news from Britain herself was uniformly awful, that index promptly doubled inside eight weeks, an event whose profound implications for students of markets will be studied at some length in chapter 12. In the present context, one factor stands out: in early 1975 interest rates round the world, led by the United States, were falling.

This single signal fact placed a floor under the depressed markets in London and New York. As soon as (because of the interest factor) a rise in the index became credible, it became anticipated – hence the astonishing blast-off in prices on both sides of the Atlantic. These events were all the more predictable, although very few people predicted them, because the mechanism of money, apparently mysterious, actually works in a basically clear manner.

The price of money is the rate of interest. As with any other commodity, the price (or interest rate) will tend to rise when the demand exceeds the supply and fall when the supply exceeds the demand. The twist with this particular commodity lies with governments.

Not only can they fix the current price of money in an arbitrary manner (because they control the central banks), they also control the supply of money, which they can ration or expand in many crude and sophisticated ways. One crude method of expansion is to spend more than they snatch from the taxpayer in revenue. Unless the government can borrow genuine savings to fill the gap, it has no alternative but to print money in various forms. On the analogy of other commodities, you would expect a sharp increase in supply to result in a fall in price. But a drop in interest rates in reasonable economic times must stimulate higher demand for the supreme commodity of money. Unless the system continues to feed this demand with more and more money, interest rates will start to rise again under the inexorable pressure of demand from the private sector and government alike.

All through the sixties the United States was feeding the world with money. Other countries, notably Great Britain, did more than their bit to help. But the United States, by persistently over-spending at home on public account, and by matching this domestic improvidence with equal over-spending abroad, was the main contributor to a global profligacy which saw the free world's money supply *double* in three years. Since world output did nothing of the sort, massive inflation became inevitable. This placed double pressure behind interest rates. The initial push came from government. As the central bankers of the Federal Reserve, faced with large federal budget deficits, tried to curb the total growth of the money supply, they squeezed the amounts available to other borrowers, mainly corporations. This placed the latter in a powerful predicament. The squeeze hit them at a time when inflation was increasing their demand for funds (this works out because stocks and machines have to be replaced at higher prices).

So interest rates went on rising – and the higher the rate of inflation (induced originally by the rise in the money supply), the more obvious it became that investors would do their unlevel best to avoid being fobbed off with the negative interest rates mentioned in an earlier chapter. The supply of funds from private sources, in other words, will initially either dry up, or wash around in great tides in search of the best rates going, if the said private sources cannot obtain a greater yield than the rate of inflation.

The efforts of governments to mop up surplus money inevitably drove up its price, at exactly the same time as investors, consciously

or unconsciously, were yearning for positive returns. As the inflation rate rose into the double-digit area, so the positive was accentu-
ated. In Britain, at a 10 per cent inflation rate, let alone 20 per cent,
it became impossible for a man to maintain the value of his investment after tax, which a thoughtful government had pitched at
15 per cent above the tax on earned incomes – and that was a *Conservative* government.

The consequences for equities could have been spelt out with
little recourse to economic literacy. As the supply of money was
squeezed, and its price was forced up, the source of nourishment
for the last stages of the equity boom disappeared. Of all investments, equities, with the disadvantage of quoted and comparable yields, were bound to be among the weakest sisters. The price
of government stocks had some kind of floor: if interest rates
doubled, the price of these securities would necessarily halve – but
no more.

Where was the stopping place for equities, whose yields had long
since ceased to bear any rational relationship to those of other investments? Would the Dow drop to 600, or 500, or 400, or (as some
of the professional pessimists argued) 300? As the London market
refused to halt its slide at 300 on the *Financial Times* ordinary index,
then went through 200 as well, similar visions of Armageddon began
to dance in people's brains. At 150, as it was, the index stood at
a quarter of its all-time high.

The irrelevance of equities in the new inflation had been signalled
well in advance by a rising enthusiasm for investments which either
bore no interest, or whose interest appeared to be of no account:
for example commodities (gold above all of them) and property.
Economic man was again proving that, however unskilful he is intellectually at reading the future, or even at recognizing what is
happening in the present, he unfailingly in the end places his money
where his mind should be.

For two decades, however, the conventional wisdom had held
that, because of high taxation, especially on investment income, the
dividend was as irrelevant as the rent roll was thought to be (utterly
wrongly, in fact) on an office skyscraper in the heart of a metropolis.
Just as property investors were drawn by the magnet of promised
capital gains, so stockholders were taught that income was no asset –
indeed high dividends were a positive liability.

Growth company management was based on the comfortable

thesis that stockholders who detest taxable dividends would far rather have green-fingered directors investing the profits, free of income tax, to make all their gardens grow. The comfort for managers is deceptive. It is much easier, true, to steal money from the stockholders before it reaches their hands than to prise the loot from their grasp afterwards. This form of raising money, true again, is by far the cheapest. But the crucial theoretical and practical drawback gets largely ignored.

Ignored truths become painful realities. The drawback, the catch 22 of the investment world, explains the disappointing performance of the large firms in *Fortune*'s roll of honour, brings our parable home to roost and elucidates the reasons for the puzzling behaviour of the seventeen stocks studied by the *Sunday Times*. Catch 22 is this: if share ratings ultimately relate more to dividend growth than to expansion of earnings, a policy of ploughing back profits, which would otherwise have been paid out as dividends, must defeat the plough-back policy's own objective – which is presumably to raise the share price.

Even in an era when people allegedly shunned dividends like mononucleosis, many investors went on holding and buying their blue-chips for those supposedly unregarded payments. But that is not the crucial point. Even for those who genuinely did shun the income, the dividend yield, whether they knew it or not, was a decisive factor in establishing value. At the end of the day, and at the beginning for that matter, investors accept low yields only because they believe, in the first place, that the crop of dividends will augment, and, in the second place, that the market will apply the same basis of valuation as today's (if not a higher one) to that crop. If (on the first count) the yield does not rapidly rise, and consequently the investors are proved wrong on the second count, too, any wise child can tell you what you get. You get investors as unhappy as the hero in the parable when his sure-fire investment proved to have a built-in drag. To put it another way, and to revert to the *Sunday Times* seventeen, you get 'consistent growth stocks out of favour', that's what.

Part III. Go-go myths

9. Why high-fliers fall

None of the broken monuments littering the investment scene in 1974 was more heart-rending than the ruins of one-time emperors of the market, like IBM or Polaroid, once the perennial idols of Wall Street. Like the poet Shelley surveying the battered torso in the sands, and reading 'My name is Ozymandias, King of Kings, look on my works ye mighty and despair', the investor can only reflect on the passing of glory – and perhaps despair on his own account.

The stocks of these two companies began to gyrate vertiginously in 1972, before the roller-coaster gathered speed on its final downward run. There were specific proximate causes in both cases. IBM faced, as it may in perpetuity, trust-busting threats from north, south, east and west. This had begun to sway sentiment against the great company, even though it was successfully weathering the computer industry's private recession (its first – an event which investors widely believed to be as likely as Chicago's Mayor Daley entering a monastery). Polaroid was hoist with the now celebrated petard of the SX-70 camera. However much confidence and publicity the company exuded, the market was nervous – and with reason. Polaroid's profits were about to be decimated. One of the soundest market maxims was thus demonstrated for the millionth or so time. The market is often wrong when pursuing a share up to the empyrean; but he who bets against the market on the way down, more often than not, is heading for a fall that will cost far more than pride.

The incidents – the so-called fundamentals – which helped to push the IBMs and Polaroids of the world off their pedestals, however, are neither here nor there. All stock-markets have their effortless high-fliers; all such astronauts are bound to have problems in orbit from time to time; and any serious shock threatens to spin them back to earth, given that they depend so heavily on psychological uplift. Avon, Disney, McDonald's, Merck, Xerox–all these suffered, along with IBM and Polaroid, the indignity of being described in the mid-seventies as 'yesterday's growth stocks'. Only a handful of years before, these were the companies which had tomorrow in their pockets. This faith in their future was what united a sufficient majority of the investing proletariat behind such stocks to make their dreams come true – for a time.

The explanation of these rises is a good deal less specific than the force which drives an apparently high, wide and handsome flier earthwards: in that case, eight times out of ten, some insider knows something you don't, and he is offloading the stock while the going is good. The upward force, in bald contrast, is the view that what goes up must go up. The stellar attraction of Polaroid for high-flying investors was the certain knowledge, locked away in the bank of history, that $1000 invested in the stock in 1938 was worth $4 million four years later. It was no use pointing out that (unless the dollar lost value at a rate worthy of pre-Hitler Germany) $4 million invested in Polaroid in 1972 wasn't going to be worth $16,000 million (that's 4000 times as much) in AD 2006. Nor would the bettors be put off by a kindly reminder that very few people placed $1000 in Polaroid in 1938; and that very few could have done, given the small scale of the outfit at that time.

The size of past gains encourages the faithful to believe, with deep sincerity, that the stock's ever-upward flight path is written in the stars, as well as heading towards them. If a 4000 times gain in thirty-four years is no longer in those stars, something much more modest in relative terms would still be deeply welcome in terms of absolute capital gains. The 1938 investor had been forced to wait for over three decades to make his $4 million. At a mere 14 per cent annual clip, his 1972 nest-egg would add another $4 million in a single ten-year stretch.

Thus the ten-year rise of ten times in the share price of the Rank Organization to 1972 was no mean figure, given the size of the company and the equity at the start of the period. Rank fits the superstar definition to a nicety. At first the company had buried its Xerox interests, acquired from America, in a corner of a factory which was making (without much success) photographic equipment. The fringe activity rapidly burgeoned into a tropical garden of profit so rich that Rank turned into the paragon of British growth stocks. It alone combined transatlantic-style growth (not surprisingly, since its success rested entirely on a licensed transatlantic invention) with a quotation on the London market.

Like IBM, Rank was a big share – big in the sense that millions of shares are available – which sold in apparent perpetuity above the market average. A tenfold increase in ten years (although the rate is mathematically much less than the doubling every year which a first glance suggests) surely justifies a premium. But how much were investors justified in paying above the odds? And what were the odds, anyway?

However splendid the results of past performance, there is doubtful logic in the relation of a price to the past, and much less logic in its relation to the future. At the end of 1972, to take a moment when Rank was still riding or flying high, the London market was worth 18 times its collective earnings. (Anybody who then predicted that the market would shortly be priced deep into single figures would have been regarded as a harmless lunatic.) Rank was selling at *double* the market's multiple, a figure that itself clearly expected great things from equity investment.

On the true, underlying base of equity investment (which, as we have seen, is yield) that 18 times multiple was the price of buying a 3·4 per cent dividend, the average going rate at the time (it rose to double figures as the market slumped). But in the period of the Big Bubble such considerations were not held to be relevant. The higher the price-earnings ratio (in other words, the more valuable the share or high-priced the market), the lower the dividend yield. And the investor didn't care, because he thought he was buying not income, but growth.

One problem clearly visible at the end of 1972 was that investors were buying much less growth than they had reckoned on. The average gain over the 1962–72 decade, in the average share and not the super-starring Rank, probably was little more than 9 per cent annually in terms of capital appreciations and gross dividends combined. As 1972 drew to its close, with the Yom Kippur War still a year away, British investors could get a safe, fixed return of $8\frac{1}{2}$ per cent before tax in standard household investments. Given that the latter guaranteed the return of the same number of pound notes as were originally deposited, even if the notes themselves had been cheapened in the interim period, the equity investor, paying 18 times earnings for the market, was logically expecting a return before tax of – what?

Logic suggests that a logical figure can be placed on the apparently illogical behaviour of the market. Suppose that you are offered a choice of two investments. The first offers you $8\frac{1}{2}$ per cent, but no prospect of capital gain or loss. Compounding the interest, you will end up after ten years with a rise in the value of your investment from £100 to £226. That outcome is certain, and no risk is attached to the exercise. The alternative affair brings risk into the equation. You have an equal chance of trebling your money or getting nowhere. In the latter, worst case, you merely receive your money back (both the risky and the safe investment are equally subject to inflation, which therefore need not be taken into account, at least for this demonstration). What will you be prepared to pay in the second case?

Half the time you will come up with nothing; half the time your investment will come up treble trumps. Thus the total payback on each £100 wagered must be £250. For that outcome you will be prepared (as a logical being) to pay something between £100 (which, invested safely, will yield only £126 of profit) and £110-odd. The latter figure arises because £110·61946, compounding annually at $8\frac{1}{2}$ per cent, comes to £250: there would be no point in investing for exactly the same rate of return as the completely safe investment.

On that logic, the price of the London market at the end of 1972 made quite good sense. Over the previous decade, over half of the two hundred largest companies in Britain actually had trebled their shareholders' money. If the 9 per cent median growth of the previous decade was going to be repeated, the collective British investor was undoubtedly wise in preferring the market to an $8\frac{1}{2}$ per cent fixed-interest yield. But the whole exercise (which is a gross simplification, but an accurate model of the only way in which the equity–fixed interest relationship can be established) falls apart in two circumstances: first, if the risks increase that the share price, instead of being maintained, will collapse; second, if the chances of a rise in the price are reduced – as they will be if, for instance, interest rates rise above $8\frac{1}{2}$ per cent. The investors of the sixties and early seventies cannot be blamed for failing to realize that stock-market catastrophe was round the corner. But since the nature of markets and mankind is to fluctuate, he who bets that the future will follow exactly the same course as the past is on to a fairly certain loser.

That outcome is not entirely sure, of course. Maybe in 1982 share prices will be found to have achieved a median growth of 200 per cent all over again. But that eventuality would be sheer coincidence. The decade ending in each successive year nearly always shows considerable variation from its predecessor. Nor does anybody invest in all the shares, even in the two hundred biggest companies. People buy individual stocks – and the logical exercise attempted above can be applied to discover what their purchase implies when it takes a high-flier to heart.

In this example you have the option of two investments once more. The first, again, has an even chance of trebling, an even chance of standing still. The alternative has an even chance of multiplying tenfold (remember, that's what the Rank Organization actually did in 1962–72). If the going rate of fixed-interest return is $8\frac{1}{2}$ per cent, you will, as established above, pay £100–£110 in the first case, when the odds are 50–50 on the equity trebling. In the second option, however, you are bidding for a return of £450: half the time you will make a £900 profit, half the time nothing at all. For that certainty you will gladly fork out over twice as much: the cut-off point is in fact some £240. Relating that calculation to Rank, the stock-market (hey presto!) comes out exactly right again at the end of 1972. It valued Rank at precisely twice the average of the market.

You might be tempted to challenge the basis of valuation on the grounds that, even without an unforeseen world recession, the chances of Rank achieving a 10 times growth in the coming decade were plainly nil. The company was too big for such pyrotechnics. On the other hand, the chances of the shares merely marking time must have seemed less than negligible – was not the whole world churning out Xerox copies with undiminished, nay, greatly growing zest? So £450 might well have been the outcome of a more painstaking assessment of the likelihoods.

One vital factor has been left out of the equation: what happens if the fundamentals of the whole market change? Again, soaring interest rates are the main example. The impact on a Polaroid or a Rank cannot be less severe than on a more mundane stock. The additional hazard for the high-flier, however, is that, irrespective of what happens to the market as a whole, the astronautic equity is subject to a fatal flaw in the valuation analysed above.

Rank was twice as expensive as the market, meaning that its latest earnings were valued by the investor twice as highly as the earnings of the great amorphous body of stocks, a mark of distinction which, we concluded, appeared to be justified by its faster growth perform-ance in the past. But 'what goes up must go up' is not a theory that will satisfy even the humblest seeker after stock-market truth. For such valuations to make ultimate sense, they must show a con-nection between the performance of the company, as a machine for generating earnings, and the performance of the company, as an equity.

If no such connection exists, then the super-star investor has flown high into the uncharted troposphere. In fact belief in the con-nection seems to be an indispensable adjunct of the investing life. Most investors, hopeless addicts, cling like junkies to their fix – the idea that stocks must have some intrinsic value. Whole platoons of analysts peddle the goods to entire armies of junkie investors, whose fixation sounds plausible enough in all conscience. The logicality follows the same pattern as the exercise in relating higher to lower growth ratings.

If a company whose earnings are growing at 10 per cent annually is worth a price-earnings multiple of x times, surely there must be a sensible, *logical* relationship between that norm and the multiple (should it be $2x$, $3x$, $4x$ or $5x$?) of a company growing twice as fast – at 20 per cent per annum? Leaving aside the argument over whether such a relationship exists, one observation can be made categorically and at once. The formula being pursued might well produce an en-tirely different result from the calculations which relate share prices to one another on the basis of past growth in the shares con-cerned. In the first case the hopeful investor is extrapolating into the future the past trend in earnings per share; in the second case he is gambling on the future performance of the share price – and that is plainly influenced by many factors which cannot be reduced to formulae.

The stock-market isn't exclusively bothered about earnings, per share or straight. It sometimes gets stimulated to fits of extreme passion by underlying asset value, or corporate rumours, or even cash flow. Two firms growing at precisely the same rate in more or less identical industrial situations may end up with very different market ratings. The reason may lie in the non-earnings stimuli, like those mentioned above. Whatever the explanation, however, the outcome is always the same: a change in the supply–demand balance for the two equities concerned.

The price–earnings multiple, it turns out, doesn't measure the relative valuation of growth rates at all. It is a statistical residual which arises from the relative movements of supply and demand. Annuals of statistics are full of mere residues into which men and women read untoward significance – and the multiple is a prime example. Disbelievers should consider the following true fable.

Back in 1968–9 the supermarket chain Tesco Stores was justly prized by the stock-market for its ability (sustained over most of the following years) to grow in earnings per share by a quarter per year. So greatly was this 25 per cent annual growth valued that the earnings were priced in the market at a multiple of about 50. In the same business of feeding the multitude was a good, solid, dull firm called Fitch Lovell. It sold at around the average of the market in September 1969. Its earnings yield (you establish this reciprocal of the price–earnings multiple by dividing the latter into 100) was almost 7 per cent, against around 2 per cent for Tesco. Its dividend yield was $3\frac{1}{2}$ times the miserable 1 per cent offered by the high-flier. But from the 1969 low to the middle of 1975, Tesco shares advanced by only a third. The good soldier Fitch marched forward by 88 per cent. If the 1969 high point is taken as the base, Tesco showed a 15 per cent decline, Fitch neither gain nor loss. As for earnings – and here is the nub – they grew by exactly the same amount, four-fifths.

It wasn't that investors, reconsidering their view of Fitch as opposed to Tesco, decided to bring the price–earnings ratios more into line. It was simply that the demand for Tesco shares at the sublime loftiness of a 50 times rating proved less than the supply from sellers who concluded (they were the wise virgins) that it was time to put the golden oil in their lamps – in the form of cash in hand.

Their decision can be expressed, with some difficulty, in mathematical terms, as one set of Wall Street analysts did when Avon Products, so great was the lust for its door-to-door cosmetics, commanded a price–earnings multiple of 64 – and that was in early 1973, well on into the saga of the Second Great Crash. This analysis for the First Boston Corporation examined 'how long the expected earnings growth rate of a stock has to continue in order to attain the same level of return on investment that could be achieved by an alternative investment in a market average'. The Bostonian prose (that's how analysts often talk, or at least write) is asking the same question that was posed earlier in this chapter, though in the context of earnings rather than of expected movements in the share price. But the answer is no less discouraging to searchers after immaculate theory. In the Avon case, the predicted growth of 15 per cent annually, as the Avon girls continued to call on the world's housewives with their wares, compared with 5·1 per cent for the market. The latter was then selling at a multiple which was only a quarter of Avon's. According to the First Boston figures, it would take *fifteen years* before Avon caught up.

Unfortunately most investors look no further ahead than three to five years. Long before Avon had exercised its opportunity to prove that the hare could catch the tortoise, investors, bored with waiting, were likely to seek faster action elsewhere. Their departure will only be accelerated if some untoward event (like the ills that befell IBM and Polaroid) disturbs the even tenor of the company's ways. No possible event is more untoward than a decline or slow-down in earnings.

What if, one year, earnings, instead of maintaining their 15 per cent clip, stand still, and then resume their advance at the same pace and with the same momentum? In theory the price–earnings multiple, since it represents the number of times investors are prepared to purchase the latest historic earnings, in the light of the projected rate in their growth, should be re-established at the good old level. But if confidence has been disturbed violently enough, the multiple, after hovering a while, may settle lower down.

When Rank was selling at its 37·7 multiple, double the market average, a fall to 25 would have meant a drop of a quarter in the stock. In point of brutal, non-theoretical fact, in spring 1975, when Rank had bounced up along with the rest of the market, more than doubling from its bottom, the low was a piddling 8·8, compared to a market average of 7·3 times. How are the mighty fallen, indeed; even though Rank's profit performance had been no less spectacular during its years of come-uppance than in those of conquest.

High-flying shares like Rank in its heyday are sustained not by economic forces inherent in the enterprise, but by psychological forces locked inside the brain of the collective investor. The world turns, not on the pivot of the actual growth experienced in the past, but on the unquantifiable strength of the expectation. Anything which, acting like Delilah on Samson's top-knot, damages that strength must have a disproportionate effect on the share price. And such damage must be rendered almost inevitable by the implausibilities on which unquantified expectation usually rests.

In an earlier chapter we considered the result of the race between two food firms, Associated Dairies, whose Asda superstores had won it a go-go rating, and Tate & Lyle, the fuddy-duddy sugar group. The victory of the latter, in the light of the above explorations, now looks like a foregone conclusion. The high-speed merchant was valued at 2·8 times as much as the sluggard (using the price–earnings multiple as the yardstick), despite the fact that the latter's earnings had grown twice as fast as the super-star's in the previous three years. Tate was then coming back from its corporate nadir; this, as usual, exaggerated its performance. Clearly the company was most unlikely to match the 35 per cent past annual growth of Asda in the years ahead. But would Asda, either? Within half a dozen years, growth on that Wagnerian scale would have seen the company valued (on the same multiple) at some £470 million, or 7 times the 1973 figure. In the present and future state of supermarket competition, that growth and that solidity of rating were about as likely as the discovery that Herbert Hoover was a secret communist.

On the other hand, it was easy to demonstrate that on perfectly safe assumptions about future Tate turnover and profit margins, the company could expect a significant upward adjustment in its stock-market rating. I make this statement with some confidence, because this was one sum which I got right. On the prevailing considerations, it was clear at the time that Tate had an excellent chance of reaching a market capitalization of £470 million by 1975; and that was exactly the same sum as Asda would reach in 1978, after achieving prodigious fantasies of growth – and while maintaining a glorious market rating that would still have to be double that of the sweet, sleepy giant.

To me, the likelihoods suggested with all the force of an avalanche that at some future date – and not too far removed – despite the huge gap between their market ratings, the high-flier was bound to fall behind. The Second Great Crash made that prediction come true within twelve months. That was only a matter of timing. The same analysis would have inscribed the same writing on the wall for other high-fliers. What was true for Asda applied to IBM; what ruined Rank savaged Polaroid – the fact that past share valuations have no bearing on past records or future performance of either shares or earnings.

This brutality brought down the market gods, deified by many who should have known better and purchased by too many who were told too little. The process fed on itself as the years rolled on. Eventually it produced the greatest disillusion in the market-place since Radio, Steel, Motors and the rest went to the wailing wall in 1929.

10. The paper for earnings fallacy

Man succumbs easily to the myth that a crock of gold lies at the end of the rainbow. No doubt this poor resistance stretches back to hard atavistic experience. There simply has to be a better way of earning a living than chasing antelopes across the deserts of prehistoric Africa, or sailing ships round Cape Horn, or driving a cab in New York City. Moreover a few fortunates do find crocks of gold at the end of their personal rainbows, and human nature will never accept that golden dreams become reality only for other people. Thus financial chronicles are spattered by glittering bubbles, of many different shapes and sizes, blown up by the desire of the many to emulate the few. The urge has obvious and close associations with the gambling fever, another nearly universal addiction to illogic. Gamblers in the mass always lose: otherwise the organizers would never make their cut, the profit. Yet the gambler, by definition, believes that he may be the exception who is going to win.

The strangest form of gamble, obviously, is one where the speculator knows there are no exceptions, and that he must always lose – or, rather, where straightforward calculations demonstrate that he must. Such high weirdness includes the stroke of perverse genius which created a whole new school of business in the sixties. It was the exchange of paper, of common stock or its cunning variations, for the assets and earnings of another company.

The first creative use of acquisitions antedated the new conglomerates of the sixties by several decades. Nearly all the corporate mammoths which emerged between the wars owed at least part of their growth, even their existence, to mergers. But these deals were not motivated by the stock-market (which in bygone Europe had only vestigial significance in the boardroom): General Motors and Unilever, General Foods and Royal Dutch–Shell, and so on, merged for mighty economic motives – ranging from the elimination of powerful competition to organizing defence against competitors who were too powerful to be eliminated.

These practitioners failed even to exploit (in most cases) the opportunity which had attracted J.P. Morgan to mergers. Quite apart from an old pirate's innate desire to corner an entire industry, Morgan, in age of lax regulation and even laxer morals, delighted in deluging the public with watered stock. If you sell more shares in a company than the company is actually worth you pocket the extra proceeds; but the price of those shares is liable to fall towards that lower underlying value – not because stock-markets possess any intrinsic sense of values, but because the balance sheet has been hideously weakened and the supply of the stock greatly increased by the watering.

Stock-markets, like all markets, are moved only at the margin. If demand for 1000 tons of copper is met by a potential supply of 1100 tons, that will sharply reduce the price. If the supply falls to 900 tons, however, the price must swing rapidly upwards, as the customers for the missing 100 tons outbid each other for the commodity. Demand (or usage) has remained more or less constant throughout this commotion, as you would expect with a commodity which industry has to buy. But nobody needs to buy a stock or share – and the generates a crucial perversion.

Actually, the entry into commodity-markets of people who have no more personal use for copper than a vegetarian has for steak tartare perverts these markets in a similar way. When a shortfall in supply pushes up the copper price, speculators will buy solely because its price is rising. The idea of actually taking delivery – getting a small mountain of metal offloaded on their front lawns – would be horrifying (akin to the fate which befell the oil-canny Gulbenkians, after some skulduggery by the Soviets, when they were stuck with an alp of caviare). By moving in on the action, however, the speculators drive the price higher still.

By the same token, if the price drops, the gamblers will dive off the high board – because their only reason for climbing up in the first place was the expectation of a further lucrative rise. That's how speculative activity exaggerates movements at the margin even in a commodity which somebody is actually turning into electric cables or frying-pans for French chefs. The balance of real supply and true demand must determine the overall pattern of the market;

but the impact of speculation distorts that pattern in both directions – up and down.

You can see why the use of paper to buy earnings had a built-in disadvantage: it automatically increased the supply of the shares. The ace conglomerators sought to postpone this black day by issuing funny money shares, or warrants, or letter-stock, which could be added to the supply of genuine equity only at some later date. But investment analysts, or their electronic calculators, were perfectly capable of working out the company's sums on the relevant basis: what its earnings per share would be if fully diluted – when all the comical paper was inevitably converted into serious stock certificates.

The device thus proved as useless as garlic in averting the evil eye. The amount of claims on the company's earnings was still being increased faster than the desire of the investment community to share in those claims. The problem (barely seen as such even by the cleverest afflicted promoters) was compounded by a defect which had crippled a previous generation of merger-mongers. This flaw is the Law of Diminishing Amalgamation Returns – the fact that the impact of a £1 million a year purchase on a £2 million company is twice as great as the effect of that same purchase on a £4 million concern.

This law, applied on a far smaller scale of corporate activity, brought down the forerunner of the conglomerates – the British 'industrial holding companies'. Even the words are all but forgotten today, along with the theory. Basically, these companies grew by brisk buys of small family-owned firms.

Ten purchases averaging £50,000 of earnings between them produced half a million, at which point the master company was in the middling leagues. At that height £50,000 purchases were no longer enough to sustain stock-market interest. Characteristically, the presiding proprietor raised his sights to bigger game, compounding the damage if (as was bound to happen, usually sooner rather than later) the hunted animal proved to be suffering secretly from some loathsome corporate disease.

With few exceptions, the industrial holding companies, like most of the conglomerates after them, fell out of market favour when they failed to sustain the earnings growth that had been their main justification. Again like the conglomerates, they then ceased to be active acquirers, because their paper was no longer so attractive to poten-

tial purchasers, and because the stock-market was now deeply uninterested in their shenanigans. Yet most of the industrial holders
survived, living a twilight existence so far as avid investors were
concerned, but settling down to the humdrum, often frustrating task
of turning their ragbags into some kind of honest cloth. So it was
to be with the conglomerates.

In basic terms, companies that consist of several ill-assorted interests have never been beloved by investors. This may seem difficult
to square with the soaring prices of conglomerates' shares – but the
high flight results not from high valuation, but from the rocket-
booster effect of large injections of earnings into a tiny vehicle. Even
if the price–earnings multiple never got above a miserable 10 (and
a conglomerate like Gulf+Western sometimes sold in the heady
days at even less), earnings growth of 40, 50 or 70 per cent a year
was bound to be translated into a leaping share price.

The progenitors and public relations men of these creations did
their utmost to engineer escape into the higher atmosphere in which
spaceships like Xerox and Polaroid spun at their magic price–earnings multiples. But all efforts to escape the conglomerate tag (public
relations euphemisms like 'multi-market corporation' abounded)
failed to enhance the public's limited enthusiasm for this kind of
investment vehicle. In any event, as we have noted, the promoters
of Textron or Litton, Gulf+Western or Ling-Temco-Vought,
Bangor Punta or ITT were pushing a rock uphill – their efforts to
promote the shares were constantly negated by their equally consistent increase in the supply of that paper.

If possible, the acquisition artist sought to avoid the problem by
using debt. Buy earnings for less than the interest charges on the
debt, and the result flows straight through to the reported profits –
even under honest accounting methods. But this merely added a
fresh and well-known hazard to the risks of buying a rotten apple.

The device of gearing is older than the joint stock company itself.
Accountancy conventions mean that, if two companies have identical profits, but one has half its capital in the form of debt, the latter
will have higher earnings per share than one which is debt-free –
provided, again, that its overall return on capital exceeds the rate
of interest on the debt.

To the untrained ear this must sound like rank rubbish: how can
an unencumbered company be rated lower than a concern which
owes not one red cent? Surely the correct valuation would be the

other way about? As so often, the simple idea is right. The supposedly sophisticated are wrongly, dangerously impressed not just
by the high per share earnings of the highly geared company, but
by the awesome impact of any improvement in profits in good times
for business.

If a company with £10 million of equity raises its £1 million
profits to £1·5 million, that's a spiffing 50 per cent rise, and that's
all. Now if the firm has £5 million of equity and £5 million of debt
and the debt costs 10 per cent a year in interest, the original £1
million of profit will be scaled down by the interest charges to
£500,000. But the returns on capital will be identical. The same
half a million increase in profit postulated above, moreover, will
raise the profit to £1 million without any rise in the interest costs.
That means profits will *double*: and the return on stockholders'
equity, 10 per cent before the profit rise (the same as for the debt-
free case), will now be a full 20 per cent (against 15 per cent for
the debtless company). Move into the higher realms of 90 per cent
gearing and a £100,000 profit gets transmuted into a six-fold increase by the same simple alchemy. The ugly reverse side of this
beautiful coin is known to any investor who has ever invested un-
wisely with borrowed money – every investor, for instance, who got
wiped out in the First Great Crash.

To revert to our examples, the debt-free dullard could withstand
a £1 million fall in profits and still pay a 5 per cent dividend. The
same fall leaves the switched-on borrower switched off: his 50 per
cent gearing means he would just cover his interest costs – and nothing would be left over for the shareholders. The blazing genius who
had jacked his debt up to 90 per cent would be deep in the black
hole of Calcutta: profits wiped out, and short by £400,000 of the
£900,000 owed in interest charges.

The paper-for-earnings wheeler-dealers of the sixties thus sailed
between Scylla and Charybdis: if they used debt, they were wide
open to the perils of gearing-in-reverse. If they used equity, they
ran into potential double trouble.

The first trap was that of increasing the supply of shares faster
than the demand. A company like ITT, increasing the number of
common shares outstanding from forty-one million to ninety-six
million between 1966 and 1972, was doing even more than expect
a 129 per cent rise in the amount of investor interest in its shares.
The object of the whole convoluted exercise was to elevate the price

per share; so the company (if it thought about the matter at all) was anticipating an even greater advance in the amounts of cash that the investing public as a whole would be willing to devote to the care and maintenance of this lovable equity. The act of exchanging equity for other companies' earnings had the unwanted but inevitable effect of making it less lovable, in case after case. There were two extremes: the company could buy another firm at a lower price–earnings ratio than its own, which was the way in which the conglomerates were supposed to earn their keep; or it could buy stock at a higher multiple than its own – which, more often than not, was how the wizards actually behaved.

A painstaking article in *Fortune* magazine, which appeared more eager to defend the conglomerates against unjust attack than to join the assault, revealed this curious habit. Few of the episodes were as bizarre as Gulf+Western's purchase of Paramount at a 70 multiple when its own stock was selling at only 8. But the general conclusion was clear. The conglomerates were growing by deals that had precisely the same effect as purchasing earnings with borrowed money at a price which meant that the bought-in profits would not cover the debt interest. The only possible logic behind this paradoxical behaviour arose if the earnings of the acquired company could be jacked up sharply and in short order (which, mainly thanks to *The Godfather I* and *II*, actually happened with Paramount). But for all their self-alleged management skills, this was a feat which few conglomerates could contrive. It's a feat, in fact, which few managements of any description pull off with consistency.

The upshot was to turn a lying boast into reality. The overlords of Litton Industries, for instance, used to repel critics with arguments that half their growth had been organic – that is, it was derived from expansion of the original businesses, rather than being simply bought in. This figure could always have been turned topsy-turvy. It sounds much less good, somehow, to assert that half of a company's growth is the result of acquisitions.

But self-styled super-managers like Litton's were anxious to establish an image of themselves as more than just pretty stock-market faces: as managers who could and would have flourished just as richly (well, almost) if the market had never existed. In fact it often turned out to be perfectly true that their earnings performance, and presumably their stock-market rating, would have been higher if, after the initial set-up by acquisition, the promoters had forbidden themselves all further purchases.

This statement applies even to those cases where the purchaser applied the traditional leverage, using a highly rated stock to buy a lowly-rated one. On the face of it, a company can't lose by swopping paper which values earnings at a multiple of 40, say, for paper valuing the selfsame dollars or pounds at 20. But look at it from the purchased company's point of view: there you were with stock priced at 15, for example, and of little interest to anybody (which is why it was priced so low). Then along comes some hairy ape of a conglomerate and offers you a third above the market price – not pennies from heaven, but millions from mammon. It is exactly as if, having sold his holding for cash, the shareholder in the acquired company had been offered shares in the bidder at a discount. True – but isn't it worth paying over the odds from the *bidding* shareholders' point of view? After all, they (through the agency of their aggressive, progressive, far-sighted managers) are giving away pieces of paper for valuable earnings. If the market values the new earnings as highly as the old, the worth of those earnings in the share price will be double the sum actually expended, and everybody will live happily ever after.

But what happens if the market changes its view of the shares? Buying in an extra £200,000 of earnings for a £1 million company, the latter being valued in the stock-market at £40 million, brings the equity worth up to £48 million – if the price–earnings multiple holds. But the potential loss of market value if the multiple declines only to 30 will wipe out all the benefit – and more. For the 'new' shareholders it will mean that the £4 million they received is worth only £3 million. For the 'old' shareholders, the £40 million with which they started out will swiftly shrink in the wash to £33 million.

Why on earth, or on Wall Street, should the multiple shrink? There are two main mundane reasons. Apart from the worsening of the supply–demand relationship which is risked by enlarging the equity, there's the unpleasant truth that the new shareholders are more likely than the old to take their money and run. Enough of those desertions, and the price must inevitably, obeying the laws of all markets, start down the slide. The tobogganing seldom happened overnight – although there was a sickening overnight slip in Rank Organization shares, when Wall Street investors reacted in savage manner to the news that the company foolishly wanted to buy a brewery. But that Wall Street reaction came in a later, better-instructed period, when investors had learnt that swopping paper for earnings worked, in the sense of generating a higher share price, only for reasons outside anybody's control. The seductive mathematics of the exchange had no basis in solid foundations: the sums rested on the most shifting of all financial ground – a market valuation. The real maths were never worked out. The takeover is in effect a fund-raising operation, in which the cash is used to buy an additional business. If the return on that purchase was greater than that on the original capital, then the purchasing company had been strengthened, at least for the time being. If not, a drag had been created on further progress.

Yet none of these thoughts disturbed the merry merchants in earnings in the sixties. As they wheeled and dealt, in fact, they and the conventional wisdom expected the mere announcement of a new earnings caper to boost, not merely the price of the victim, but that of the aggressor as well. Even as they mouthed and acted on this foolish wisdom, professional investors must have noticed aspects of a contradictory reality.

For example a standard procedure in such cases was to arrange a little friendly support for the prices until the deal went through. If the operation was so wealth-enhancing for the shareholders, how come the market needed propping up in this manner? It was a gambit that in other circumstances would have been condemned, and possibly punished, as cooking the market. It is small comfort to the investors who suffered as a result to know that many of the chefs of this particular market dish in the end got thoroughly cooked themselves. The greater comfort lies in the contemplation of conventional wisdom and its disasters. These arise because conventional wisdom represents the ideas foisted on the masses by leaders who can see only what is in front of their noses. As we are about to discover, the truly wise individual looks backwards as well as forwards to find and profit from not the conventional but the unconventional truth.

11. Fallen stars and busted flushes

Murderers may revisit the scene of the crime. Investors generally resist the temptation, and investment advisers find the resistance still easier, and still more necessary. If there is a dead body in the safe or deposit box or home filing cabinet, either it is given a hasty pauper's funeral, or it is left there to decompose: sometimes in the usually vain hope that it will rise again from the dead.

But only the rare intrepid soul seeks to recapture the mood and mental processes which led to the buying decision in the first place, even though such an exercise is the best way of revealing the shoddy reasoning and the too easily accepted premises on which the myth of performance rests. The mistakes stay buried in old papers and old files – including newspaper files, from which, however, educational exhumation is readily available.

Ever since I initiated the practice in 1963 the *Observer* has published a Christmas list of the leading share winners of the year on the London market, together with potted descriptions of the men and the marvels which had brought investors to the year's richest monetary rewards. The proceeds from £1000 invested equally in the ten winning companies listed in 1963 would have amounted to £3229 in the week after an exceptionally merry Christmas. From that fact alone, one conclusion can be drawn at once: that 1963 was a bull year in the market, one of the golden stretches that prolonged the myths of the go-go era.

That, indeed, is the first lesson learnt from a stroll down (or up) Memory Lane. Gee-whiz boys and miracle companies may come, and gee-whiz boys and miracle companies may go (as most of them do); new managements may wield new brooms, and old companies may dust off old stories; new stars may appear on the stock-market horizon, and new meteors may flash across it. But overall the rewards and the kicks are dealt out by that impersonal, impervious and all-powerful entity, the economic cycle,

with its sorcerer's apprentice, the long-term trend of the stock-
market.

No other study in the entire field of investment will yield students
more benefit than the contemplation of such cycles. However, most
people prefer to contemplate, not the skies, but the stars that shine,
and investors are no exception. In 1963 the cycle had carried
upwards an interesting bunch of not especially heavenly bodies:
'bodies' being a word whose double meaning, with its cross-
reference to the graveyard start to this chapter, is deliberately
chosen.

A number of the 1963 stars ended up in the market morgue. That
was the fate of the bearer of the leading torch in the *Observer* list:
John Bloom, a skinny, skimpily bearded young man who made a
modicum of money from door-to-door selling of cut-price washing
machines, but coined a veritable mint from selling shares of his company to investors who fell over themselves to believe in the Bloom
legend. If one leg of the investing public can be pulled, it follows
that so can another, and Bloom also floated a firm called English
& Overseas Investments, whose main asset was a holding in Rolls
Razor, and whose main attraction was the unknown.

The paramount virtue of an unknown attraction in any stock-
market is that it defies quantification. So (as we know) does an
apparently concrete feature, like a historic growth rate in earnings
per share. But there are some limits, however far apart, to the valuation that can be placed on a 15 per cent compound annual growth
rate. You might find some spiritualist misguided enough to pay 100
times the earnings: but not 200 times. The figure to be placed on
English & Overseas, however, was a matter of whether the promised
land would be reached, or how much milk and honey would flow,
if and when the borders of Canaan were penetrated.

The promise lay in the presumed relationship between Bloom
and a much older, many times wealthier entrepreneur, Sir Isaac
Wolfson. The latter, with one of the country's biggest mail-order
and retail groups in his back pocket, not to mention family investment interests worth much fine gold, had no visible reason to
become involved in the Bloom saga – save for the small but profitable matter of financing instalment purchases of the washing
machines through a Wolfson financial company. The tales, however, hinted at far deeper, psychologically tinted motives. The older
man, a canny septuagenerian whose love for wheels and deals had

been preserved undiminished by the years, identified young John, so it was said, with the young Isaac of earlier decades. The enthusiasts drew unflattering contrast between Bloom, evidently bursting with energy and ideas, and Sir Isaac's reticent and industrious son Leonard, who minded the Wolfson stores (which was all, hinted the Bloom claque, that young Leonard was good for).

Did anybody ever hear this story confirmed from any non-Bloom source? Had, especially, Sir Isaac himself ever told the tale? If so, those who heard have for ever kept their peace. But it doesn't matter whether a market tale is true, so long as it is good enough to be true. That is one unfortunate reality of stock-market swingers, swindles and swan-dives: they make such marvellous reading and telling. Bloom that year was an endless source of copy. Even his fiascos were good copy – the home movie kits that didn't move, the bum Bulgarian holidays (in a country where a WC was then allegedly called a *was ist das*?). In a strange way, the flops strengthened rather than destroyed the uncritical adoration which Bloom, as he expected, even demanded, received from the world. After all, it took a man of imagination and initiative to bombard the public with new offers, even hollow ones – and a man of courage to admit to his mistakes. And a man with imagination, initiative and courage – that was a man to back. No wonder Sir Isaac Wolfson supported him.

Or did he? Bloom's English & Overseas had soared by 800 per cent in the year, largely on hopes that Wolfson would take a major stake in the company. Its big fascination was thus the unquantifiable bounty which would flow when the unconfirmed deal took place at an unspecified time in the indeterminate future. As history (a more sober judge than the stock-market) recalls, Sir Isaac stayed coy, Rolls Razor caved in under an oppressive weight of sweeping mismanagement, and English & Overseas survived into a Bloomless future only thanks to heroic work in the intensive care unit.

Other dreams from my past swam out of that 1963 newspaper file. There were two brothers by the name of Richards whose company, an agglomerate named Brayhead, promised much promise, duly contradicted by a savage and awful price collapse. The brethren then proceeded to disprove the old saw about heavyweight boxers and market high-fliers: that they never come back. The second time round of these cut-price Muhammad Alis came at the tail end of the Second Great Bubble, and was a far better tale, imaginatively speaking, than the first. This last fable was a *mélange* of disc stores for computers, exotic United States connections and (the clincher at the time and in retrospect) avuncular interest from Bernie Cornfeld's IOS. Cornfeld played much the same role as Wolfson in the Bloom saga, except that the less genuinely canny IOS got firmly stuck with a wad of shares of little worth when the second tale proved no more worth telling (or at least hearing) than the first.

Another double-comeback was that of Klinger, riding high in 1963 on an apparently irresistible tide of demand for a marvellous invention, machines for texturizing nylon yarns. In its previous disaster, in stockings, Klinger had been saved by these wonderful engineering designs. Its admirers the second time round knew not that Klinger was driving full speed ahead into a business disaster of almost beautiful finality because of its interest in making the textured yarns themselves. Its impresario invented high production targets for the machines and set lofty sales targets to match. When the machines couldn't be sold to anybody else, he took them into his own factories; and there they proceeded to churn out far more textured yarns than Klinger could sell.

In the awful calamity that ensued, one story was that the stock couldn't be properly counted for some time, because it was physically impossible to force a path into the warehouse. The can of yarns, or rather worms, ended up in the unwilling arms of the biggest investor in the company, the great Imperial Chemical Industries. That only served ICI right for its policy of taking stakes in textile firms to keep them independent both of one another and of the rival giant Courtaulds – a policy derided as 'balkanizing' the industry by a maverick industrialist, Joe Hyman, whose Viyella textile group was also among the stars of 1963.

His Viyella creation turned out to be the only substantial corporation in that 1963 bunch. However, nobody could have forecast that the recently forged connection with ICI, which had propelled Hyman upwards so swiftly, would have so strange and convoluted a sequel. Hyman, the most creative manager whom the hidebound British textile industry had ever seen, fell out first with ICI and then with his boardroom colleagues. They ousted him at night just after a vast celebratory cocktail party, at which the conspirators, like the assassins waiting on the Ides of March, circled round the doomed Caesar with sickly smiles on their faces. Eventually the company was thrown in with another ICI holding, whose troubles were only slightly less desperate than Klinger's. And at that point the Viyella of 1963 finally ceased to be.

The truth to be drawn from these textile tales is that investors in the Klinger case didn't understand the fundamental economics of the business. Since there is some doubt whether the management did either, the shareholders can be forgiven on that score. But could they, or should they, have been able to uncover the management's uncertainty? More specifically, could investors have found out that textured yarns, not the marvellous machines, were the main force behind Klinger's booming fortunes? If they had done so, would it have made any difference?

No similar risks were taken by backers of Viyella, who might justifiably have shied only at the obvious fact that Hyman was abnormally prone to publicity, a tendency from which most stayers in the business field are notably free. The wary might also have considered the inevitable downside risks in an industry such as textiles, which is subject to its own abnormally severe cycles within the business cycle.

At least many investors knew Viyella by its shirts, whereas few Klinger fans could have recognized a textured yarn or explained its uses. But few purchasers of equities have ever bothered to check their temptation against the realities of a company's products. In some cases the wrong initial decision would have resulted – the first Ford car, the first Polaroid camera, the first Haloid Xerox copier or the first electronic computer would not have created much confidence; but, except with the private Ford company, there was plenty of time, after the product had been perfected, to join the equity hit parade. In many other cases, however, the billing simply fails to live up to the goods at any time. Bloom's washing-machine range was genuinely inferior to Hoover's, which made his long-term ability to compete with the American subsidiary deeply suspect.

Back in 1963, for another example, a new star had appeared on the furniture scene in the shape of Williams Supermarkets, a British forerunner of the one-time miracle of Levitz in the United States. An almost legendary operator named John James had fallen in love with the Williams concept; and those who recalled the stupendous monetary results of James's love affair with Sir Arnold Weinstock's Radio & Allied, later enveloped into the General Electric Company's financial apotheosis, were happy to follow the new star. The supremo of this business, however, was no Weinstock, and one look at a typical store was enough to raise grave doubts about whether any sizeable number of British homemakers would let the stuff on offer into their living and sleeping rooms, even for a fee. So it transpired: a decade later James offloaded his far from super supermarkets.

A sadder story lay behind BM Group. This was the less risky alternative to Bloom's Rolls Razor vehicles and consequently showed a substantially smaller gain in the boom year of 1963 – a mere 300 per cent. By convoluted reasoning, which illustrates the essential irrationality of markets, the riskier situation often commands a premium over the more secure; which is surely the reverse of logical thought. The product was another washing machine sold door to door, the Imperial automatic. Since it was several cuts above the Rolls Razor offering and sold to a more affluent group of customers, the Imperial looked a safer bet. Moreover, the whole operation was master-minded by that pabulum of the investing classes, a computer.

Door-to-door selling suffers the inherent disadvantage that expensive salesmen have to be supported by costly newspaper advertising: without coupons clipped from the ads the salesmen wouldn't know which doorbells to ring. The Imperial answer was to gear the level of expenditure on advertising to the level of actual sales via the magic computer. The method worked excellently so long as sales rose or varied within reasonably narrow limits. When sales slumped sharply (they always do, when the ranks of the eager coupon-clippers and door-to-door buyers have been depleted), the computer can't cope – except by closing down the business. Imperial ran into the same cycle of over-selling and under-earning that brought down Bloom. The founder's private interests never were injected into the BM Group, as hitchers of their waggons to that 1963 star had hoped.

There were much sounder businesses in the *Observer*'s 1963 bundle, in sober lines of trade like sugar or gas cookers, building or upholstery fabrics. They were all second or third rankers, however; and none survived to become, as their backers hoped, tickets to the everlasting paradise. The list as a whole smacks in retrospect of greedy men being avidly fed by a market hungry for bull-period profits; it is redolent of reputations founded on nothing more than the movement of the share price (which then, of course, completing the typical cycle, fed off the reputations which had been created by its own rise).

Another bygone of 1963, not on the *Observer* list because it was so small as to escape unnoticed, was an outfit called H.W. Phillips. Its capital gain in the year was even greater than that of Bloom's vehicle. Close – actually even perfunctory – examination showed that it contained very little except some small interests making artificial fur, some allegedly miraculous but unrevealed processes for revolutionizing the textile industry and a fast-talking proprietor of unconvincing antecedents. His subsequent business demise left a number of first stunned, then outraged creditors looking foolishly after their lost money. Phillips was a British equivalent of the no-hope penny stocks which have never quite lost their allure even for the harder-headed American investor.

The moral goes deeper than the valuable instruction that bull markets bear to their top not only froth but scum, and that the sage investor learns to look beneath the surface. In some ways the excesses which this journey in the time machine back to 1963 revealed have been curbed since, not least by the shocks to people's purses that followed in the Second Great Crash. But most of the horror stories of that era, a decade or more back, could be repeated with minor variations today. That is in itself one cautionary thought.

Another is that these blotches on the face of capitalism, these minor pustules, bear an ominous similarity to the legends of much greater companies: like Litton or Ling-Temco-Vought. The principal difference, as fantastic in retrospect as it should have seemed at the time, is that these operations, though founded, just like Bloom's, on telling the tale, rose to gigantic scale and genuine might. Even in 1974 Litton was the fifty-third largest corporation in the United States, L-T-V the twenty-ninth.

Those who backed them were no more likely to understand what Litton's management meant by 'systems' than Klinger's backers were to grasp the mysteries of texturizing. If Litton's non-technical top management spun a non-texturized yarn about their new technologies, investors believed because they wished to believe. If they were informed that the 'systems' approach explained Litton's past phenomenal growth, they not only accepted the tale, but thought it entirely reasonable that 'systems' management could be applied to make further fortunes even in a profitless business like shipbuilding.

Then, since James Ling was plainly a genius, even his mistakes (like Bloom's) had to be a mark of distinction. Like the Richards brothers of Brayhead, Ling on his far larger scale even managed to pull the same trick off twice – double-twice, in fact. His Omega Alpha corporation was one of the last casualties of the Second Crash, falling to a collection of corporate vices which were identical to those that all but bankrupted L-T-V.

The master-plan was to buy and refurbish dingy companies, which could then be resold to the public, thus generating proceeds which would be used to buy still more properties ripe for refurbishing. Just as Ling brought L-T-V close to its knees by his foolish foray into the United States steel industry, so this time he gave OA a deadly karate chop by venturing into financial services. The operating losses on this buy forced Omega Alpha into huge write-offs and loaded it with $96·8 million of unserviceable debt. And thus Ling's end-of-the-beginning ended.

Murderers not only visit the scene of their corporate crimes, it seems, they repeat them. Both Litton and L-T-V, moreover, were sustained in their triumphant years by a touch of the unknown: Al Jolson's message that 'you ain't seen nothing yet'. Since the past in terms of the share price and sheer conglomerate growth had been literally so fabulous, what wonders could not be performed in the as-yet-unwritten future?

Through all the speculation and mystification, the principals of the two great star conglomerates talked – and talked. Their candour was almost as engaging as their loquacity. No journalist ever left the maestro's side, any more than anybody left Hyman's, without good copy. No investment analyst ever went home to Wall Street from Dallas or Beverly Hills without feeling warmer inside. They were not deceived in one respect: James Ling and Roy Ash and Tex Thornton, like the other heroes of the years before the Crash, were clever men, far brighter and more businesslike than most British heroes of 1963. The businesses which they bought and built were sounder affairs, too, than the rickety structures teetering at the top of that British bull market. But like those transatlantic fly-by-nights of 1963, the three Americans and their corporations were not what they were seen, or cracked up, to be – and nobody was sufficiently interested in truth to explore behind the façade.

That in itself is no great offence. Explorations of this kind are difficult to pursue, however dedicated the seeker after truth. When

Fortune looked into International Telephone & Telegraph, the supreme monument to the corporate empire building of the sixties, with its $11,154 million of sales, tenth largest in the United States in 1974, its assiduous scribes could find little to criticize or question, even in ITT's advanced ideas about accountancy. Yet the magazine, justly famed for its brilliant in-depth probes of murky situations, was visiting the company at the very time when, on top of the Chilean and Dita Beard scandals, ITT was about to run into crucial earnings setbacks at the Hartford insurance subsidiary, which it had bribed the Republican Party to keep.

The offence of the deceived investor does not lie in the failure to look for, still less to find, the truth. It lies in the fact that, even though the truth was neither sought nor found (because its discovery was impossible), investors chose to value Litton and L-T-V as if they not only knew the truth, but knew the truth to be wondrous. All stock-market meteors, with few exceptions, are made of the same base metal. The beginning and end of wisdom is to know that the meteors will fall from grace one day, probably sooner than you think, and to ensure that, whoever else is hurt in the crash, it will not be you.

Part IV. The basic truths

12. The movement of markets

Rain or shine, there's one question which anybody purporting to knowledge, genuine or otherwise, about the financial and investment world must expect to be asked first and foremost. Relatively few people inquire into the chances of the latest hot-shot share, such as those revisited in the previous chapter. But the highest-octane investment banker in Wall Street, the suavest City merchant banker, the little old lady with her all in AT&T or Shell – everybody wants to know: will the market go up or down?

Short of recourse to the Delphic report of the sage Bernard Baruch (who merely replied that the market would fluctuate), the expert is reduced to the usual run of two-handed commentary. On the one hand, markets will rise; on the other, they may fall. Thus neatly removed off the hook and replaced on the fence, the expert can go about his business, safe in the knowledge that nobody can hold his ignorance against him. For the fact is that, faced with this apparently simple question, most experts have fewer clues than the bumbling police officers whom detective story authors provide as butts for the likes of Hercule Poirot, Nero Wolfe and Sherlock Holmes.

Why is it fair to describe the problem as falling into the non-exacting category? Only because the man is being asked to predict in very general terms how a broad market will behave in response to certain known forces over a limited period of time. If he can't express a useful opinion on this score (to be fair to him, nobody can), then are his predictions on individual stocks likely to be much use? (As the reader knows, they aren't.)

Yet the questioners are on the right track. The most important factor in the movement of individual share prices is probably the general direction of the market. If you had a magic lamp, a greedy mind and one wish there is no doubt what you as investor should rub for: an infallible knowledge of when the whole market will turn, and in which direction.

No more forceful and beautiful proof ever occurred than that shock boom in the London market early in 1975. Although the skies were thick with economic storm clouds, even though business confidence and political confidence were racing one another downwards, elementary financial economics could have revealed that the conditions existed for a sharp revival in equity buying. Here they are. First, a falling trend in interest rates. Rates which had gone belting upwards in 1974 were now coming down. Second, the piling up of uninvested funds in the hands of the big institutions; these had gone on amassing insurance premiums and pension contributions undisturbed while the storms had lashed down on the City of London. Third, historically high dividend yields and abysmally low price–earnings ratios were available on many key stocks; great international names like Unilever and Shell were selling for the price (comparatively speaking) of a well-established peanut vendor. Fourth, at a composite price of around 150, the thirty stocks in the *Financial Times* ordinary index had little further to go – unless, that is, the world was coming to an end.

The rationale behind this fourth argument is that the index can never sell at zero, unless all the constituent companies go bankrupt simultaneously. Although the Labour government of Harold Wilson was intermittently doing its best to achieve this objective (more by inadvertence than malice), business managers were resisting the government's efforts with tolerable success. So a zero-worth market was out. (Some pessimists so far forgot their senses as to predicate a *minus* figure for the index, with shareholders actually paying others to take their property away. But this could happen only if liabilities were attached to owning shares; and that, thanks to the blessings of the limited liability company, is not so.)

However, this misguided pessimism pointed in a sane direction: the cheaper shares got, the less people were likely to sell them. After all, if your possession is worth a large fat zero, be it a stock certificate or a Guzzi motor-scooter, you have no incentive to sell – so you won't. As the *Financial Times* index sank further towards the ocean floor, anybody not forced to sell by the previous price collapse was increasingly certain to stay on board. London saw an epidemic of 'bed-and-breakfast' operations which emphatically proved the point.

'Bed-and-breakfast' is one of those eloquent British phrases, coined by some unknown genius, which passes into the language.

It means that the holders of deadbeat investments, rather than cast the offending articles into outer darkness and face the losses like men, sell the shares, establish a tax loss and promptly buy the self-same offenders back. As the London market reached its nadir, many investors preferred bed-and-breakfast to outright sale. The implicit belief that their shares would one day show higher prices demonstrated a clear refusal to believe the world was indeed ending. This refusal, since markets are moved by psychology, was itself an omen of much significance, to those who were prepared to believe the oracle. Human beings, however, find it understandably difficult to move against the crowd, and it is a safe bet that very few investors, professional or amateur, got in at the bottom of the Second Great Crash. Equally, however, men find it hard to avoid being carried along by a mob.

When the first feeble buying of equities began in that economically bleak winter, no equivalent volume of selling occurred (because investors, as noted, were still disinclined to offload at sub-bargain-basement prices). So prices shot ahead; the crowds then rushed to buy before prices moved away from their clutching hands completely; thus the price sprint accelerated further.

Even though the boom which doubled the ordinary index in a mere two months still left the London market, in relation to its previous high and in terms of constant money values, far down in the depths, these stirring events deserve detailed analysis. The analysis is built of hindsight. But its value to the investor extends far beyond the limited reach of the backward view. Observe again the clear, uncomplicated factors which might have been picked out as encouraging portents for the market.

The first is that the national economic performance, and the even more execrable behaviour of Her Majesty's ministers in this instance, have nothing to do with the case. Markets move according to their internal forces; they are not an economic weathercock, sensitive to every wind that blows. Markets may indeed react to a given gust – but that is entirely a matter of market choice; and markets may choose, quite perversely, to move in the opposite direction to the tornado. The forces which actually did influence the market in those two miraculous months were the permanent factors which are the genuine, underlying makers of markets.

To put first things first, we have observed before that the level of interest rates on fixed-return stocks, such as government bonds, has a perverse but decisive effect on the level of equity prices. The relationship between the two is by no means fixed and immutable, like the movement of the stars. But movement holds the key to understanding: that is, if interest rates are moving in one direction, equity prices, sooner or later, must move in the other. It's the stock-market's law of gravity: when one goes up, one goes down, and vice versa. To which can be added the original Newtonian law of gravity itself: rates which go up must come down. Again the reverse also applies. Those who disobey these grave laws are the stock-market equivalent of the young officer ('Where's he buried?') in A. G. Macdonnell's *England Their England*. That young man ran round putting out fires in ammunition dumps. His equivalents plunge into equities when interest rates are rising.

Conversely only those who are constitutionally prone to look gift horses in the mouth neglect to buy equities once they become convinced that interest rates are on a downward slope. Unfortunately, both the folly in the first case and the over-caution in the second are encouraged by refusal to accept that a ball thrown into the air must come down again – investors congenitally feel that booms and slumps will go on for ever, and lack the conviction or the courage to advance against the temper of the times. In doing so they ignore the existence of historical guidelines. Because the evidence is there for all to see, we broadly know when the market, or an individual share for that matter, is expensive by past standards, and when it is cheap. We also know by definition that the market reaches its point of greatest expense, of super-costliness, just before boom turns to bust. So equally shares must be at their cheapest shortly before the tide turns, and money comes flooding back into a Sahara of desiccated stock prices.

Finally, the institutions have become more and more important in determining the volume of buying. J.H.C. Leach has shown the massive impact of the swings of institutional buying in London, where they regularly account for two-fifths of all purchases. In 1972 £1400 million of new money was poured into equities; in 1974 a scant £100 million was spent – quite enough to explain the strength of the former year and total collapse of the latter. It has become possible, within wide limits, to calculate how much uninvested money is available to enter the market – and the sum is in the thousands of millions.

It also follows that the bigger this pile grows, the smaller the supply of stock on which it can be expended must become. That is because, if the big buyers are holding back, prices will decline. In 1973 Leach's figures show that £537 million of net buying by the institutions had to contend with nearly £2000 million of selling by individuals who had soured on the equity cult. The 1974 gap between institutional buying and private selling was just as huge – small wonder that prices dropped so shatteringly. The fall went so far, however, that individuals (as we have seen) became reluctant to put their depreciated holdings on the market. Sooner or later institutional buying power a) must come into collision with b) investor unwillingness to sell at a loss. At that point the accident becomes a happy one – prices will be raised by a) until b) gives way: and the only question left for the investor to answer is: when?

To know that the market must turn is easy: it always does. (The day when it doesn't will mark a new era, ushered in by the Red or Yellow Revolution or some other catastrophe. Anyway, the fact that the world may end is no reason for not investing in stock-markets – you'll be wiped out in any event, so you might as well play the odds.) Calling the turn, however, is a different, far harder matter, because it involves more psychology than economics. Any calm, cool and collected professional should be able to read the signs and give an accurate diagnosis and prognosis of the market's clinical condition. But nobody can tell exactly when or why the first fund manager will reach for his telephone and utter the incantation that starts the avalanche.

Indeed ignorance goes still further. The professionals, the experts, the gurus are mostly none too sure whether the turn has actually come. Often they discover that they have been luxuriating in a bull market, or agonizing in the throes of a bear phase, only months after the event. Like weather forecasters who resolutely forecast a sunny day while hail is clattering on their windows, market pundits often warn of calamity while stocks are driving upwards, and vice versa.

The same man who, when the great British stock boom burst into flower in early 1975, warned that the bull market had not yet begun, a couple of weeks later was proclaiming its definite arrival – just in time for the boom to expire in a surfeit of miseries about the local hyper-inflation. This particular writer was a chartist, one of those seers who plot the movement of shares and markets on graph paper in the hope of discerning a pattern which, past experience tells them, foretells or establishes a trend. Sometimes their lucubrations are correct, sometimes not – in this they are no different from anybody else. But the psychological drive behind their efforts is patent, as in the willingness of intelligent investors to take heed. In this the latter in turn are no different from the cultured intelligentsia who take the arrant nonsense of astrology seriously. If only there were a magical external guide to the uncertainties of the present and the future, in life and stock-market alike, how much less unendurable the uncertainty of both would be.

For those who find charts too esoteric or far-fetched, other omens loom large. Some New Yorkers swear by the movement of trading in odd lots, the theory being that small packages of stocks are favoured by small investors. A pick-up in odd-lot demand therefore means that the small man, like the first swallow, is signalling summer, while his departure has opposite connotations. Other elaborate theories are based on the relationship between trading volume and price movements – these, alas, are particularly useless on the London market, which managed to reach the last quarter of the twentieth century without any accurate figures on its own daily trading volume. Any figuring extrapolated from market performance, anyway, suffers from one plain defect: the fact that history is being asked to tell the future. This it can never do, even when the history is as recent as yesterday's trading.

Unfortunately this defect affects even my own favourite indicator, which is that the number of new highs and new lows recorded each day is an important guide to the market's temper and trend. This purely empirical observation, which demands checking by some researcher armed with the requisite files and computers, has much appeal. The idea is that a decisive move by the highs to outnumber the lows portends a cheerful change in markets; and, conversely, if the lows outnumber the highs, then no matter how strongly the market is rising, investors are still firmly stuck in a bear trend.

There is a sensible explanation of why the theory should work. In glooms it takes confident buying to push a share to a new peak; in times of affluence, determined selling is needed to force a share down to the bottom. So a surplus of buyers or sellers at the extremes of the market, and against the market trend, may signal a wider and ultimately decisive change. But in reality my highs and lows say nothing about the future; again, they merely describe things as they were yesterday – and what the searcher for signals urgently hunts is evidence of how things will be tomorrow (if not the day after).

The weakness of watching the past was proved inadvertently by one wise and good lady pundit who subscribed to the engaging idea that investors in the mass (by which she meant the market) always knew more than the individual investor. It followed that you should only buy shares which, on the evidence of low dividend yields, massive price–earnings ratios and peak prices, were favoured by the buying masses. Only a good fairy saved this counsellor from total disaster, because the invariable truth is that the market chases its favourites up too far and reacts in savage, sometimes overdone fury when they disappoint.

By a slightly different token, however, the market has an uncanny instinct for truth in the opposite direction. If a company's share price plunges downwards, despite the tips of the columnists and brokers, the protestations of its ebullient chairman, the announcement of wondrous figures and marvellous bids – don't, however much are you tempted, dream of buying the shares. One time out of ten, you may miss a bonanza. The other nine times you will save all your shirts.

What applies to shares applies to markets. All booms are overdone; all busts go too far – but only a fool bets against the market when it insists on going down. The argument that there is no reason for the fall is akin to saying that your brakes should not have failed when your car ploughed into a brick wall. They *did* fail; the market *is* falling, which means that there *must* be a reason. The only problem for the disbelieving spectator is that he can't discern the explanation even after the event; and for this there is much less excuse than for being unable to identify the cause beforehand.

The latter feat requires less brain than nose: the same kind of educated sense that dogs and pigs in the Périgord bring to unearthing black truffles from beneath the immortal oaks. I once found an infallible nose – the brilliant investment banker for whom a friend worked. Every so often this obsessed man would telephone his junior at home of a Sunday, full of desperate gloom about the market. This was invariably the signal for a full-blooded boom in prices, and I grew to rely on this somewhat back-handed tipping off. Alas, my Cassandra-in-reverse resigned in a huff one day, leaving me to fall back on mere facts in the unending battle to beat markets to the punch.

Basic economic analysis won't work as well as a nose, but economic data are the beginning of prosperity. The level and trend of interest rates; the relationship between stock-market dividend yields and fixed-interest returns; the proportion of savings going into the various investment possibilities; the relationship of price–earnings ratios and dividend yields to historic norms; the rate of growth in the money supply – all these are factors which must determine (and always have done) the bounds within which markets move. Markets move, moreover, in great sluggish cycles, interspersed with violent, short and sharp intervals, rather like a monumental gestation period. In London, for example, shares moved upwards for three years to 1955, fell for three to 1958, boomed again to 1960, stayed flat for six years, shot up between 1966 and 1968, flopped back until 1970, whipped up until 1972 and slumped until early 1975. In these wider cycles, investors had opportunities to double their money in two to three years, not by buying wonder stocks, but by backing (as opposed to bucking) the market. That's why the foundation for any intelligent investment programme is an alert appreciation of the market's bearing and general direction; and a readiness to change that appreciation, equally intelligently, when the evidence shows that, once again, you've got it wrong.

13. The equity tightrope

The great plurality of the investing public never needs advice on the stock-markets – because most people never go near them. The plurality, thereby earning itself the collective name of sucker from those who think themselves sophisticated, resolutely deposits its reserves into the keeping of dull banks, dreary savings institutions, hidebound insurance firms and the lacklustre like, where the rate of return ranges from less than nothing to a pittance.

The less-than-nothing phenomenon – which we earlier identified as 'negative interest' – arises from the inability of the guardians of the people's money, at times of inflation, to offer rates of interest that over-top the speed of decline in the value of that money. But even at times of monetary stability (which have been few and far between in modern times) the small investor, who collectively makes by far the largest investments, is lucky to get away with any true return on his money in real, concrete terms. It follows that the smart guys, the men who know how to butter and honey their bread, are those who sneer at savings banks and marvel at the penchant of the naive West Germans for pouring their abundant personal wealth into fixed-interest deposits in good times and bad; and who goggled in even greater amazement when the 1975 Britons, passing through the most prolonged hyper-inflation of any advanced industrialized society in many decades, abandoned the initial urge to fly from money and flooded the savings institutions with their funds.

Since the populace was being offered 7 per cent yields at a time when prices were rising by 25 per cent a year, the savers were rushing to lose 18 per cent of their money in a twelvemonth, without any hope of redress or recovery. Presumably they argued to themselves that 18 per cent down was better than losing a full quarter by hanging on to banknotes. And hanging on to currency, when inflation was eroding your purchasing power, suddenly seemed better sense than buying consumer goods which, however fast prices were rising, could not be turned back into cash of the same denomination in an emergency.

The history of financial markets, however, shows that the suckers have often been smarter than the wise. There have been years on both sides of the Atlantic when the non-interest-bearing savings certificates known as pound notes or dollar bills have been better investments than the supposedly fertile documents known as common or ordinary shares. Slumps in stock-markets are frequently sharper than the 25 per cent inflation rate with which the United Kingdom celebrated the mid-point of the seventies. Any smart investor heavily committed to equities in the off-years is the true sucker. Those invested in savings accounts at these times leave the wise ones gasping at the post – if not behind it.

The equity investor walks a tightrope, and on a tightrope it is easier to fall off than to get to the other side. The would-be Blondin begins from the point of necessity: he must do something with his money, even if it is only to wish it luck as he waves it goodbye. If he chooses to leave his savings in cash or near-cash (the latter having the advantage of paying interest), one decision has been taken, perhaps wisely: not to place the trembling foot on the rope.

The risk isn't simply that of the one off-year. Over considerably longer periods of time, the laws of mathematics, which govern all markets, may make it extremely difficult, if not impossible, to get to the other side. Let's take November 1972 as a convenient date. It was neither the best nor the worst of times for the stock-markets. Wall Street in the middle of that month had pierced the 1000 mark on the Dow Jones industrials, to general if somewhat uneasy rejoicing; and the blows that were to strike London in the years just ahead didn't even figure in stockbrokers' nightmares.

At the end of 1972, anybody who had invested in the London market five years previously would have shown a gain of only 17·8 per cent (coming down to $12\frac{1}{2}$ per cent after application of the local capital gains tax). Compare that with the situation of a nervous character who kept off the tightrope. The compound growth of an investment in a building society returning 5 per cent annually would have been 27·6 per cent free of income tax – and higher rates than 5 per cent were available over most of the period. At certain points in the five years, the record of an investor who came in at year 1 would have been still more inglorious: this is because the market had off-years in years 2 and 3. Years 4 and 5 were better – they showed substantial rises of 21·3 per cent and 13·4 per cent respectively. But the glory of this performance was dimmed by a catch which even I spotted. I wrote at the time. 'It will take only a market setback of 18% in the next 24 months to drop the return of a *four-year* investor (who had the advantage of a lower starting-point than a year 1 entrant) to a building society level.'

The cold breath of the Four Horsemen of the Apocalypse must have been hissing in my ear. In harsh actuality the market collapsed to a quarter of its previous peak before the tragedy bottomed out at the very end of 1974. These cataclysmic events are not needed to underline the point – that the magic of compound interest works in both directions. As con-men down the ages have known to their benefit and the victim's cost, the mathematics by which 7 per cent per annum over ten years adds up to an increase of nearly 100 per cent, and not a measly 70 per cent, is virtually irresistible magic.

Many investors probably don't realize that this is the rubric by which they are living (or trying to). Even conscious compound-interest fans tend to appreciate the happy miracle of accelerating absolute growth more than its unhappy companion: the damage done by a break in the chain. Serious unhappiness can follow, for example, if the 7 per cent curve is stopped dead – not reversed, just checked – for only a single year. If it resumes its 7 per cent rise, they must wait not ten years for their money to double, but a dozen. Put another way, to get back on target if the off-year comes halfway through the cycle, they will need a growth rate, not of 7 per cent, but of almost 10 per cent – a very different matter of magnitude, and a target which even an equity hot-gospeller, or a keen fund manager of the kind who took Wall Street by storm in the sixties, would hesitate to guarantee. As a matter of historical fact, investing in the market and sitting there has been bad medicine for most of the postwar period, precisely because the fat years are followed by lean ones with such monotonous regularity and with such debilitating effects on the phenomenon of compound growth.

At this juncture the over-initiated will dismiss the whole concept of 'the market' and point out, rightly enough, that this is something which nobody ever buys. Wise men pick selected shares which will grow faster – much faster – than the common herd. We have noted before, however, that there is a flaw in this otherwise delightful theory: selected shares, those in the super-star, high-valuation league, may also fall far more rapidly. Here, too, there is a knowing riposte. The object of the exercise is not to select shares at their zenith, but to find a stock in its early, unnoticed days and to stay with it, not to the end of the road (because, unlike the Golden Road to Samarkand, this one never ends), but into the everlasting tomorrow.

A book published in February 1975 under the encouraging title *You Can Still Make Millions in the Stock Market*, for instance, extolled the fortune which the writer, Samuel Mitchell, had made from a modest investment in Xerox Corporation: by complete coincidence, the equity chosen for analysis in my chapter 4, 'The tale of two growth stocks'. That chapter noted that whether you made an acceptably large profit out of Xerox or not depended entirely on the moment of purchase. If you got in on the ground floor (as Mitchell did) – fantastic! Starting with a purchase of a hundred Haloid (the predecessor of Xerox) for $30 a throw, Mitchell worked his way to $4 million in under two decades – or rather, Xerox worked his way. Several times along the route, Mitchell checked with the management to ensure that he was still on course. Each time he was satisfied, intellectually and financially. But the story does not have a happy ending: the whole Mitchell thesis – that Xerox, 'like "Ol' Man River" ... keeps rolling along at a growth rate unprecedented for a multi-billion dollar corporation' – was about to be tested and found wanting. When Xerox acquired the Californian computer firm, Scientific Data Systems, Mitchell 'casually said to Peter [McColough, the Xerox boss] some time later "We paid a helluva price of SDS" and he added quite casually "We needed it, Sam".'

They needed it like a hole in the head. In 1975 the $900 million computer buy was erased from Xerox's future in one of the costliest write-offs and most expensive acquisition failures in corporate history. To *Forbes* magazine, quoted approvingly by Mitchell, McColough had said: 'It was absolutely essential for Xerox to have a computer capability to reach the objectives we have set for the Seventies.' Unless the brave decision to axe the computer division had been taken, Xerox would have been unable to meet any objectives in the seventies, or in the eighties for that matter. As it was, the total return to investors in the 1964–74 decade was a feeble 5·34 per cent annually. It wouldn't even have doubled Mitchell's money over the period; and Procter & Gamble, a giant long before Haloid's early, unnoticed days of growth began, had a better growth record for investors over the decade.

Mitchell's story, the days of wine and roses no less than those of dismal reckoning, is a cautionary tale. The sky, or at least the penthouse, is indeed the limit for ground-floor entrants. But joining the lift on the fiftieth floor or higher gets you a much shorter and less rewarding journey. Somebody some time is going to book a ride at penthouse level, only to be sorely disappointed when he finds that there is nowhere to go but down. And at that point somebody who stayed in the lift too long will feel a sinking situation as the floors he passed on the way up meet him on the descent.

It's still true that ground-floor or low-down purchases are the order of the day – the problem being that there are so many ground floors from which to choose. The statistics of growth sagas like that of Xerox *née* Haloid read so seductively in retrospect that only the wariest readers remember that Haloid was one, not in a thousand, but in several thousands of runners. And only the wary and thrice-warned know that statistics can deceive, that the magic of maths can produce the phenomenon of non-existent super-growth – something like Bigfoot, the man-like giant gorilla, who is alleged to inhabit the American West, who leaves vast footprints, but is never actually seen by any trained observer – although he is believed in passionately by credulous laymen.

The statistics show, say, that a £100 investment has grown by 30 per cent a year to reach a wonderful £1,380 in ten years. But suppose that this investment has galloped up nine-fold in year 1 (by no means an unknown or exceptional feat for a well-lubricated stock in the take-off period), and then slows down to a still excellent four-fold trot in year 2. Supposition can now yield to stubborn fact. The stock can then *decline* by 62 per cent over the next eight years and *still* hit the 30 per cent compound growth target for the whole decade. Yet on any criteria, for eight years out of ten, such a stock has been a total bust.

The number of such busts is legion, ranging from the big bombed-out conglomerates all the way down to the Haloids that didn't make it. The statistical truth applies to earnings as well as to returns. In case after case, of which Xerox is only one example, the ten-year growth in earnings per share looks wonderfully high for such leviathans of American industry and commerce. But a glance at the starting-point of a 20 per cent compound growth rate usually shows how small the beginnings were; and a company that in five years quadruples its earnings (32 per cent per annum) and then takes ten years to double again (7 per cent a year) will still show a fifteen-year compound growth in earnings of 18 per cent.

For a long time companies have ranked high in the *Fortune* or *Management Today* ten-year growth comparisons solely on the strength of early rises from a tiny base. The key is simply that a pound stock which appreciates to £10 has done nothing special when it limps up further to £11; but that 10 per cent gain is, of course, 100 per cent of the original purchase price, *mirabile dictu*, and the proud possessor can now claim, perfectly correctly, that his capital has grown eleven-fold instead of ten-fold.

The lesson has not been lost on the true, wised-up growth addict. Despite the teachings of the Xerox-loving Mitchell, the best course after a year or two of super-growth is not to hang on in perpetuity, but to seek another home for your super-profit. This unfortunately raises the formidable difficulty of persuading lightning to strike in the same place (your bank balance) twice. The plethora of investment opportunities produces acute problems of choice. How can you tell which Haloid is waiting to metamorphose into Xerox, or which of the numberless nameless corporations will stay that way?

The little company that will make it exceedingly big is rarely marked out by any distinguishing features. At the height of Wall Street's long, hot period, the keen young investor used hopefully to identify these animals by the very absence of the normal signs of credibility. If a company (preferably as far away from Wall Street as possible, in the Deep South or on the West Coast) operated in an expensive new area of technology, needed large, unspecified and non-existent development funds, had a long string of losses and had so far failed to realize one of its many golden hopes, the fanciers would be overjoyed. I remember one of these explorers telling me in just such a case: 'I've found my Xerox.'

Like punters who back only rank outsiders on the track, these Wall Street wanderers seldom won. The game is no easier if the choice alights on a company which actually has a track record and is still full of running. Many an exercise conducted by the shrewd has proved not only this point, but also the supreme shrewdness of keeping the neck well stuck in. In 1967, for example, an eminently well-informed observer publicly named five entrepreneurs whose equities, it was hoped, would collectively multiply 200 times in twenty years. The mind-boggling figure is another of those compound sleights of statistics. It translates into 30 per cent a year, which I take to be the most that any mortal investor could hope to achieve over any significant span of time. After a five-year span the Fearsome Five were all but bang on target – no mean achievement, even in that relatively lush period. But the individual year-by-year figures fill in with bald historical fact the fancy theoretical statistics rehearsed above.

The great bulk of the gain was made in only one year, when the five shares appreciated by 180 per cent. Over the next four years, even though the portfolio advanced against a falling trend in the market, the gain was so small, at 28 per cent, that after capital gains tax it worked out below the going tax-free returns on a building society deposit. Once again, the central, certain postulate is reinforced. Gigantic gains made in early years, when a tiny equity capitalization meets the full force of a powerful surge in earnings from a tiny base, see the investment through many years of subsequent decline or stagnation.

Of the five entrepreneurial selections, only one achieved super-growth in any later twelve-month period between 1968 and 1972. Super-growth is defined for the purposes of this exercise as more than doubling the share price over the span of four seasons. The best achievement of the other four was a 63·8 per cent rise in one year by a financial conglomerate – and that was a recovery from a pronounced individual setback in the bear market, not a surge forward to new glory (which, in fact, never transpired).

The conglomerate's comeback was in year 4 of the phantom portfolio, when the market rose by a fifth, and nearly all shares (by definition) rose with it. There is a compelling lesson from this experience about smaller growth stars – only the conglomerate at the start of the portfolio had a sizeable market capitalization, and its value even then was a mere piddle in the international or even national leagues. Such undersized rockets are bad investments in declining markets, good buys in bull markets – and there is some empirical evidence to suggest that they are the leaders in heavy market setbacks.

A bear trend is usually at its strongest, scattering all before it, in the initial decline. It then settles on a Plateau of Stagnation (two stages better than the Valley of Despair which was explored in the

First and Second Great Crashes). Stagnation is psychologically and financially an awful phase for a stale growth stock. Those who invested for a fast ride get bored with a sluggish slide down and jump off the trolley. Conversely, the market commonly picks up rapidly from the plateau, as do the battered rockets: only, the latter fail to maintain their momentum. (Those investors, would-be easy riders, who hung on through the stagnation are prime candidates for speedy departure once the trolley begins to move again.)

As for the Fearsome Five, none of these trolleys moved much after 1972, except in the wrong direction. A firm which specialized in finding holes in the ground and filling them with sludge disappeared into a larger group, and was thus preserved from any possibility of vanishing into a hole in the ground itself. But the purchaser's equity went into a swoon which cut the price by three-quarters, to the discomfiture of taken-over enthusiasts who had stuck with the new shares.

Another member of the fivesome, a minor conglomerate, managed to decline in price in two years by over 80 per cent. At the start of the portfolio the price had risen to an astounding level 27 times higher than the eventual bottom of 1974: at which trough the equity had fallen about as far as a share can drop without passing into the happy hunting-ground of stock-market skeletons.

The bigger conglomerate hung on grimly by a series of just-in-time liquidations of assets, barely surviving in the process an almost equally cataclysmic fall: down to a grisly tenth of the 1972 peak in two years. Only the sole solidly based industrial stock in the group, a chemical outfit, came through in reasonable shape. Its share price came down close to a third of the 1968 peak, but revived strongly with the market in early 1975.

As a statistical curiosity, both conglomerate and chemical firm still showed delectable advances over a decade, thanks to the necromancy of early gains from small beginnings. But the hard-pressed survival of the one and the enduring qualities of the other left the portfolio started with such high and ambitious hopes in 1967 in frightful shape – without even taking account of the Fearsome Five entrant so far left unmentioned.

This was a modest-sized financial outfit which had grown by prodigious leaps and beatific bounds from the ribs of an even smaller investment bank. Neither the leaps nor the bounds were especially easy to follow, since they veered from banking to insurance, from property to films – indeed to any port of call where, with seemingly effortless ease, vast and growing profits could be taken on board. True, the group did seem to wander into legal and quasi-legal controversy with equal ease. But that is sometimes a characteristic of companies which can't wait to move on at the cracking pace which is their *raison d'être*.

Old sages recalled an adage even hoarier than their heads: in a situation where newcomers are blazing ahead in a market, and established firms, in this case the conservative investment banks, are trailing behind, the *prima facie* case is that the trail-blazers are moving into uncharted and dangerous territory. This must be true. The Establishment has the benefit of funds which have been entrusted to its care since time immemorial, while the outsiders must offer extra inducements to attract money, and therefore need to earn considerably more, when relending the booty, in order to cover the prime cost of their material.

This is the style of analysis which Samuel Mitchell sets out brilliantly in his book to explain why he never believed the stock-market claims for the Levitz firm. Basically, Mitchell examined and rejected the Levitz case on the foundations of common sense applied to his general knowledge of business and what he could glean in particular about the furniture trade. Mitchell couldn't understand how, selling at cut prices, Levitz could make bigger profits than firms selling at the full amount on the ticket. Levitz couldn't: which is why the shares plunged from a peak of $60 to a low of $4.

If Mitchell had been as rational and fearless about the Xerox buy into computers, he could have saved himself much pain. His instincts were plainly trying to warn him: that's why he suggested to the Xerox chief that 'we' paid a helluva lot for Scientific Data Systems. But the 'we' was his weakness. Past success and present pride had bound him personally to the Xerox cause. His judgement was warped, because in the case of Xerox it couldn't be brought directly to bear any longer. Xerox, however much it grows and prospers in the future, is most unlikely ever again to be the stock that Mitchell knew, loved and called 'we'.

At that, he fared better than anybody who stuck with the Famous Five, which were hopefully going to wax 200 times bigger in twenty years. After only eight years, two are no longer with us, one is on the brink, one is insignificant and only one has in any way lived up to its billing. Let that be two lessons for tightrope walkers who put their investment faith in balancing rods made of little growth stocks. First, one success in five is an excellent batting average. Second, don't sit on your first year of phenomenal capital gains if the stock or the market turns rancid – get out fast and switch to the investments which are most likely to withstand a bear onslaught (if that's what is happening); or which have greater staying power, if optimism continues to rule the exchanges.

The tightrope walker, however, has a problem not known to the earliest investors – the capital gains tax. This fiendish device is difficult to cope with intellectually. Everybody knows in their heart of hearts that an unrealized 1000 per cent gain carries within it a tax liability that is in no way lessened (except by inflation) if the winner holds on. But the gain, equally, is reduced by inflation, even if by nothing else. The reluctance to sell, pay the tax and pocket the residue has a minor financial aspect and a major psychological explanation.

Financially, taking the profit and paying the British rate of 30 per cent appears to weaken the investor's leverage. Instead of £1000 working for him at compound interest, he is reduced to £700. But this argument depends entirely on the stock continuing to grow. If it stagnates, then the £700 placed in another investment must produce a better result, if it generates any gain at all. Those who pretend to hearken to this financial argument are really heeding the psychological one.

The mind sees the original investment gain at its full value of £1000 and forgets about the gains tax altogether. The switch investment, since it begins at £700, appears to start well behind the line in a competition with the original unsold purchases. But the comparison is misleading. If the switch investment doubles to £1400, and the £1000, left alone, would have advanced to exactly the same point, the capital gains tax liabilities are respectively £510 and £420. But the respective *profits* are £1190 and £980 – the £700 gross gain on the switch investment is competing with a £400 extra gain on the unsold stake.

That is an outcome in theory, not in real life. And theory also notes that a new investment must outperform the old, so-far-untaxed stake by 1·4 : 1 to produce the same absolute net return. But if this fact is allowed to reinforce the investor's deep psychological attachment to his own successes, the equity tightrope can only lead from a rock to a very hard place – for the decision to let capital gains

ride is as likely as not to result in mediocre to miserable performance
in subsequent years.

The simple antidote is to subtract the capital gains liability from
all valuations, so that at least you are staring reality in the face and
are psychologically prepared for the pain of parting with some of
the profit to the Revenue for no good personal end. That simple
step is a giant stride towards showing the tightrope walker where
he is going : and that, as we are about to establish, is the essence
of successful investment.

14. Investment objectives

Once upon a time there was a troubled investor. He saw in the prints what any reader will always find: to wit, that the rational policy for the amateur is to hold a limited number of shares, probably no more than a round dozen. This gentle soul wanted nothing from life except a little capital appreciation to provide extra income. But he owned no less than forty-one assorted stocks and shares: a figure which, at an educated guess, is probably par for the course among amateur stock-market fans (or professionals, for that matter). What puzzled this investor, however, was that, by his own lights, he was reasonably successful: how could he be so right if he was so wrong?

He belonged to the 'Heads I win, tails I don't lose too much' school of investment. When any particular share prospered mightily, his habit was to skim off the cream, and to reinvest the skimmed cream in another promising churn. If a share went to sleep, or began to die on him, he automatically sold, hoping to limit the loss to 15 per cent. This fate visited one purchase in four: an excellent rate of striking in a world where, as Damon Runyon once observed through the mouth of Louie Liverlips, all human life is six to five against. As for holding forty-one shares rather than twelve, this was another safety measure: the investor felt there was safety in numbers. Since one in four would go awry even in a smaller portfolio, because of bad selection or worse timing, the bigger number gave him thirty-odd potential winners, the smaller only eight.

Two things now troubled his former serenity: whether he would have done better, all the same, by restricting his purchases; and whether his proliferation had inserted too much money into his broker's large silk purse. (This was in the days before the purse turned into a sow's ear.) Given the random behaviour of shares in stock-markets, the doubts were quite unanswerable, the kind of worrying question, like the identity of the Dark Lady of the Sonnets, that people carry to their graves. But the policy by which the investor lived in part simply rationalized a well-attested fact: the inexorable tendency for portfolios to grow, if not in value, at least in number.

Too few investors have the courage and self-discipline to obey a selling principle (like the 15 per cent rule cherished above). Any self-respecting and self-deceiving person can always find a good excuse for clinging to a share, and some tempting titbit is always around in the stock-market (especially in a rising market). So the investor retains the sleeping beauty and buys the titbit, thereby increasing his number of holdings by one. That is the virtue of imposing a limitation on size. It forces the investor to be truly selective, to ask whether the share at which he is shooting seductive glances is truly more desirable than the investment which must be sold to make room. In other words, restricting the portfolio is a valuable discipline – in the right hands.

However, investment is an undisciplined pastime. My troubled investor could have spared himself any anxiety. He was, after all, following a policy – never mind if, by the pundit's rules, it was misbegotten. If an investor's methods work out, then he should by all means praise the Lord and continue to pass the ammunition. The only rational policy is the one that meets rationally selected objectives, regardless of theory. However, it helps to venture along your chosen path with an eye, preferably both eyes, open to the pitfalls.

The drawback to the Heads and Tails policy is so obvious that, as with large holes in the ground, many people fall right into it. Suppose one investment blossoms like a flowering cherry, yielding a +10 per cent gain. If the portfolio is equally split between forty-one stocks, the net result of this magnificent stroke of selective genius is a 10 per cent rise overall. If the front-runner is only one of ten, however, the whole portfolio bounds forward by +1 per cent, bringing far more cheer to one and all.

That is the less attractive reverse side to safety in numbers. However, if one investment is a total write-off, the forty-one-strong portfolio comes into its own. It drops by some $2\frac{1}{2}$ per cent; the smaller portfolio suffers a 10 per cent slump. The critical question is whether the chances of a spectacular success or a catastrophic failure are increased by raising the number of throws.

If you hold the academically respectable view that stock-market investment is a game of pure chance, theoretically the odds must favour the larger portfolio. But that, alas, is only theory. Let us return to the Pin Test again. A pin stuck in a newspaper's list of share prices may or may not come up with a winner. But it doesn't follow that, if the first pin fails, a further twelve or twenty-four, or twenty-nine pricks of the pin will do the trick. Those who enjoy testing theories can select random portfolios in retrospect. Find an old edition of a newspaper, prick in the pin and compare the selections with the latest prices. A typical exercise of this kind, using my own pin, threw up one set of a dozen stocks with a 29 per cent gain, only two of which were above the average performance of the set. But the soaring pair included one fellow who leapt ahead by 265 per cent (as the result of a timely bid by Radio Corporation of America – but you can no longer rely on Bobby Sarnoff, RCA's prodigal chairman, to pull investment chestnuts out of the fire: he's been ousted). Another set of twelve pin-pricked stocks, to return to the argument about random stock selections, included four above the average for the bunch, which this time came to 20 per cent. Continue sticking pins in the paper for a hundred more random dozens and all you will get are similarly random results. What else would you expect?

In any event, the investor is supposed to bring thought rather than pins to bear. The difficulty lies in finding where reason lies in the market and how you may recognize rationality. The Heads and Tails investor described above, who plainly accepted the rule of reason, had actually chosen an irrational course – and in one of the few areas where logic can be scrupulously applied. His success ratio (and his failure rate for that matter) should be precisely the same, no matter how few or how many the stocks he buys. He admits as much himself in describing his theory.

But think again. If the same amount of money is divided between forty-one stocks instead of a dozen, the total in any one stock will be much less. While it is great fun and good for the morale to have a 100 per cent gain on any investment, the pleasure is far greater if the profit is £200 instead of £50. This alternative formulation of the mathematical drawback of proliferation emphasizes yet more tellingly that, if your judgement is worth anything to you, it is worth backing with a reasonable amount of cash: putting less gold behind the judgement won't make it any better. Moreover, he who insists on trying to persuade two-score stocks to hatch, as opposed to sitting on a dozen, has so hard a task that he is not surprisingly driven in the direction of some mechanistic device – like selling the whole investment if it fails to perform within some specified period, hopefully before the price decline has reached some cut-off point, like 15 per cent.

The mechanism obscures an essential limitation of logic which is even clearer in the Top of the Milk Technique favoured by many amateurs as another alternative to thought – that is, turning any substantial paper profit into real money and letting the original stake ride. The stock-market logician, confronted with some such plan, shakes his weary head and observes that the investor is starting from the wrong point.

The place to begin is some overall target for performance. With that decided, the investor can deduce what individual gain over what time span will enable the target to be hit squarely in the middle of the bull. For example, assume that he wants a 35 per cent gain per annum after capital gains tax: that means an overall rise of 50 per cent in twelve months, or about 4 per cent clear of expenses on an individual investment held for a month (compounding can be left out of the argument over such short time intervals).

Since half the investments made are likely to disappoint, losing half their value, the good eggs have to hatch out double. In other words, it makes no sense, from this angle, for the investor to sell for less than an 8 per cent gain in a four-week period – net of all selling and buying costs. To be on the safe side (and safety is an essential part of the investment game), 10 per cent is a more sensible target, which has the added advantage of offering easier arithmetic. However, it makes not a jot of sense to sell every investment automatically once it has passed the magic 10 per cent – or any other benchmark. The true question should be engraved on every investor's wall. Are my chances of maintaining this rate of appreciation in this particular investment greater or less than in any other investment to which I might switch? If the answer is 'greater', you don't sell *any* of the holding. If it is 'less', then what sense is there in selling only part, as in the Top of the Milk Technique? You should dispose of the lot and seek that other, cosier home.

The question can be rephrased, possibly more helpfully. Ask each time you review your portfolio whether you would, at the *current* price of each of its contents, be prepared to put the *current* value of your holding into those shares. Thus the rational attitude. But investment, in addition to being undisciplined, is a most personal matter. The policy to be pursued must be one that fits the investor's personality as well as his purse. Most investors, however, are torn between their emotions and their intellects, and this affliction by a mild form of schizophrenia pervades all their decisions with a misty cloud of confusion. Mostly they end up seeking that contradiction in terms, maximum safety and also the greatest conceivable capital gain: a combination which is rarely given to man. The disease can be mitigated by fresh thought about the language in which objectives are formulated. That 10 per cent per month figure, for instance, relates solely to the share price. Now the basic axiom of stock-markets is that share prices conform to no known law. In other words the 10 per cent objective is as rationalistic as aiming, when tossing a coin, to see it turn up heads. Nobody can escape from the uncomfortable truth – that investment is a game of hazard – wriggle how he may. But the hazard can be reduced to more manageable terms.

First, a small digression is necessary. When company directors moan about the low standing of their shares, they don't mean its actual price in the market so much as its relative price. For example when Philip Morris officers were bending the ear of the Los Angeles Society of Financial Analysts back in 1973, they couldn't understand (with good reason, as later events were to prove) why their securities had a price–earnings ratio of 24, compared to 65 for fashionable, hot-shot bets like McDonalds, let alone 99 for Polaroid. Philip Morris, in contrast, was a resolutely unfashionable company in many respects. An American academic has written an article which purports to describe the amazing success of the United States tobacco majors in their efforts to diversify away from their medically insecure business. But the figures attached to this study proved, beyond a peradventure, that the most successful by far of the professor's three guinea-pigs was Philip Morris, which had diversified by far the least.

While all the others had been busy minding everything else except the original shop, Philip Morris had set about doubling its market share of the domestic weed in eight years – and serve the others right. There is something fundamentally unglamorous, however, about a business which puts in first place its basic priority, although that must be the business from which it derives most of its revenues and where by definition it has its greatest strengths.

In any acquired or new endeavour, in contrast, the management is forced to learn new tricks; and learning (as the payers of private school fees know only too painfully) is an expensive process. Philip Morris was not above diversifying itself, with the usual concomitants of pain. ('We have made rather sweeping management changes [at Miller Brewing]' was its 1973 version of the standard euphemism for firing virtually everybody in sight.) But hard graft in its own hard market explained the growth rating which Philip Morris didn't have.

Its aggrieved directors erred in concentrating on the misery of its relative price–earnings ratio, down in the dumps at the time, not only against the instant camera and hamburger kings, but standing 60 per cent behind the rating of Avon Products, whose 14 per cent growth in earnings per share over five years lagged visibly behind the 19 per cent for Philip Morris. But the stock-market is not concerned with relativities between A and B; the relativity that counts, as we have stressed before, is between C and D, the price now and the price then, when the investor comes to sell.

The same growth rate in earnings can translate (and always does) into wildly different share price movements. Nobody would ever have quarrelled with the selection of IBM as a 'growth company', for example. But given that the five-year growth rate for earnings back before the deluge, in 1973, was 14 per cent, what would be the intelligent guess at the five-year share price gain? Am I bid 200 per cent? Or would the conservative punter stick to a mere doubling? Either way, it's a wrong bet. At that point IBM had appreciated by just 28 per cent in the five years, barely preserving the real value of a purchaser's money (if that).

If examples of injustice are sought, Polaroid's experience is even more instructive. Its multiple of 99 belied the fact that the shares had actually fallen by the odd percentage point over the five years. Since earnings per share had also declined (by 5 per cent) Polaroid shareholders at that moment of equipoise had got off lightly. The figures had only begun to measure the consequences of the new camera, and the 99ers were about to see their faith rewarded with sackcloth and ashes.

McDonalds, on the other hand, had at least grown twice as fast as Philip Morris, at 37 per cent per annum, and its shares had also risen twice as nourishingly, having boomed by 961 per cent. (Which raises the interesting question of what on earth the Philip Morris management, after an astronomical rise of 431 per cent, thought they were complaining about.)

That rough mathematical equivalence – double the earnings per share rise, double the share growth – should not be allowed to mislead. For all these cases point unequivocally in a different direction. The growth that truly counts for the investor is not earnings per share, nor any other figure in the control of management: *the growth that counts most is that of the price–earnings ratio.*

The moral of our digression through the case of Philip Morris and its more favoured contemporaries is thus established. The reason for IBM's disappointing gain is that its price–earnings multiple moved backwards. If McDonalds had then dropped to the same multiple as IBM (which happened in due course) its share-price gain would have been almost halved. As the Philip Morris directors had noted, if their shares merely sold for the same multiple as Avon (surely only justice after performing better than the cosmetics company over the past five years), the tobacco firm's share price would have been 2½ times higher.

But there are always sound, or at least psychological, reasons why one price–earnings ratio should outsoar another. The future of any tobacco company is shadowed by cancer: its prospects, on any extrapolation, don't seem as sure as those of some drug company which might (for argument's sake) come up with a cancer cure one day. So the well-clad investor would not have reacted like the Philip Morris managers. It would have been as clear to him as the unwisdom of eating shellfish in Naples in August that tobacco firms would not turn into market pets this year, next year or ever. Which means that their price–earnings ratios, relative to the market, are unlikely to rise, but have a fair chance of falling.

Since earnings times the price-earnings multiple equals price, it follows that the key dynamic factor is missing – for the ratio is much more likely to be decisive than the earnings. In a marvellous year, earnings may double as the result of heroic, unexampled feats of management. But a halving or doubling of the price–earnings ratio (which has precisely the same effect) can take place in mundane circumstances when nothing in particular is going on.

The objective investor first inquires, when evaluating a share, whether the historic price–earnings ratio is liable to rise, stay level or drop ('historic' in the investment context, as we have seen, means any figures at all, since they all relate to the past, immediate or not).

Only when this exercise has been completed is it worth taking a view on the earnings prospect – because only then can the objective mind evaluate what an earnings rise is worth in share-price terms.

At this point bold theorists who learnt no lessons during or after the Second Great Crash will interpose an objection: that there is a casual link between earnings performance and stock-market rating. One year's decline in profit will sabotage a high multiple more effectively than an IRA bomb; three years of super-charged profits will do wonders to any laggard rating – other things being equal. The twice-bitten, thrice-shy can retort that other things never are equal – as witness the contradictory performances of the shares studied in this chapter. Full many an investor has come ungummed through the false belief that splendid profits must ineluctably lead to a prestigious share price.

A more intelligent way of sidling up to the issue is to question how the rating will perform given a steady earnings performance, and what would a steady performance be? To revert to McDonalds, the educated answer – as we saw in chapter 1 – is that it sure as hell won't be an earnings increase of 37 per cent per annum, doubling every two years. So the investor must postulate a considerably more modest growth figure – and with that done, he could see all too clearly that the multiple of 65 wasn't going to be topped, at least for long, by that share in this world; and that a return to less exalted levels was as good a bet as that world has to offer.

A drop of one-third in the price–earnings ratio, in fact, stood to cancel out a 50 per cent gain in earnings per share – which, as I pointed out to anyone who would listen back in 1973, made McDonalds a far from juicy mince of sirloin. Time and again experience confirms theory; yet just as often investors ignore both. In particular they always tend to underestimate just how low high-flying stocks can dive. When the Australian mining share Poseidon was on its £100 and upwards flight, even the most cynical of stock-market gamblers didn't dream of it falling below £50 – let alone the £5 chasm into which it eventually plunged. Unless the investor takes a considered view on the future price–earnings ratio, however, he isn't flying high, but flying blind.

The ideal investment – and some of these paragons have existed from time to time – would be a company with a good-to-stunning earnings growth and a modest, stable multiple. The investor could be certain that no nasty surprises were in store: as the earnings performed, so would the shares. Where these treasures can be found, however, is invariably where they cannot be easily discovered. The solution of that enigmatic sentence lies in the fact that these are companies which the market for some reason or other has failed to notice. Once they are spotted, the alchemy of greed takes over: the investor starts to prefer future earnings to present ones, the management begins to share the same illusion, and before the bell has even had time to toll another fallen growth star is in the making.

Proof of this postulate can be found in the very example considered in this chapter – Philip Morris. By October 1975, when again parading their charms before the financial analysts, the management had far less reason to worry about its relative stature in stock-markets. The share price had risen by 135·6 per cent since 1970, compared to a 52 per cent decline for the Avon whose rating the Morris men had once so envied. Over ten years the 487·1 per cent Morris gain stood against an 18·1 per cent decline for Polaroid, another of the former envied.

The reason was that the Philip Morris multiple of 14 in 1975 had budged only one iota from 1970, when it was 13. In consequence, the full increase in earnings over the period had flowed through into the share price. Avon, in contrast, had suffered a catastrophic decline in the multiple from 48 to 19. As for Polaroid, the former 99er was now selling at 30 – so, even on stable earnings, the camera company's shares must have fallen by two-thirds. Philip Morris had been saved, so to speak, by its Achilles heel: the tobacco curse had averted the market's greedy attention from a 20 per cent ten-year growth in earnings per share.

The objective investor can be greedy too, but he must be wisely greedy. He makes his price–earnings assessment first, and doesn't buy unless he sees an excellent chance, in the prevailing market context, of the multiple either keeping its level or rising. He sets a limit for the multiple beyond which he is not interested. He ignores the seductions of those who argue that you should forget about the historic multiple (the one based on last year's reported earnings) and concentrate on the current one (based on the projected or expected current year's rate). He shuns this advice because he knows that the historic figure already takes into account a view of the future. So when the multiple reaches his cut-off point, no matter how enticing the vista of the future, he takes his money and runs – if not to the nearest tax-free erogenous zone, at least to the nearest bank.

When the Second Great Crash resounded round the world, far fewer smart money men were found jumping out of windows or perched on the sills than in the First Version. That's partly because they were less extended on credit; but it's also because some of the professionals whose credentials are now to be examined had enough sense of self-preservation to follow the above advice, while encouraging less witty investors to chase the high price–earnings ratios into Never-Never Land. Thus does money flow from weak hands to strong. It's no part of the naked investor's role, however, to play Mickey Mouse to somebody else's Charles Atlas.

Part V. The professional touch

15. I'm OK, I'm OK

'Professional' is one of the English language's most abused words. In its simplest and most direct sense it signifies anybody who performs any activity for pecuniary reward, no matter how ineptly. However, the presumption is that nobody gets paid for his or her labours unless he or she is above a certain respectable level of competence (an unsafe presumption in many fields, notably politics, bureaucracy and business management). So the word 'professional', at its highest level, has come to describe a special order of excellence: the performer who knows to a fine point what he is doing; who understands precisely how to go about those well-known actions; and who sets rigorous standards for his own performance. To such a model pro, the word 'unprofessional' sums up everything that is sloppy, and personal sloppiness is something which he cannot abide.

That is why a Jack Nicklaus, after finishing high in a field of champion golfers, will head off to the practice course for three hours of hard work because he is dissatisfied with some aspect of his game. That is why a supreme chess-player (like Bobby Fischer before his eccentricity turned to impossibility) undertakes a rigorous physical training routine for the world's most sedentary sport. The professional leaves nothing to chance: unfitness might cause fatigue at a fateful moment.

Establishing how the concept of professionalism meshes into the stock-market is a task which requires the analytical powers of a Fischer. First, everybody playing in the market must be in the game for the money (although you wouldn't believe it from some of the deeds and the consequences). The pro differs only in that he spends the majority of his working hours at the game, normally in the company of other full-time players. The Wall Street or Throgmorton Street circuits thus have a similarity to the pro golf or tennis circuits – except that the level of physical fitness is lower and that of argumentation even higher. But the assumption that the pro achieves a higher and more exacting standard of performance than the amateur is unsupported by any factual evidence. There are demonstrations of wondrous intelligence (like the two Wall Street backroom boys who spotted that a bond issue by American Telephone & Telegraph, of all companies, provided them with the opportunity to make several millions without risking a dime). But for every one of these triumphs there are several stories of total goonishness, like the addiction of one-time hot-shot Fred Mates to the worthless bits of paper called letter stock. Just as the pro is often the first to follow a hot stock to perdition, so he tends to fall for the charms of the market's latest human marvel with all the nous of a First World War general stumbling on to the couch of Mata Hari.

Objective judgement of pro players in this market game is formidably difficult. When a golfer consistently fails to qualify for big competitions, a tennis player gets eliminated in the first round of Wimbledon or a batsman consistently fails to connect with the ball – then the dud results are plain for all to see and judge by. But the results of most investment by most professionals are seldom seen. If they handle private portfolios only the private owners know whether the handling has been competent – and that presupposes an owner who has some standards of competence to apply. If they manage the great holdings of insurance companies, only their boards of directors are in a position to make any judgement; and since the boards share in the decisions and the responsibility for the decisions, they are in part sitting in judgement on themselves – and in general that is an exceedingly comfortable posture.

Yet any informed person, introduced at a cocktail party to a lean, bespectacled, well-tailored gentleman, and advised that he manages several millions of other people's money, immediately feels in the presence of abnormal shrewdness, expertise, sense of timing and encyclopedic knowledge. Why, the cocktail guest may very likely ask his new acquaintance for a hot tip – or at least a hot view of the market, hopeful that some of the millions will brush off on him in this painless manner.

Like most illusions, this one is based on the same phenomenon as that to which Sigmund Freud attributed the origin of dreams: wish-fulfilment. We want the world to contain infallible investment geniuses, modern Midases, for then we can hope to accumulate easy fortunes for ourselves. Fiction encourages the fancy (which, after all, is fiction's job). Ludwig Bemelmans's wonderful tales of hotel life in the pre-Crash days of the twenties include a marvellous piece about the perfect waiter who, after years of being tortured by a sadistic manager, while ministering to a fastidious, germ-phobic Wall Street adviser to great fortunes, discovers that his own market gambles have made him rich. He then executes a worm's turn, insults and assaults the overbearing manager, as he has long wanted to, and leaves the Hotel Splendide in retributive triumph. The manager, however, repairs to the market Merlin, whose wizardry rapidly reveals that the elderly waiter will find Nemesis waiting round the corner of Wall Street. Sure enough, the old boy is back, ruined, tail between the legs; he is humiliated, but then forgiven, though only because the wizard is unhappy with any other waiter.

The story is irresistible nonsense from beginning to end. But it perfectly conveys the dominant image of the secret, powerful man of money, who invariably knows something you don't know, and who may, if you throw yourself on his favour, vouchsafe you a glimpse of Aladdin's cave and all the fabled treasures therein. Any myth attached to human beings is bound to explode: in this the stock-market differs not at all from any other athletic pursuit. But the components of athletic myths include visible signs of prowess and preparation. The stock-market does include people with astounding memories and a preternatural gift for mental arithmetic. But while these faculties can be exceedingly helpful, like having a good eye for a ball, they have lost much of their obvious advantage with the advent of calculators and computers. In any event, it was never true that high intellect or lofty numeracy went hand in hand with high market profits.

The American market in particular includes many operators who have passed through business school. But nobody on Wall Street would attach much virtue to this type of qualification in itself: at any rate, not in competition with practical work. Probably any poll of market men would place experience far above any measurable natural aptitude or qualification.

Since stock exchanges are markets, and since all markets move according to their inner forces, the market men are probably right, in a limited sense. The truly experienced professional does acquire a fingertip knowledge from the experience of dealings, successes and failures, which can give him a sixth sense. He can develop the instincts which in pro tennis produce the percentage player: the man who knows which shot has the highest chance of paying off and which risks are not worth taking. In the stock-market, however, those who listen most to the voice of their own experience tend to be over-canny; and many don't listen at all – they tumble like any tyro into every pitfall on the path.

The mathematical marvel, the gnarled old hand, the newest *Wunderkind* and the most irrepressible punter all agree on one thing, however: that performance is the ultimate and only criterion, separating the men from the boys – but not the pros from the pros. The full-time investment manager, adviser or broker can never lose his professional status, except by leaving the game. Be he never so hopeless, the man remains a pro, a fully fledged member of the circuit in good standing, until he drops out, either of his own accord or at the instigation of a receiver in bankruptcy (or some other representative of affronted creditors or regulators).

All pros, moreover, know their own performance, even if the world does not. In judging themselves, however, the pros are as likely as the amateur to exploit man's large lode of self-deception. All investors like to believe that they have performed better than the facts are prepared to reveal. Investors don't on the whole claim that the portfolio has appreciated by 50 per cent when they have managed only 10 per cent – not deliberately, that is. But very few pros should ever be prone to the common, terrible disappointment of amateurs when, after a glorious year, with this one doubling, that one trebling and the other rising by 80 per cent, they tot up the whole portfolio and discover that the overall rise is no more than a third.

The explanation contains no magic. If one-tenth of a portfolio trebles, as we saw when condemning over-large portfolios, that is a gain of only 20 per cent on the entire package; and one share's 80 per cent advance, admirable in itself, is a mere 8 per cent overall. Moreover, the investing mind tends to ignore the small setbacks – 12 per cent off here, 9 per cent off there – which eat into the lovely fat triumphs of the investing art. Simple psychology directs the oversight. Most investors regard profits as positive, potentially to be taken, and losses as a mere temporary inconvenience, which will be righted and eliminated in the fullness of time.

This is, incidentally, the reverse of the time-honoured market maxim, take your losses and let your profits ride. Whether the converse practice is any the worse for contradicting hoary lore is another question, since time often honours nonsense. But the fact that pros are wont to mouth such wisdom may possibly indicate some degree of immunity from the above simplistic deception. In fact the necessities of the game of portfolio management force them to make comprehensive and accurate assessment of their invested values, and they should know to the last digit on their electronic calculators how the latest assessment compares to its predecessor. Self-deception takes over only with the professionals (and then with several vengeances) when it comes to working out not how, but *how well* they have done.

The professional believes that all's well and has ended well if he has performed better than 'the market': 'outperformed the index' is the favourite phrase in London, where the pro has two indices to choose from – the *Financial Times* ordinary index of thirty heavy-weight stocks, or the *Financial Times* actuaries index of five hundred stocks, which weigh in at many and various poundages. You can outperform the index when both pro and market are on the way down, according to this theology. Thus the pro will even express pride (one of the most successful post war financiers and market jugglers committed this sin not long before his pride had its inevitable fall) because his wretched fund has dropped by less than the market.

If the market is down by half, I for one find it small consolation that the genius to whom my funds are entrusted has reduced the value of my savings by only 40 per cent. Exactly the same crime is perpetrated by stock-market tipsters in the media and elsewhere. Even the most aristocratic pundits compare the performance of the make-believe portfolios which they offer to readers with the movement in the indices over the period concerned – although as an exercise in comparison, this is nothing more than a weak joke.

A less heinous example is provided by Thomas J. Holt, a Park Avenue investment advisor who, according to *Business Week*, 'has called every major market turn' since 1967 – including such phenomenal feats as predicting an 880 peak for the Dow Jones industrial average in two to three months from April. It peaked bang on schedule on 15 July – at 881·81. The extraordinary thing about this most prescient of men is that the hypothetical portfolio into which he places his tips hasn't set the Wall Street world on fire. A man who has called every major turn in such violently fluctuating markets should have more to show for the turns than 173 per cent in four years. But the impressive point, all the same, is that Holt's hypo-theticals did hit the 30 per cent growth rate which is probably the ceiling for pro ambitions. What is not at all impressive is that he beat the New York Stock Exchange composite index, which fell by 15 per cent over the period.

Deep technicalities are not needed to demonstrate the point. A selected portfolio, composed entirely of stocks which the tipster or the fund manager – both of them alleged experts – believes will rise, is being compared with a wholly random selection of industrial equi-ties, compiled for no better reason than that they are thought to mirror fairly accurately the overall behaviour of the whole market. What's more, these poor standards of comparison possess inherent and great disadvantages. The fund manager can put his invested money wholly or partly into cash whenever he chooses: he can switch investments, casting out swine and bringing in pearls; he can take a winner at its peak, and buy in a sleeper at its bottom. In contrast, the index is always fully invested in equities and never changes its composition – except when some stock (like Rolls-Royce or Burmah Oil or the Penn Central or W.T. Grant in sad days gone past) disappears through a hole in the market.

Any professional who can't beat this competition, regularly and by a noticeable degree, isn't worth much desk space. Of course it is exceedingly difficult to climb when the market is sinking, especi-ally if, as during the Second Great Crash, it is falling from heights of fantasy. By the same token, however, it's very easy to soar when everything is leaping upwards – a fact which most pros are some-what more reluctant to stress. In sunny days, even if they did noth-ing but invest their patrons' money in the components of the Dow Jones or *Financial Times* indices, the pros would do fine. But since professionals tend to favour certain classes of stock, characterized by high earnings growth and lofty price–earnings ratios, which prosper disproportionately at certain stages of bull markets, they should quite naturally out-soar the index, without exercising any cleverness at all.

The evidence is, however, that pros over the long run don't con-sistently outperform a large stock-market index like the Standard & Poor's five hundred at all – not according to professors John H. Langbein and Richard A. Posner of the University of Chicago. They found that very few managed funds have achieved this trick – indeed in 1974–5 the averages had beaten the pros handsomely – and hence gave their support to the 'market fund' concept. These funds simply invest in the five hundred constituents of the Standard & Poor's in exactly the same proportions as used in compiling the index, and never expect to sell a stock. This may be as good an idea as Langbein and Posner believe – but it does, of course, sound the death knell for any idea of professional expertise. If all pros invest in the same shares in the same proportions, who needs them? And how can their abilities be compared?

In fact relative performance is simply not a suitable standard for the judgement of investment skill – a paradox shortly to be explained. True, the man whose fund achieves a higher return for its investors than all or most others must have something going for him – even if it is more luck than judgement. On Wall Street, as the Crash was covertly gathering its momentum, the leading trust managers were the gun-slingers who took outrageous risks, placing large sums of money in tiny markets, with the inevitable result that the markets rose. But self-fulfilling prophecies are more feats of manipulation than acts of measurable analytical intelligence.

In London, as the unit trusts proliferated there came to be a fashion for highly specialized offerings. This one specialized in gold shares, that one in high income yielders, the other in commodity shares, another still in investment trusts. Investment moves in waves from one market sector to another. In Wall Street in 1975, for instance, pollution control, truckers and coal were in favour; rails, finance and small loan, and savings and loans were out – right out. At other times, these positions might well be reversed. It therefore followed that at some time each one of the British specialists would come into its moment of glory, during which the managers could pat themselves on the back until their arms ached with the contortion.

One group, for example, began offering an investment solely in the Australian market. Initially, as the fund languished, nobody had the faintest idea that new nickel wealth would before long transform Australia into the hottest pot (well over boiling point) in world financial poker. But when the heat struck, the fund's management inevitably seemed to be financial luminaries of the brightest order.

That is why who does best may not tell the observer anything about who actually is best. The good manager is he who consistently, taking one year with another, provides his investors with a return which preserves the value of their capital as a base, donates to them at least the equivalent of a 3 per cent compound annual return in non-inflated money, and gives them on top a substantial bonus in clear capital gain. Fleshing out this target with figures depends on the rate of inflation – and one of the underlying factors behind the Second Great Crash was that the accelerating decline in the value of money opened up a yawning chasm between realistic investment targets and actual performance.

A minimal objective might have been doubling a portfolio's value (with cash dividends reinvested) in ten years, or 7 per cent per annum. We concluded that this became totally inadequate as rates of inflation climbed above 7 per cent and went on in some countries to three or more times that level. But even before inflation went into its vicious upward spiral, several major trusts and funds had failed to make the 7 per cent grade, which hardly validated their claims to be capable of handling other people's money. Doubling every five years (14 per cent compound) is a more acceptable target in more reasonable times – although that too would have failed to finance an investor through the great inflation of the 1970s.

This kind of long-term target figure is the true touchstone of investment performance, and the one which gives the lie to the hot-shop operator. The odds must always be heavily against a rate of return as high as 25 per cent compound (which doubles an investment in about three years). The manager who achieves this end truly does deserve congratulation and remuneration, however the market has been behaving. But anything less than a satisfactory mathematical return at any time is no grounds for praise or loud cries of glory, no matter how much the manager has clobbered the index of his choice, or how much he boasts about the clobbering – especially if the boasts are based on dubious valuations or unrealizable book worths.

Most professionals never meander into such murky depths. They merely live comfortably off the fact that, so long as they score at all, the chips (that is, the customer's bank notes) will probably still roll in – largely because few among the clientele know what the real score is, or what constitutes a good or bad score card. London was even inhabited until quite recently by trustees who had contrived to decimate substantial fortunes by leaving them largely invested in undated government stock: a step about as wise, in the postwar condition of the British economy, as throwing a match into the tank of a car to see if you are out of petrol. The so-called beneficiaries of the trusts didn't even notice that their fortunes were burning up until it was too late.

In making an honest assessment of performance, anyway, time rears its ugly head. Let us imagine that you have £1000 (or £100,000, or £10 million) invested on 1 January, which is worth a quarter more on 31 December. That cannot be the end of the story, or of the calculation. How have you accounted for fresh sums of money injected into the portfolio and the market at different dates? Many amateur investors don't account for it at all, because most don't want to face the sad truth that they are not such desperate magicians of the market after all. The discovery shouldn't truly cause them so much pain, because in this respect at least they are no different from most of the pros – certainly no different from those who couldn't even outperform the Standard & Poor's five hundred.

16. How pros make out

The previous chapter suggested, uncharitably enough, that the professional investment manager, meaning the investor of a publicly financed portfolio, doesn't necessarily have to establish any excellence at his job. Nor does he set demanding standards by which excellence, or its absence, may be measured. This insinuation might seem to spare another and larger group of market pros: the men, mainly the brokers, who man the stock-markets of the world, and who are commonly supposed by their customers (or some of them) to possess much of the same expertise, in knowing when to buy or sell which investment, as the managers of the great pension funds, mutual funds and the like. Nor is it clear that the investment managers are a superior grade to the brokers, somewhat in the relation of cardinals to bishops – that is, unless cardinals are often in the situation of gratefully accepting advice from bishops. The stock-broker on both sides of the Atlantic counts it a fine day, and a substantial step towards his next car, loose-box or yacht, when he persuades a fund manager to follow a share recommendation. In that case the fund will place its buying order through the broker, who will pocket the commission – a handsome one, since funds seldom buy in small numbers. And if the tip proves successful, the broker can count on a steady flow of unsolicited orders, possibly for ever more.

The courtship of those who buy and sell by those who stand in the middle is a familiar form of economic conduct. The lowest financial specimen of this life is the insurance salesman, and the highest is the banking go-between who brings borrowers of gigantic sums into contact with their possessors. Other recherché forms include the man who can find a buyer for a Boeing (let alone a Douglas or, as recently demonstrated with some lavish revelations of graft, a Lockheed). But the brokers come well up the league. Any favour, from a blazing tip to a case of lukewarm Scotch, that can preserve the favour of an investment fund is a passport to the good life.

Brokers need such passports, because their profession is singularly at the mercy of the market. Even if cocoa prices suffer a slump because some pernicious bug maliciously fails to destroy the crop on schedule, the actual quantities of cocoa consumed don't vary that enormously from year to year – and cocoa dealers still make a living. When stock-market prices decline, however, the volume of trading falls catastrophically, too. The unhappy broker gets caught in a three-way squeeze. Lower prices mean that commissions charged on a percentage basis become smaller in amount: squeeze 1. The volume of trade on which commissions of any size can be charged diminishes sharply as well: squeeze 2. Finally, the broker's own investments suffer along with everybody else's: and that is the final turn of the screw.

The world may contain knowing innocents who believe that brokers, with their noses pressed close to the market and thus honed to a fine degree of sharpness, always sense when to get out (or in), and are thus sitting on the sidelines when their customers are being rubbed in the dirt. It is true that the members of the New York Stock Exchange have shown something suspiciously close to pre-science by stepping up their sales of shares they don't possess just before market booms boil over. But this accumulation of short selling at the peak almost certainly reflects, not unequal wisdom about where the market is heading, but the greater tendency of professionals to speculate at all times; and in the higher zones of bull markets, short selling is the most obvious speculation around.

A little careful thought reveals that brokers are unlikely to possess prescience in any uncanny amounts. A professional who was expert at playing the market to a phenomenal degree would have to be a masochist to drag himself daily into an overcrowded and fundamentally arid district like Wall Street or the City of London. He could just as easily sit out in Southampton, Long Island or Malmesbury, Wiltshire, enhancing and safeguarding his fortune with a few adroit telephone calls to the less brilliant brethren left behind in the Big Apple or the Smoke. The great Warren Buffet, after all, managed very nicely without shifting his base from Omaha, Nebraska – and that is a good deal further from the action than Scarsdale.

Brokers are in much the same position as racehorse tipsters, or (no offence intended) promoters of fraudulent investments. If a tipster truly knew which horse was going to win, he would be certifiably insane to pass on the information to the world at large. The only result would be to raise the odds against himself, preventing him from getting any more bets down at the best price. The fraudulent promoter comes into the argument because he purports to offer the public an irresistible opportunity to make money at a staggering rate of return with no degree of risk at all. He, too, would have to be some kind of philanthropic lunatic to share wealth which he can create so effortlessly.

The racetrack and the con often go together, in fact, since infallible systems of winning on the horses or the hounds have long been among the favourite offerings of the con-man. However, the broker meets the con artist only at the point of suspended credibility. The customer who asks a broker for a good stock to buy needs a generous supply of innocent faith. He too assumes not only that the principal knows more than the inquirer, but also that the former is quixotically willing to share the knowledge for nothing – or for the relative peanuts of his commission.

The magic word, commission, holds the key. The tipster lives, not off the certainty of his tips, but off the security of his sales of tips. The broker goes one, if not a dozen, better. If he consistently lands his clients in the financial mausoleum, no doubt commissions from the aggrieved source will become fewer and further between. But very few citizens of the investing world follow their broker's suggestions exclusively. Normally their purchases and sales are composed of an amalgam of tips from the broker, figments of their own imaginations, items dredged up from the media or the social round, crumbs from the rich man's table. By and large, the clients that a broker has, he holds – and not by virtue of the superior power of his advice.

He has a built-in incentive, which may or may not be resisted, to persuade his clients into the market. If they sit on their hands, or on a large pile of cash, the broker cannot earn a commission. His *raison d'être*, which is officially to help the customer deal, is in practice to make him do so. The motivation, as with most manifestations of economic activity, is more blatantly and sedulously observed in the United States than in Britain, where the national penchant for understatement and self-deprecation extends even to the allegedly hustling and bustling business of the stock-market.

In London there lives at least one lugubrious broker who seldom sees any joy in the market at all, who attempts to deter clients from investing in any share they happen to fancy, who advises them to wait until he gives the signal – and then either forgets or fails to run the flag up the pole. The British broker isn't normally this self-denying; but, when asked for his opinion on a share, he tends to climb up the fence with smooth speed, and to sit decorously thereon. Across the Atlantic, fence-sitters have about as much chance of making the big money as flagpole-sitters. The selling side of the securities business is uppermost, as it should be, since without selling there can be no profit. In good times, for instance in the curtain-raising years before the Second Great Crash, the profit was abundant. John Thackray has calculated that for the 1971 outlay of only $300,000, a New York Stock Exchange member of strictly limited intelligence could reckon on taking home $200,000 a year to Westchester. When the market slumped, amid scenes of distress in brokerage houses that were in some respects more painful than those of 1929, the price of a New York Stock Exchange seat slumped, too – until it must have been more of a bargain than any of the offerings on the Exchange.

By the time the dust of the Second Great Crash had settled, many fewer brokerage houses were competing for the business, the missing brethren having crashed largely because of the kind of commercial mismanagement that would normally be expected only of those of strictly limited brainpower. As business and share prices picked up in 1975, brokers could again be dreaming of $200,000 incomes, and thoughts could be turning once more to the yachts and other hallmarks of fame which had sometimes been forcibly sacrificed on the altar of past follies.

Any broker's advice *may* be good. Then, so may the postman's. The odds strongly favour the broker, of course, if only because he moves in the world of markets and manipulation. Some of the rumours and rumblings reaching his ears could conceivably be based on profitable truth. Where there is smoke in the stock-market, there is usually some fire – the knack being to avoid getting burnt by wandering, moth-like, too close to the flame. But most stock-market denials contain within them the seeds of their own contradiction. As a picker-up of these considerable trifles, the broker should lead the field. But as an intellectually strong analyst of the fundamental and superficial factors that will determine the movement of markets and individual shares, the broker seldom gets beyond the qualifying rounds.

The big broking firms, it is true, employ batteries of analysts to do 'research' into stocks and industries. Firepower like that of Merrill Lynch, pre-eminent giant of the industry, which used to spend $6 million on a hundred analysts, has tended to increase as a result of the 1975 change in commission payments on Wall Street. As a result of the switch to fully negotiated commissions, the big institutions apparently halved the number of brokers with whom they deal – and the desire of the big brokerage houses to build up their institutional service has been met halfway by the desire of researchers in independent companies to come in out of the cold.

The other factor was the 1975 uplift in prices and trading, for the number of boys in the industry's backrooms rises and falls with the tides of stock-exchange business. In part their employment is necessary window-dressing to persuade the institutional clients that these houses have something to offer other than a glad handshake, a dry martini (or a gin and tonic) and a ready eye for a commission. The research work may be immensely detailed and full of goodness, like a well-cooked steak and kidney pie. But the high hurdle comes on the bottom line: the dreaded place where the analyst must make his recommendation – buy, sell, hold or (occasionally) switch – and where he often falls down.

Take the interesting case of William O'Neil, who sends 263 of the highest-ranking institutions in America 5 pounds avoirdupois every Monday of logarithmic graphs charting seventy-five performance factors of ten thousand-odd stocks. The thousand weekly pages, which cost up to $48,000 a year, almost certainly represent the most detailed research effort anywhere in the world; and *Business Week* quoted results in August 1975 which did indeed seem to indicate that the O'Neil Datagraphs gave an excellent guide to purchases and sales. But in the same article O'Neil gave hostages to fortune on that old bottom line: he named five stocks to buy, five to sell. On 31 October I had the unkind thought of checking on the Datagraphs results. Of the five buys, three had dropped by half or more; one was down by about a fifth; the other was down a few points. As for the five sells, one was marginally up; of the

three I checked which were down, none had fallen by anything like
the decline of O'Neil's three bad buys.

To quote O'Neil himself, 'You can't kiss all the babies.' But you
should do better than miss most of their faces entirely. Once the
analyst arrives at that bottom line, all the analysis and research, including the ritual visits to factories in the industrial heartland for
reception and flattery by the directors, are only slightly more useful
than a fairground crystal ball. O'Neil claimed to *Business Week* that
he had discovered an entirely new way to evaluate shares, based
not on opinion but on facts, and nothing but the facts. The disproof
of the pudding is in the eating.

In the end, everything boils down to a subjective judgement of
which way the shares are likely to move. Beavering away at the discernible facts of an industry or a firm may or may not have some
bearing on this movement – and the analyst never knows which way
the cat will jump, or won't. There are brokers and researchers who,
contrariwise, study the movement of the shares rather than the
characteristics of the company; and they too can sometimes be
blindingly right – whenever, that is, they are not being shatteringly
wrong.

These home truths about stockbrokers are well understood by
anybody who ranks as an experienced (or burnt) hand in securities
markets. Yet the populace persists in asking for recommendations
of a 'good' stockbroker – goodness presumably meaning the ability
and willingness to put his clients on to and into good things. But
asking any more of a broker than the faithful execution of an order,
and the transmission of any information which has a bearing on the
client's portfolio or investment plans, is like expecting the caddy
to have the same playing skill as the master golfer whose clubs he
carries.

But are there any masters in the investment world? All available
evidence suggests that the low handicaps are very rare. A spotlight
on this paucity emerged from a study of pension-fund performance
conducted by some British actuaries, Bacon and Woodrow. The
pension funds are the kings of the investment market. Yet the study
showed that their reigning managers, with £1500 million flowing
into their coffers in 1974 alone, mostly stuck with shares during the
worst year of the Second Great Crash – when they should by all
rights have adhered instead to cash. The actuaries concluded, looking over a five-year time span, that about the only thing for which

managers of these funds were paid was to get their timing right in switching from the stock-market to fixed interest – and most of them seem to have botched even this comparatively simple job.

The average performance in seventy-six funds was remarkably close to that of the big London stock index, the one with five hundred components. Now that is by definition mediocre; but it is also far from surprising, when you consider how professionals actually invest. There is one investment trust in the great and grand City of London which on one day not so long ago held 448 separate investments in its £53 million portfolio – just fifty-two short of the number in the above index. It occurred to me at the time to wonder why, since this proliferation guaranteed mediocrity, the managers didn't just spend their time at home playing golf, investing the entire £53 million in the index and leaving it at that. Little did I know that, as reported in chapter 15, this would be seriously recommended in 1975 as the correct and sound procedure for fund management. Certainly it made and makes more sense than attempting to manage 448 different stocks.

Allowing a forty-hour week, with no time off even for Christmas, these wizards could devote precisely 4·64 of their collective man-hours per year to the survey of each of the subsidiary investments. The number is wildly excessive on any basis of calculation. Over so wide a range, with so small an investment in each unit holding, results achieved must be strictly a matter of chance. It is impossible to have any positive control over performance. Yet such are the workings of fate that this particular trust managed to rise by 111 per cent between its 1962 high and the pre-deluge date of 1972.

Some studies I conducted at that time among the investment trusts of London provided some curious insights, rather like observing tropical fish through an underwater window, into the life and habits of professional investors. Because the trusts are closed-end – that is, they invest a fixed amount of capital and can increase it only by a fresh issue of shares or other securities – their operations have greater clarity than those of unit trusts or mutual funds. Their only mystery is why London should boast so many of them (their numbers are comparable to the 448 investments held by the example quoted above.)

Their nomenclature is no less intimidating. I found it impossible to decide whether Beaver was to be preferred to Delta; or London & Lennox to London & Lomond; or Dualvest to Triplevest; or

Updown to Outwich. A decision on their collective investment
merits was no easier, since the results varied enormously. Out of
three random specimens chosen for examination, one had grown
by 198 per cent in the decade under review, another (the 448er)
by the 111 per cent already reported, and the third by only 71 per
cent. The natural reaction to these discrepancies was to see whether
they could be explained by any differences in animal habits. Before
starting on that inquiry, however, one conclusion was already
obvious – that only the 198 per cent-gainer fell into the realms of
professional respectability, offering an 11·5 per cent compound
annual growth rate. Even that verdict requires some qualification,
because investment trusts are supposed to enjoy the thrills and
pleasures of this so-called gearing (which is why people bother to
invest in the things at all).

The directors can borrow money at fixed interest to bolster the
shareholders' funds, which in theory should enhance the return on
the equity. If a trust portfolio jumps by 198 per cent in ten years,
and half the portfolio is financed by fixed-interest debt which is
covered by the dividends, the equity should jump in value by 396
per cent. Even given the well-known disadvantage of gearing (that
it works just as effectively, but disastrously, in reverse), the presumption would be that trusts are heavily geared. Not so my three-
some. Admittedly, the most successful had the highest gearing, at
24.7 per cent of its capital in the shape of loans and preference stock.
But the second most rewarding had only 8·8 per cent gearing. The
worst of all weighed in, on this scale, at 14·2 per cent.

Another popular theory is that the trusts know Wall Street down
to the last paving stone, and therefore derive greater horse-power
from their United States investments. The champion of the three
had a particular United States reputation (which is no doubt why
it is called British Assets); but its 35·1 per cent United States holdings wasn't that much greater than the 28·9 per cent which the
second runner had invested in its dollar basket.

That left only one avenue unexplored. Were the discrepancies
explained by greater concentration? The leading trust is administered by some canny Scots under the name of Ivory & Sime, who
operate from the well-heeled precincts of Edinburgh's Charlotte
Square. At the time, however, Mr Ivory (or it may have been Mr
Sime) had invested British Assets in thirty-six different sectors,
none with more than 13·1 per cent of the portfolio. Even the 448-

stock cornucopia contained one sector less, at thirty-five. Since there are only some three dozen sectors listed in the *Financial Times*, it turned out that a pin wasn't a scandalous weapon with which to pick an investment trust: results would hardly have been any different if the trusts had used the same weapon.

The only shared policy seemed to be the belief that too few eggs spoil the basket – thus these pros picked an egg, or two, or twenty from each available basket. The sad conclusion has to be that, whether because of the size of their funds, or because of the limitations of their managers, or because of the basic hostility of markets to reason, professional investors tend to make the same mistakes as the eagerly rank amateur. They buy too many shares, hold them too long and buy for too many reasons. The sensible policy for the amateur is quite different. Hold no more than a dozen to a score of investments at a time, move in and out of the market and investments as conditions dictate, and operate on strict screening criteria which suit the requirements of the portfolio and your own temperament.

Unfortunately the policy is exceedingly difficult to apply – that is if you are a hired gun who has to keep a fund of many millions invested at all (or most) times. A £20 million portfolio, for instance, is by no means one of the heaviest loads which an investing management has to carry. But if it holds only twenty stocks, the average holding would be a cool million pounds. If a trust as a matter of principle never holds more than 5 per cent of any equity, that would limit the choice to £20 million companies at the very least. Those dimensions present something of a problem in Europe, but not in Wall Street; except that the Wall Streeter, while he has many more substantial equities from which to choose (which is partly why the canny ones like Ivory & Sime like investing there), also has far larger sums of money to deploy.

Multiply the above figures by ten, and the extra nought begins to explain why Gerald Tsai's investment performance collapsed under the weight of the money poured into the Manhattan Fund. You also begin to understand why, according to a study by Peter Williamson, only one out of 180 mutual funds outperformed the market as a whole in 1961–70. Another study, by three experts at the Wharton School, showed that 136 funds averaged a 10·7 per cent compounded annual rate of return from January 1960 to mid-1969; a hypothetical fund which invested *equal dollar amounts* in all the common stocks on the New York Stock Exchange would have returned 12·4 per cent.

Whichever way you look at the evidence, the answer comes out the same. By trying to achieve better results, the professional manager, taken as a whole, seems to end up with worse figures than if he had made no effort at all. Confronted with the bleak inevitabilities of his profession, in other words, the manager produces performance that belies his visiting card, but which rewards him just as satisfyingly as if the deeds lived up to the billings. The statistical necessity we have described is very possibly the mother of moderate performance. But, that being so, for what is the purchaser of professional investment expertise paying?

Part VI. The real beating

17. Gentlemen *v.* players

The amateur investor, on the hard and brutal record of fact, has no need to feel at either a practical or a psychological disadvantage against the pros whom we have been studying. The amateur's engaging habit of begging for crumbs of advice when confronted with a *soi-disant* expert on equities or economics is a conditioned reflex, which doesn't even serve the purpose, like the twitchings of Pavlov's dogs to the sound of a bell, of preparing the victim to receive sustenance.

The pro's principal advantage is that he can make money out of securities (by dealing on behalf of other people with their cash) without showing any demonstrable investment skills himself. If the amateur makes any money from the market, it's because his own money and mind has worked for that reward. In itself, that is a greater advantage than might be supposed. It removes all extraneous factors. The pro, when jockeying to persuade his customers to take yet another crack at IBM, cannot be interested in its investment merits alone. So long as they buy, he earns – and IBM is merely one of a long list of investments which nobody can be blamed for recommending (even though, from mid-1970 to mid-1975, the advice would have cost the recipient 18 per cent of his capital). The companies are unlikely to blow up, and whether or not you consider the buy a bad egg depends on that marvellously elastic quantity known as a 'time horizon': in other words, how long you are prepared to wait before the pay-off.

Most amateur investors have very distant and almost infinitely elastic time horizons. They thus throw away an indispensable crutch: the knowledge that the uncertain future is worth less than the certain present. This is for two indisputable reasons. First, time is worth money, because the funds can usually be invested as an alternative in some medium that yields higher returns than an allegedly blue-chip security like IBM. Second, even moderate inflation gnaws away at the true rewards year by year. In any event the investor who buys with no clear target in terms of either time or gain is being no wiser nor more sophisticated than a French peasant who buries his coins in the ground. Such an unthinking investment is of roughly the same kind as the squirrel's store of nuts – except that the careless amateur's store may never be eaten.

That is just one of the ways in which amateurs fritter away their assets. We can scarcely be blamed in one respect, since investment is generally on or beyond the fringe of our lives. Most people are principally interested in their businesses or professions, from mining manganese to mastering the law of torts, and they are unlikely to devote sustained thought and action to their savings. Pastimes like golf or bridge probably get more attention, mainly because they are not overloaded with the fears of risk and childhood inhibitions which make handling money a matter of anxiety for the majority. If an investor can lose his or her inhibitions entirely, operating like an amateur but concentrating like a pro, the personal status rapidly changes, anyway: the investor may even become a super-star of finance.

The annals are full of worthies and unworthies who, having made a few honest bobs in some game or other, proceeded to expand them mightily by something that the biographies often refer to as 'judicious speculation'. The list ranges from the supreme John Maynard Keynes, who was a dab hand with equities and currencies as well as economics, to the heart-warming tales of the two Joes – P. Kennedy, father of the president, and Hirshhorn, the uranium king, both of whom supposedly sold out shortly before the 1929 market went into its fateful nosedive.

It's small consolation for the envious to set against the Joes the distressing experience of Cyrus Eaton, the late Mr Krushchev's favourite capitalist and the only man extant in 1975 with personal experience of every panic this century. He saw a fortune of $100 million sliced down, like so much salami, to $5 million as the First Great Crash crashed. Not that $5 million in the valuable currency of the 1930s would fail to keep its owner warm during the long cold nights: as it happens, Hirshhorn's killing from selling out in good time was reputed to be $4 million – or rather less than poor Eaton's post-Crash residue. The comparison only goes to reassert that stock-market performance is relative, not absolute.

The two Joes both began their careers as dealers in securities, which put them firmly on the professional side of the fence, where sat another mighty North American speculator, the Canadian Lord Beaverbrook. But the interest of all three in the exchanges was purely passing: they used the markets as means to personal fortune and moved on to higher things as soon as higher sums beckoned. They were promoters, not mere sellers on commission, and their main promotions were initially themselves. Their professionalism lay in exploiting the opportunities afforded by possession of an inside track to create still more opportunities and still more money. They were entrepreneurs, who happened to use the market in stocks as others employed the market in wholesale groceries or carbonated soft drinks. The only lesson that the rank amateur can absorb from their cases is to note the unwavering concentration on the objective, which is the accumulation of wealth; and their exploitation of the knowledge that a profit does not exist until it is taken (witness that crafty selling out in 1929).

No, the amateurs who cause most pain to the careless investor are people like the retired British arc welder who accumulated £500,000 by stock-market speculation in his retirement; or the American widow (one of countless thousands) who, left with a large young family to support, greatly magnified her husband's pittance by the same expeditious route. The stock-markets, the investment columns, the investment banks, the newsletters are staffed with people who believe they know far more about investment than any arc welder or widow, dead or alive, but whose half-millions are nowhere to be found, unless, that is, you count excuses for their failure to enrich themselves, of which they have a good half-million ready and waiting.

The widow and the welder had one asset, of course: time. Neither had the distraction of other work, and they could thus set about their amateur investing with that desirable combination of professional concentration and amateur assets. What have these amateurs got that the average or even the top professional hasn't?

In the first place, they have the besetting virtue of ignorance. They may know little or nothing about 'fundamentals', possibly not even what a fundamental is. Tell them that the phrase includes the extrapolation of the past year's earnings per share in the light of the latest quarterly statement and the projected outlook for the economy and the industrial sector concerned, and these wise amateurs will still be none the wiser, and none the happier. As for the technicalities, a point-and-figure chart leaves them as cold as the differential calculus. Advise them not to buy because a share has formed head and shoulders, talk to them about necklines and triangles, or some other gobbledegook, and they will simply have another cup of coffee. Even such basic concepts as the price-earnings ratio may strike little response in these bosoms.

Nothing confuses these investors in their devoted search for a share which appeals to their instincts; and there truly are people with an instinct, not for the market, but for a good investment – just as some travellers can find their way to the red-light district of a strange town with the accuracy of a homing pigeon, just as one collector of Spode consistently picks up the bargains which another misses. It is a great error to suppose that these intuitive, innocent investors are ignorant. A colleague of mine on the *Observer*, Anthony Bambridge, once discovered in a share register an exceptionally well-provided shareholder who, despite his possession of a fortune in the Tesco supermarket equity, lived at an obscure and unlikely London address. The assiduous reporter repaired to the home and was referred to the local pub: and there the Tesco capitalist sat, tucking into his pint of beer. The investor (one of the Tesco founder's founding employees) was not only aware of his riches; he also knew that day's value of his holding down to the last penny – which is more than most private investors know about their portfolios. And that is another of the ways in which they literally fritter away their good fortune.

The basic rule for the amateur is to set aside a fixed time – once a week, once a month, even once a day, according to taste – and to devote that time to a thorough review of what investments he holds, whether he has more cash to invest, what he wants to sell, what he wants to replace, and what, if these thoughts have any positive results, he will consequently buy. There are amateurs who successfully flout this rule: buying and selling when inspiration visits them, like Archimedes sitting in his bath. But they have a touch of genius – and you can legislate only for the norm.

Beyond that rule, lines are difficult to draw. The problem is the same as that of advising budding authors. Each one must work out his own system of transferring thoughts into written words. But the investor, like the writer, needs to work out what kind of animal he is. It's no use spending hours polishing classical periods if your bent is towards Mickey Spillane plots. Nor does it produce anything save grief to pursue highly speculative shares if the past has produced plenty of evidence that in such respects you possess the suicidal instincts of the lemming.

There truly are some investors whose instincts work in reverse, whose entire career in the stock-market is equivalent in its certainty of judgement to that of the prewar German tycoons who were sure they could control Adolf Hitler. In the first place, this class of purchaser is attracted (and then magnetically) only by outright speculations: so outright as to be far out. One medical investor of this ilk (doctors, no doubt because of their scientific training, are especially prone to wild gambling on the stock-market) had only to buy a share for the company to go into liquidation. Once he even succeeded in messing up an accurate piece of inside information. The informed insider had advised him to place his Sea Island cotton shirt on Canadian Eagles. The doctor duly rang his broker and sat back to collect the profits. The shares soared according to plan, and with his money up, so he thought, by some hundreds of percentage points, the investor rang to sell. He was profoundly put out when the broker commiserated with him over his *loss*. In his excitement, this sure-fire wrong investor had said *Mexican* Eagles by mistake.

He had only one rival in my experience, a foreign trade expert who bought the shares of Britain's most spectacular flown-by-night, door-to-door selling company, Rolls Razor, *after* the receiver had been called in. Had he waited to pull the same caper in the same circumstances with Rolls-Royce, as not a few Wall Street punters did, the trader would have handsomely recouped his losses.

But the Rolls-Royce purchasers, apart from those with a sentimental attachment to the shares, were gambling that the British government would find it impossible to shuck off all its obligations to the workers of Derby, the Lockheed Tristar builders over in Burbank, California, the Royal Air Force *et al*. The nature of that particular gamble explains a great deal about the true context of speculation.

To the Rolls Razor buyer, speculation means buying something not only far out but dirt-cheap. That is certainly speculative; but it is the most dangerous variety of the genus, akin to betting that the last ace will turn up just when your hand needs it – what the biographers would be forced to call injudicious speculation, because the speculator has no good reason to suppose that he will win. Unfortunately the word 'speculate' (maybe already part-devalued by its close relationship in sound and spelling to 'peculate') has been further debased by apocalyptic events, like currency crises and bank failures, which have imparted an aura of shadiness, of gnome-like intrigue, even of rank treachery. But the verb merely means wondering what will be the further course of events if some particular event occurs; and the investment policy of the speculator is to act on that musing analysis. This is proper policy for all thinking investors. The act of investment is the logical consequence of studying the present to discover what factors are likely to shape the future, and in what form. If the investor (like most amateurs and pros) has no thoughts on the subject at all, he is reduced to random choice.

Pros actually go one worse: they look over one another's shoulders and attempt to safeguard themselves by copying each other's decisions. Thus they break the cardinal investment principle that the richest prices go to the hero who bucks the stream, not to the cowards who bob along together until they all reach the same stretch of white water.

The Rolls-Royce case was the simplest of speculations, which is why those of us who didn't jump on the running board should be thoroughly ashamed. As soon as it became clear that the government of Edward Heath, despite its early dedication to the dismembering and disembowelling of commercial lame ducks, was itself crippled by the obligations in the Rolls-Royce case, there was only one question to answer: how much money would the receiver be able to recover for the shareholders? With a valuable car company to be sold off, and with the government compelled to buy the engine business, the price was plainly going to be far higher than a miserable few pence a share. The next question was how long before the pay-off; it took years – but all along the route chances abounded for an easy cash-in. The old Joes would have pounced on this one like hawks.

In another case of classic simplicity, the United States dollar, it had been clear for over a decade before the Nixon devaluation that the old $32 an ounce price for gold could not be held indefinitely – not when a gusher of unwanted United States currency was spewing forth across the frontiers in thousands of millions year by year. No profound knowledge of international economics was required to understand this point. Even cursory following of the business news day by day added to the certainty that one of those days would be the day of reckoning.

More than one pro justified his label by seizing on this point as the only refuge from the dust and destruction of the Second Great

Crash. One broker of my acquaintance resolutely placed all his own cash, and the money of many clients, into goldmining shares. The gold bug was simply backing a well-founded judgement of events, and thus deserved every penny of the fortune which he earned by such eminently judicious speculation. (He spoilt it later on by continuing to extol gold and mines after the United States had begun to turn the dollar tide – the borderline between single-mindedness and monomania is dangerously thin.)

The judicious man, however, must do one injudicious thing. As we have emphasized before, he must back his judgement to the hilt: half-measures, like each-way bets on horses, yield lower profits. Most private investors, emulating the 'I would, I dare not' hesitations of Macbeth, are half-hearted in every move they make with their money. They want to double it, true, but they also want to keep it intact. They feel that their choice is sound (otherwise they wouldn't be considering the purchase at all); yet they fear that some factor which they haven't considered will make their choice most unwise. Thus they either miss the boat entirely, by delaying the decision, or they under-invest in the situation.

In a sense the half-heartedness is perfectly correct. Equity investment *is* a chancy activity. But there is no point in entering the lists unless you are prepared to take the chances. If you are prepared to run those risks, then they should be run wholeheartedly. Most of us, however, speculate not only with half our hearts, but with half our minds. We do not think through decisions or indecisions. Remember that the main difference between professional speculators like the two old Joes and the common-or-garden amateur is not just that the former win much more money, and not merely that they are luckier. The good pro gambler simply works at his game.

In that respect the successful amateur investor has to be as dedicated as Damon Runyon's late lamented Harry the Horse. Much can be learnt about speculation from that unlikely encyclopedia. Although Runyon's Broadway characters preferred to bet on a fixed race (which is the *ne plus ultra* of speculation) they were not averse to a bet on an honest proposition. Here they were not directly concerned with the fundamentals (i.e. with whether the past form indicated which horse stood the best chance of winning), which are the equivalent of stock-market analysis. Their main interest lay in the niceness of the price. In other words, if a horse at 2 to 1 was three times as likely to win as a rival gee at 8 to 1, they would back the latter animal. For they knew that horses, like shares, are unreliable beasts (if not, why quote odds at all?), so the best gamble had to be the cheapest. By much the same reasoning the tennis buff who thought Arthur Ashe had any chance at all of beating Jimmy Connors in the 1975 Wimbledon final must have fancied the odds, which at 4 to 1 were far too high for a two-horse race with any uncertainty in the outcome.

The above analyses all depend on some degree of lore. The best way for the amateur to acquire that knowledge, that experience, that training of his fingertips is to record, each time he reviews his portfolio, why he took each decision. Then the reasons can be compared with the results – accurately measured, all expenses counted in and with total ruthlessness. That way he can get some idea of what works for him, what doesn't, which sources of advice have been most profitable, which disastrous, and what factors he has found it most useful to watch and follow. If you know what you have been doing in the past there is, after all, a better chance that you will know what you are doing in the present.

On this foundation, the amateur can build up a much more secure investment strategy than most professionals. The amateur has only himself to satisfy in the first place; second, timing (unless he needs cash in a hurry) is a matter of total option; third, he can (and should) choose objectives which make personal sense – whereas the pro is often forced to chase after growth goals which are strictly unintelligent in the given circumstances. For example during the worst period of the Second Great Crash, even under double-digit inflation, cash was best. That's a justifiable course for the private investor; but what possible rationale is there for paying a pro a commission or management fee to place your money in an instrument you could perfectly well buy direct? (The appearance of funds on Wall Street which did precisely that, and nothing else, was the final evidence that the equity god was dead.)

As with a regimen of exercise or diet, an investment course needs dedication and self-discipline, which the amateur may not be able to muster. But the regimen is worth trying. Take the £1000 test. Name the growth you would like the nest-egg to achieve in six months' time. Then invest rationally (as above) on the first of the month, reviewing each subsequent first. If you meet your objective, not only will you out-do most pros – but maybe there's a *third* old Joe in the making.

18. Mind your own business

We have established the truth that an investor, if he wishes to emerge from nakedness into full dress and prosperity, should find out what kind of investor he or she actually is. Everybody in the ultimate analysis has only one investment adviser, and that is himself or herself. Even if the secret and sage Felix Rohatyn of Lazard Frères whispers his latest intelligence into your whorled ear, you and only you can decide whether to follow his advice and to what financial extent. Even if you have entrusted your entire $33,756, 892·66 to Felix with full power of attorney, you had to sign the legal instrument. There is no escape from this responsibility.

That paramount principle raises the very reasonable questions of what the investor should demand of his resident expert (i.e. himself), and whether there are any rules and regulations which the investor as dealer should apply to the investor as adviser (the punishment for breach of the law is axiomatic and automatic: if the advice goes wrong, you lose the money). The rules will vary somewhat from case to case, but there are certain semi-eternal verities, or temptations, to be avoided. One is to avoid buying any shares on the strength of other people's personality, a vice to which journalists and stock analysts are especially prone. Both categories meet far more businessmen than the average purchaser of equities; and both are more easily impressed than the outsider would suppose. The reporter is generally thought to be a cynical, hard-boiled and hard-bitten character, possessed of no wool which could be pulled over his eyes. But a man's judgement is always much influenced by his profession, and the journalist's profession (like the psychoanalyst's) is to get stories. It follows that the man who has a good story to tell – as recalled in chapter 11's walk down Memory Lane – will endear himself to any reporter. But does it follow that the best story is the best investment?

The answer is plainly negative. Financiers, whether they realize it or not, also always appreciate the value of a good yarn. One, Jim Slater, now reduced to cultivating his garden, was quite explicit on the subject. He described his problem to me at a time that was out of joint in all respects, including that of his share price. As the wizard outlined the problem, his first story had been that of a minor young industrial figure who had developed a highly lucrative passion for equities while bedridden by illness. His second story had been that of converting the equity passion into lucre by peddling advice to other investors. The third story was building an industrial conglomerate (which happened to be the time of the ex-maestro's most lucrative gains). The fourth tale was the conversion (markedly less successful, except in terms of sheer survival) of the conglomerate into a multi-multi-millionaire bank. Now, said the master, came the tough problem. What did he do for a fifth story?

The only answer I could suggest was to tell the truth. Fate came up with a better reply, from the point of journalistic copy: Jim Slater's decline and personal fall. But whatever less painful answer had evolved, some journalist would have lapped it up. The satellite pets of the money world do swallow more than they should: they are too prone to flattery, partly because of the precarious contrast between their own fortunes and those of the mighty men they meet. Equally, an unbelievably incompetent board of directors can put on an impressive show for a visiting fireman. Nor need a friend or golfcourse acquaintance go to much trouble to persuade you of his extreme ability – after all you probably know little about the man himself, and still less about his business.

Never buy because you like, respect or are impressed by the top magus or magi is a sound rule at all times. There are exceptions: when the man is a dependant in some respect, supplying you with goods or needing your money, the connection is likely to strip away pretence, and to reveal competence, if any – so you are better able to judge fundamental quality.

That was how John James, then a West Country proprietor of radio shops, spotted the abnormal qualities of the then obscure managing director, Arnold Weinstock, who went on from supplying James with television sets to reshaping the General Electric Company, to the eternal profit of all parties. The business relationship provides a far sounder basis for judgement than friendship, for friends, as a basic fact of life, always impress when talking about their vocations – even writers.

Think how hard it is to assess true quality when interviewing a candidate for a job. In that context the interviewer not only knows exactly (or should know) what the interviewee will be required to do, but can cross-examine the victim to the heart's discontent to establish whether he can fit the bill. Even with this advantage, hunch ultimately plays a greater role in successful selection than rational judgement.

In the investment context, nobody outside the company has full or even partial knowledge of what the managing director's job entails. And nobody (not even, or perhaps especially, a stockbroker's visiting researcher) can bracket the said executive with a particularly withering cross-examination to demonstrate his fitness or unfitness for the job.

One expert financial journalist's personal assessment of the most exploded financial bomb in postwar Britain, which led him to call the offending company 'a must for every portfolio', is only a single example of a multifarious sin. Every writer has at some time or other fallen for a pretty talker, in much the same way as susceptible and sexy men fall fatally for pretty faces; and financial commentators are nothing if not sexy and susceptible, figuratively speaking. In any event, the personal judgement is irrelevant to an investor. You are not buying the man, but the equity; and your sole concern is whether the price is going to rise within your time horizon. The quality of the man at the helm will have an influence on this prospect, but not necessarily the decisive influence: nor is success necessarily permanent.

Edwin Land was as impressive in the years when the SX-70 camera savaged the company's performance as in the era when the first instant cameras created his and his shareholders' fortunes. The sole difference was that with the SX-70 Land had 'over-extended the risk–reward ratio in a number of ways, ranging from the pressure on his manufacturing resources to the inadvisability of producing a high-budget item in a highly optional market at a time of cyclical economic downturn' (to phrase the matter in the language beloved of the researchers – in other words, the Polaroid boss took too many risks at once).

If somebody known to you personally starts a new venture, or brings an established one to market, and you back him, the ball-game is different. Getting in on the ground floor is as sound a principle in investment as in anything else. But it is this – the entry via the basement – which gives mileage to your judgement of the man. There is no comparison with the blind faith of investors who back some personage known to themselves only by reputation and newspaper or magazine stories.

One investor of inherited means, who was in a position as a top journalist to be far better informed, told me once that he had divided his substantial all between Shell and Mercury Securities, the parent of the S.G. Warburg merchant bank, on the grounds that Lord Godber, the Shell chairman, and Sir Siegmund Warburg, the chief conductor of the bank, could look after his family money better than he could personally. Closer investigation would have revealed that Lord Godber had long since ceased to have any executive role with the oil group, and that the bank was well past the dynamic stage of its earnings growth, which (note the ground-floor factor again) had coincided with the period when it was making its way in the world. A hungry fighter, as is well known, tends to win – and fight – more bouts.

All judgements made on personal grounds must be subjected to two acid tests: one, how much do you really know about the gold-creating ability of the alchemist in question? two, if you were totally ignorant on the latter subject, could you still make out a convincing case for purchase of the shares? These two deceptively simple questions lead on to another often broken rule: never buy on insufficiently considered impulse. Many investors time their buying on no better grounds than the hole that spare money is burning in their bank accounts; or the fact that the market has been galloping ahead strongly, and they feel like going along for the ride. Now impulse may be an invaluable motivator for those whose intuition is in good working order. But the soundly based common investor, when in the buying mood, and when the mood has fixated itself on one or two particular securities, asks himself, as honestly as possible, whether in a less euphoric state he would have been interested in the investment under scrutiny.

The test is the same in both instances: can you substitute an objective viewpoint for the strictly subjective and come up with the same answer? Here the investor has to resist the temptation to cook his own books. On any matter of decision, it's easy enough to tip the scales in the preferred direction. That is why psychologically astute decision-makers, caught on the horns of personal dilemmas, draw up lists of pros and cons. Not because they think they will produce an accurate balance sheet of the factors for and against (they know they will not), but because their subconscious will automatically tilt the outcome in the truly preferred direction.

So it helps to have underpinnings to the objective assessment. One is to search for some defensive factor which may put a floor under the price (the technical name, if it helps, is 'limit the downside risk'). The possibilities include a heavy discount on asset value, a low price – earnings ratio and a high dividend yield. When the three are found in combination you have a defensive share, which is not identical to a defensive position – risk still exists. A case can be made for buying these triple non-threat equities; but even here the principle of seeking some other underpinning should be observed. In other words, just because a share price is over-filled with assets, rich in dividends and abounding in earnings cover, the job of selection is by no means complete.

The would-be purchaser of these jewels should search for the explanation of the (by definition) lowly rating of the equity. If the cause is likely to continue to wreak its havoc, then the downside risk is unacceptable. If, on the other hand, the reason looks likely to disappear or diminish with time, the work is over; you possess your underpinning.

A second safeguard is that the company, at the unpretty price you are considering, should have a substantial market capitalization. If the market values the whole company for peanuts, it may not follow that it is good only for monkeys; but unless the investor wishes to compose a wholly speculative fun portfolio of busted flushes, or recovery stocks which may never leave the sanatorium, he should shun all-but-worthless offerings on principle.

Another way of investigating the status problem, and of underpinning the choice, is to assess whether the market price is based on some feasible degree of corporate performance, and isn't discounting miracles into the hereafter. In an earlier chapter I briefly described why I concluded that the sleepy Tate & Lyle sugar giant was a surer investment than a wideawake superstore star. I simply assumed a modest rate of growth in turnover which I thought would easily be attained, and applied to that growth a net profit margin, equally modest, which the company had actually achieved in the recent past. My highly encouraging projection, as I expected, proved to be conservative – and it confirmed that the share price was *under*estimating the future.

This is a sacred principle, because the more the future has been discounted, the less that future can offer a purchaser in the here and now. This defensive rule is especially hard to obey, because it insistently rules out the front-runners in any bull market. So the fast-draw investor on the hunt for an exhilarating shoot-out will ignore the warning; on the other hand if, as with most investors, your time horizon is reasonably long, years instead of months, you really have no excuse for walking out into a street full of flying lead.

The first rule of investment is to find out what considerations are most cogent for you, which principles work best in your individual case; then stick to them – no matter what heartrending profits are missed because the rules eliminate the wonder stock of the moment. The cautious long-term investor remembers that for every long-term wonder performer countless other stocks possessed of roughly the same configuration become burnt-out cases and end-year tax-loss candidates. The individual's rules and regulations need not preclude buying a wonder stock entirely, since any worthwhile code of investment conduct must contain provision for exceptions. But remember the rule again: those exceptions must be justified, by anyone who is not a golden-fingered genius, on some more material grounds than passing hunch.

In other words, our well-bred aversion to shares with high price–earnings multiples (based on the worsening of the ratio between downside risk and upside potential as the multiple moves upwards into space) needs to be leavened by the full knowledge that in every list of a year's best market performers, some will have multiples of the kind that induce insomnia in the prudent investor. To avoid an excess of nightmares, the kind of solid evidence to be sought is a sign of genuine and determined buying interest on the part of the big institutions, who are going to determine the price anyway.

Not only does the investor need rules for buying: selling is vital – an integral part of the act of purchase. Just as every fat man is supposed to carry within him a lean man screaming to get out, so every purchase holds within it an implied sale begging to be made. If the purchaser has no idea what that implied sale may be, he may not recognize the moment when it arrives; and there are few agonies in the world of might-have-beens more galling than the contemplation of the profit that got away. It is run fairly close by the profit that, in the seller's estimation, was taken too soon. Some would argue that a profit can never be taken too early. And it is true that

moaning about the 200 per cent profit you missed by taking one
of 100 per cent possesses the same element of nonsense as groaning
about the shares you could have bought and didn't. A beautiful old
New Yorker cartoon shows a patient on a psychiatrist's couch reciting a list of lost opportunities – 'I could have bought ...' (Today
that same patient, very probably, would be reciting a different sad
refrain – 'I did buy ...')

The decision to sell and take a profit has the same connotation
as a decision not to buy those same shares at around the price realized by selling. The fact that the investor was already on board,
but left the ship at his chosen destination, makes no difference –
even if the argosy does sail on into uncharted and richer waters.
You have to end every journey at some stage. But the destination
should not be fixed in automatic rigidity. The seller needs some
general indication of the type of gain for which he is prepared to
settle. As we have noted, this came to mean so impossible a target
at a time of double-digit inflation that the investing public simply
abandoned the game, leaving the investment industry to stew in its
own unkeepable promises. The rule of thumb lays down that there
is seldom any point in accepting less than double the going available
net rate of interest, after capital gains tax.

Thus if 9 per cent after tax is available as a fixed-interest return,
the investor should be thinking of 18 per cent net of all buying and
selling expenses and the capital gains tax – at an annual rate, naturally. After allowing for the inevitable failures and semi-failures,
the net result probably wouldn't vary much from the 4 per cent clear
profit on a portfolio in a month, or around 50 per cent in a year
on a simple arithmetical basis, which we previously identified as
a suitable objective.

The time-worn thesis, honoured in chapter 15, of cut your losses
and let your profits ride does have the advantage of removing the
necessity of decision, but at the price of sacrificing logic. Every time
a share reaches the glorious point where a sale could theoretically
be worthwhile, the gloriously logical mind asks honestly whether
the precious object has any chance of repeating the gain. If the
answer is no, or don't know, the logician takes his profit (not forgetting, again, to allow for all buying and selling expenses). If the
answer is more hopeful, then the logician is prepared for a further
ride to the profitable end of the line.

But in the real world the questions about a potential disposal have to do with loss as often as profit. On the law of averages, often the logical problem will run on these sadly different lines: what to do when a share, far from recording a gain of 20, or 30, or 40 per cent has shown a like or worse fall. The right question is unchanged – although the answer is usually prejudged. Few people readily accept that they were unbalanced or unintelligent enough to buy a share (or anything else) at 20 per cent over the odds. *Ergo*, the share is bound to rise to the level at which the purchaser, clever fellow, bought the thing.

Holding on to a fallen share is often simply the erection of a hasty defence for a vulnerable ego. In ordinary circumstances, although not in the totally bizarre conditions created by the collapse of the seventies, whatever price a share has seen, it will generally see again – even if the wait does take almost as long as that for Godot. But hanging on to a loser on that excuse is tactically incoherent. The business of investment is to maximize what can be managed with the money, not to leave the cash sitting there to prove that the investor is less of a sucker than sometimes, on that law of averages, he is bound to be.

Once in a while the market may have turned its back on a favoured share in a fit of collective imbecility, and the maverick investor, sitting on his loss, will be proved right. But don't count on finding these Koh-i-noors. A weird kind of inverted logic is applied by born losers in this situation: they argue that, since so many thousands have already gurgled down the drain, it is tantamount to a bargain to send more money the same way. In investment, this becomes translated into the view that if the share was cheap at 100, and has fallen to 50, then the burnt offering must be still more of a bargain and you should load up with many more. The Charred Stock theory has been transmogrified and dignified into a technique known as pound or dollar averaging: as the share moves down (or up) the averager puts in an equal amount of currency, meaning that his average cost is never the highest or the lowest price paid, but has a bias towards the latter. He acquires more shares at the lower prices, fewer at the higher. The device will save the unwary from the temptation of chasing a rising price too ferociously or crucifying themselves by clinging to a wholly undiluted disaster. But dilution is the only good end that is achieved; and the averager only deceives himself if he thinks that by this mechanical device, or any other, safety can be plucked from the nettles of danger.

Remember that self-deception is an inherent aberration in the psychology of investment. Those who recognize this fact, and then learn to understand their own psychological profiles, have a flying start. Unfortunately self-analysis took Sigmund Freud several years and the process is highly unlikely to be faster in anybody else's case. The game of getting to know yourself in this field may be considerably more expensive than it was for the father of psychoanalysis, unless, like Freud, the self-patient – knowing that his own experience is that which he must know best – is prepared to draw heavily on his own personal casebook. That means keeping an honest one. And it should end in imitating the honest men whose careers in the stock-markets are an example to us all.

19. The fail-safe fallback

The fault with criticizing the foibles and follies in the mass of the men who brought down the Temple of Mammon in 1929 and of their sons and grandsons who all but managed to achieve the same demolition in 1974 is that the criticism extends unfairly from the general to the particular. Even the Wall Street of 1929 contained sober and safe citizens who understood the truth about markets, who were wiser and calmer than their contemporaries and who played no significant part in the excesses that cracked the pillars of capitalism. Even in the long deception which destroyed postwar savings no less thoroughly, the world of money contained many astute and impressive men, most of whose actions were as shrewd as their well-stocked minds.

To debunk the myths of the stock-market is not to destroy all reputations made by or in the market. In investment, as in other trades, arts, professions, sciences and rackets, there are geniuses and exceptional performers, noble whales amid the shoals of lesser fish. The stock-market, alas, has the unfortunate habit of seeing genius and brilliant achievement in every rising price. Which means that, at times of boom, so many bubbles swell, only to be pricked later, that the outsider has few means of guessing which is the hero, which the future has-been. But the many long, distinguished and honour-able careers made in the securities business have been founded on the attributes needed for success anywhere else: hard work, applica-tion, honesty, the talent for picking and developing associates, the ability to learn from experience and to pass it on, the power to distin-guish good thinking from bad.

The masters of the game, men like George Ross-Goobey, whose role in changing the pension funds of Britain we discussed in chapter 2, or Lewis Whyte, who handled the Sheikh of Kuwait's millions before the Arabs had learnt to handle their gotten gains for them-selves, or Ed Johnson, the Bostonian who set the standards for the

United States mutual fund industry, or Ben Graham, the ace of security analysts: all these gentlemen would have made a mark anywhere, but happened to magnify their fame in markets.

Their distinguishing characteristic, however, is not electrifying brilliance and the sudden, Napoleonic coup. Rather they are marked out by the qualities of patience and modesty. Conservatism is the keynote. Graham, for instance, holds that the prime (and modest) target of the investor must be to avoid actually *losing* money. It is tempting Providence (or whatever else looks after investors) to aim for lofty targets – like, say, the 31 per cent annual compound growth chalked up by Warren Buffett, a Graham disciple made famous by his feature role in Adam Smith's best-selling *Supermoney*. The Buffett partnership ran its $105,000 grub stake up to a $105 million feast in thirteen years by turning its back on the very investments which, according to the conventional market wisdom, were required to produce that degree of growth.

These conservative gentry search out situations where the downside risk is small to non-existent, no matter what happens to the market as a whole. This automatically precludes the euphemistically named 'growth stocks': that is, on our previous definition, equities whose past record encourages investors to believe that their future earnings rise will support a present price far higher than can be justified on any present values. Never forget the two howling hypotheses contained in that definition: 1) that future trends can be extrapolated from past figures; 2) that the same value attributed to the company's future today will always be applied tomorrow. Neither hypothesis is remotely tenable, which explains why growth stocks are as likely to grow backwards as forwards.

Getting turned on at full juice by the past rise in a share price is the exact reverse of the rational policy beloved of Graham, Buffett and other good and true gurus. They are far more concerned with dividend yields and operating results than with market movements, in which they are profoundly disinterested. So they seek out shares where, for one reason or another, earnings are undervalued. At one point Buffett found a couple of insurance companies, according to Adam Smith, which were selling at *1* times earnings. Others, with similar beneficial results, have sought situations where assets were vastly greater than market capitalization.

It's this undervaluation which gives the investor his base, his assurance that the money will still be there tomorrow morning. And, of course, all true undervaluations get corrected, which is when the capital gains should start to flood in. Nor is it at all bizarre in highly taxed times to insist on dividend yield as a guide, akin to the little birds which guide earnest seekers to honey. A host of implications flow from a high, well-covered yield (other things, including the continuation of that dividend, being equal). They are that 1) the company's price–earnings ratio is low; 2) its cash position is excellent; 3) the investor's capital is earning its keep in two ways, generating income as well as prospective gains; 4) since there are always upper limits to dividend yields, here is yet another insurance against a downwards movement of the shares and of your nest-egg.

Two classic instances of conservative brilliance quoted in *Supermoney* are Disney and American Express, the latter in the wake of the Great Salad Oil scandal. The stock halved as investors worried about claims for the non-existent salad oil with which Tino de Angelis had worked one of the century's finest frauds. Buffett found that in Omaha the banks were still selling Amex traveller's cheques copiously and that credit-card holders were still using their Amex cards. So he bought incessantly as the stock quintupled in five years. With Disney, Buffett saw in 1966 that the company was valued at only $80 million – which was no more than the value he placed on the great cartoons, from *Snow White* and all seven of the dwarfs onwards.

These are prize specimens in the menagerie of Nice Fat Anomalies, where most stunning stock-market successes are to be found. The NFAs may be individual stocks, they may be whole sectors. Once the socialist millionaire and cabinet minister Harold Lever spotted that the great British clearing banks, among the stuffiest investments known to man, had one and all fallen to childishly absurd price–earnings ratios. This was because, for the first time, the bankers had removed the heavy drapes from their secret reserves to reveal their true earnings, previously hushed up as effectively as the sexual misdemeanours of live presidents and princelings. Less astute investors than Lever simply didn't know what to make of the new information. Lever, being a generous soul, pointed out the realities to a mass television audience; and in the subsequent months even so true-blue a chip as Barclay's Bank duly rose by 60 per cent.

The gurus, however, are trained Anomaly hunters, with all manner of sporting equipment denied to the average investor. The latter can't, as the Buffett boys once did, actually take over a situation entirely to unlock the earnings which they were sure lurked within. If British brains less financially attuned than Lever's didn't understand bank profits when they were cooked, they can't be overly blamed for failing to understand them raw. But the Anomaly can be found in many less impenetrable thickets; and nothing more is needed to effect a capture than a reasonably good eye and an awareness that the Anomaly is what is being sought.

One such example is the basically stable company whose shares fluctuate, often for neither rhyme nor reason. A millionaire acquaintance of mine made steady pocket money for years out of J. Lyons, which had an annual tidal rhythm. In the first wave the market thought it impossible for the presiding families, the Salmons and Glucksteins, to produce yet another set of dreary results from their nutritious food and hotel interests – on which notion the price duly shot up. It then duly sank down again as the S and Gs showed their perennial capacity to disappoint. Steady money in these situations requires steady nerves; taking profits when all around are hailing new peaks, and going back into the market a second, third or fourth time when the share has returned to the sludge.

With the tidal share, there is always the latent fear that the tide will start to flow in one direction only. That is an unworthy inhibition, even for non-millionaires who can't afford to drop a few thousands here and there: unworthy because the risk is quite small as market hazards go. The tides flow most profitably with big steady-state companies, where bankruptcy or pronounced change of character are so unlikely as to be ruled out of any court in which the investor might appear. The signal to the alert-minded sounds when a good heavyweight share of the fluctuating variety is flat on its back, as witnessed by a feeble price–earnings ratio.

If a company like Unilever, with splendid businesses ranging all the way from detergents in Germany and frozen peas in Britain to Good Humor ice-cream in New York, sells at a single-figure multiple, something is likely to be wrong, not with Unilever, but with the market. It happened in 1964, and the events of subsequent years are of absorbing interest to Anomaly fanciers.

Three years of net profits round the £63 million mark followed, then four years in the £76–£86·5 million range, then a jump to over the £100 million mark in 1971. Earnings per share rose by 69 per cent over the period, certainly not enough to set the Thames near the group's Blackfriars headquarters on fire. Yet the shares gyrated from a low of 132·5p in 1966 to a high of 423·7p in 1968; after which they fell back to as low as 185p in 1970-only to touch 406p in 1972.

The price–earnings ratio oscillated correspondingly, from under 10 to around twice as high. This skittish and erratic market behaviour by a sedate and consistent industrial performer is as manna from heaven to those in the financial wilderness. As a matter of academic fact, £500 invested by a tax-exempt fund to Unilever at the 1966 low, and then sold at the high, with the process repeated every year thereafter, would have been worth £12,000 in six years: a performance worthy of the redoubtable Buffett partnership, and one which could not have been bettered by many 'growth' stocks in which the capital had been left untouched.

By comparison, a straight investment in Unilever at the 1966 low, held until the 1972 peak and then sold, would have swollen the £500 to £1500: not bad against the background of only a 69 per cent rise in earnings per share, and further evidence of the defensive value of buying stocks at the anomalous point in their cycle. However, to exploit the Anomaly to the full, frequent buying and selling are required. No investor born of woman, of course, can expect to hit a precise high or a low, even in a single year, and the capital gains tax will erode some of the benefit from switching into the investment and out again-yet the point is perfectly clear. And yet again it contradicts the conventional wisdom.

This treats the Du Ponts and Unilevers of the market world as 'lock-aways', as conservative holdings on to which the investor should hang as a base. The above is a recipe for nullity. Stocks such as these provide a do-it-yourself go-go kit, although as with any do-it-yourself operation, the process does require extra work. A managed investment will normally perform better than one which is left lying, either fallow or fertile; it is poor policy to ignore the price pattern of shares; and it is the ultimate of soundness, the very essence of investment, to buy blue-chips when they are cheap and to take the profit when they are dear.

Hunting the tidal Anomaly demands the other half of the guru's formula-the patience that goes with the modesty. The investor must wait for the moment to strike, just as he must bide his time on the trail of any other anomalous type. With the tidal share, the moments come when the price–earnings ratio is approaching its all-time high (sell) or low (buy). With the sleeping situation, the first necessity is to spot the out-of-line valuation. Then the assets and earnings have to be investigated as thoroughly as possible. If satisfied, on both scores, the investor may need even more patience while he waits for his perception to be recognized by the market and thus by the share price.

Occasionally the Anomaly will turn into a far less charming beast, the Nasty Surprise. American Express could conceivably have been up to its ears and beyond in absent salad oil; the Disney brothers might have massacred themselves with Disneyworld or some other grandiose project. Research is intended to reduce this possibility, and the object of the research is to answer that single mighty question we have posed before: why is this share standing so low?

In the tidal cases, the answer is simply that the big buying institutions have become bored with the things, of which they hold millions, and in their sheeplike way have all been abstaining. Their teetotal action becomes self-fulfilling. Since nobody else in the market has much buying power to speak of, the shares in question decline, and some off-loading begins. But when the institutions have somewhat reduced their lodes of Unilever, and the price has sunk to the bottom of the mine shaft, they look again. Their clouds of boredom lift, and they reopen their purses. The sheep dutifully flock in the same direction until the share is expensive once more, at which point the flock again no longer wishes to know. The action of the tides is thus explained by something a good deal less celestial than the gravitational pull of the moon.

Once the Anomaly is satisfactorily explained, the investor is on safer ground. Indeed he is on fail-safe territory, where at the very worst he should, just as Ben Graham advises, avoid actually losing money. There can, however, be upside Anomalies as well as downside ones: that is, a share which for no apparent reason begins to move against its sector of the market until it is standing at a substantial premium compared to the surrounding crowd.

There are only two possibilities (in human life generally, there are very seldom more than three). They are 1) the Somebody-Knows-Something-You-Don't phenomenon; or 2) the market is wildly, ingloriously wrong. Either way the case for jumping on the anomalous bandwaggon isn't strong for those with weak nerves or poorly developed speculative instincts. The only upside Anomaly which deserves to be hunted is that which arises from an undeclared bid for the company's shares. We shall be discussing the role of mergers and acquisitions in stock-markets in the next chapter – but note for the time being that a bid can strike just as easily (indeed, more so) at a downside Anomaly as at an upside one.

The seeker after profitable truth (bearing in mind that most take-over approaches are vigorously denied before they are confirmed by events) looks for the underlying anomalous position. For example one of the most lucrative twists in the saga of Ford of Britain concerned the large British minority holding in the company. At least in the eyes of the Ford moguls in Dearborn, the existence of this single large local shareholding in an otherwise totally controlled car empire was an obvious Anomaly. As for outsiders, the more United States Ford denied the very idea, the more logical it seemed.

The pay-off, when it eventually came, was most gratifying; and the brighter Londoners realized to their future profit that when an international firm, especially a United States one, buys a local outfit, it always pays over the odds, partly as an insurance against political opposition. The bias of the courts and other interested parties in favour of minority shareholders also helps, as witness the Ford-like events when another Anomaly got corrected: the oddity of two Barclay's Banks – one which counted the money of multitudes of British citizens and another which traded most profitably overseas.

Once the idea of combining the two had occurred to the collective consciousness of the Barclays (UK) hierarchy, the profit for the minority holders in the foreign operations followed inevitably. An anomalous portfolio of minority holdings in firms controlled by larger companies, provided that other aspects of the subsidiaries are up to snuff, meets the fail-safe considerations in every respect, especially if the rumours of rich rationalization have already started to circulate in the stock-market's bloodstream.

A mere mention of takeover possibilities is not enough – not at all the same thing as a nice, meaty Wall Street or Throgmorton Street rumour, well dusted with breadcrumbs and denied to a turn. Whether these whispers actually start from genuine information, derived from the chauffeur's mouth as opposed to the horse's, is irrelevant, given the high accuracy ratio shown over the years. Nor is everything lost if you have ignored or not heard the rumour. The offer may be contested. In that case, there is usually more to go for. Many an investor has sat there foolishly swearing at his missed opportunity each time some bauble being fought over in the market rises by another 20 per cent.

Again, there are only two possibilities. Either the defence will
succeed, which can only mean persuading holders that the shares
are worth more than the bid price. Or the defence will fail, in which
case the shares will be bought for at least the current price. That's
fail-safe spiced with a pinch of adventure: the best of all possible
worlds.

The profitable Anomaly must normally be hunted in less glamorous thickets. The anomalous element in contested bids for a
company's stock lies in the fact that the bidder is willing to pay
above the market price, possibly (see Ford and Barclay's) because
an underlying business Anomaly exists, possibly because the bidder
is embarking on a flight of fantasy. But as 1975 came to its end,
evidence accumulated to show that the most humdrum Anomalies
of all repay hunting – these being the companies which, while perfectly sound of wind and limb, offer high dividend yields.

Tabulations of the performance of British unit trusts showed that
those specializing in high-yielding shares had outgrown other
varieties by a convincing margin (while, of course, providing higher
income as well). The explanation preferred at the time was that such
shares always do best in the early stages of a recovery. But these
securities had also led the market during its recession, in the sense
that their declines had been substantially less than those for trusts
invested in low-yielding stocks selected specifically to produce capital gains.

You couldn't ask for a more anomalous result than higher capital
gains from the stocks selected with a totally different end in view.
It is in such dreary lists that the Anomaly hunter can find his fail-
safe reward. If he fails to find an Anomaly that will be corrected,
his high dividend yield should leave him safe. If the correction does
take place, the hunter has in practice achieved the theoretically impossible: that perfect combination of high yield and abundant capital gain.

Part VII. Shareholders *v.* the rest

20. No bids are bad news

The years that galloped up to the disaster of 1929 were the years in which speculation gripped first a nation and then indirectly the world. The Second Great Crash was preceded by less outright gambling than in the late twenties, when so much of the play was with stakes that didn't happen to belong to the gambler. The prevalent mode of the sixties was more the merger. Throughout this latter, heroic phase of capitalism, equity values were kept buoyant in part by the seemingly insatiable appetite of corporations for one another. The colossi, save for the conglomerate rampagers, were on the whole kept out of this feast by political or legal pressures; but below the snow-capped peaks of capitalism, the world of business had never seen such a torrent of amalgamations, forced and voluntary.

Private companies, public firms, family-controlled enterprises, widely owned corporations, small outfits, big brothers – the enthusiasm for corporate purchases at one time or another embraced them all. In the United Kingdom, a socialist government, of all bodies of men, at one point threw its muscle and money into encouraging mergers, for the greater future good of the British economy (which in nearly all cases failed to materialize), and for the immediate good of the affected shareholders (which materialized without any trouble at all, if they had the sense to take their money and run). Even in the United States, where successive administrations found antitrust activities a convenient way of proving their populist laurels, the merger wave went on unabated lower down, while the big actions, against the likes of ITT and IBM, rumbled on in the upper regions.

On one possible line of argument, the Second Crash was partly caused by the peaking out of the amalgamation boom. The takeover executed by exchange of shares, as we saw in chapter 10, introduced an element of phoniness into markets, in much the same way as watering the stock did in more innocently crooked days. The amalgamation merchants issued great gushes of securities, far more than the market would have absorbed in any other circumstances, in exchange for the paper of the desired company. It was an apparently painless method of raising money (the cash value of the company being purchased) without actually having to test the willingness of the market to offer a certain price for a further supply of the purchasing company's shares. So attractive was this manoeuvre, which had the often far from incidental benefit of adding more earnings and prestige to the purchasing potentates, that the latter were often prepared to settle deals on a flimsy basis – just so long as settled they were. By the time that a succession of corporate disasters, in which 'acquisition strategies' exploded like land-mines all over the managerial West, had made even stockbrokers wary of mergers, the political and public temper had also turned against the deals.

The bid fever died from a cause that reversed the rationale which had originally promoted this unheard-of intensity. As the stock-market boom (cause) faded, so did the lust for mergers (effect). Those who believe that the higher reason must govern markets should ponder why the pitch of amalgamation activity always rises when stock prices are at their zenith. Surely the wise corporation, like the wise investor, would buy companies when they were cheap, not the other way round?

If all acquisitions were in exchange for high-priced shares, the paradox would be easily resolved. Smart, slick entrepreneurs would be using grossly over-valued pieces of paper to acquire stupidly under-valued firms. In effect, the slickers would still be buying cheap. However, we have seen that the smartest and slickest gentry around (at least in their own estimation) habitually paid prices that were expensive in relation to their own stock.

The statistics of the London market illustrate the buying-dear phenomenon with peculiar intensity. When the *Financial Times* ordinary index peaked at 543·6 in 1972, so did the number of mergers – they reached a record 1100. Then the rains came, and the index dropped to 363·9. Keeping faithfully in step, down came the merger total as well: it fell by over a quarter. And in the following year, when many companies in London were truly dirt-cheap, buyers showed near-total lack of interest in the bargains – just like investors. The paradox can be elucidated by psychology and monetary economics. First, the share boom is contagious, and managements get sucked into the action, and into the desire to contribute to that action. Second, at the same time, all market booms are fed by easy money. Firms as well as personal finances are awash in the monetary flood, and thus the joy in acquisition is financially unconfined.

In market depressions, the engine goes into reverse. The psychology of managements is darkened both by the contagion of financial misery and by the worsening business conditions which accompany the market fall. Those conditions almost certainly include a clampdown on the money supply and rising interest rates. When the business cycle has rotated still further and credit is easy once more, corporate managements, licking their wounds, begin to move into merger action only slowly, until general confidence returns both to the stock-market and to the economy.

In the previous chapter we noted that the uninvolved investor can hope to take a free ride on the merger swings and roundabouts. But what about the investor who is already on board, either with the attacking pirate or on the galleon loaded with gold? Attitudes tend to vary sharply depending on which side the person striking the attitude happens to stand. An Otis Elevator threatened by a marauding United Technologies reacted in 1975 in the time-honoured offended style: an affront which could be assuaged only by more money. When a long-awaited, much-canvassed bid arrived for the fine old British emporium, the Army & Navy (which had once made its wherewithal by providing the gear on which the sun of the British Empire never set), its chairman too waxed notably indignant. People who had toiled not, neither had they spun, he suggested, would reap in a moment all the benefits for which the valiant troops of his store had been sweating away for years. But the essence of a property-owning democracy is that what's owned can be disowned, what's bought sold, what's offered accepted. If the job of directors is to maximize the shareholders' wealth, and the job of the shareholders is to pocket the proceeds wherever they find them, then the Army & Navy had reason to congratulate themselves on a good fight won – as did their investors.

The matter of mergers is by no means as one-sided as liberal economists believe. True, the public interest is defended by preserving small-scale to medium-scale enterprise and by preventing the weighty from waxing over-mighty. But the public interest is also defended by keeping a sword of Damocles hanging over the heads of boards of directors: a sword that will descend in the shape of an unwelcome pounce if their prowess fails to satisfy the share-holders. Better still, when a board has failed lamentably for long and dusty years, an offer for the shares, preferably from a rich foreigner or some native whose attentions are unwelcome to the in-cumbent, may accomplish as much good for the shareholders as decades of dynamic expansion. There's simply no substitute for an over-generous bid when it comes to lining bare pockets.

When, in 1974, Rockwell International bought Admiral Corpora-tion, it was one of the few conglomerates still buying. The pur-chase – Rockwell's twenty-third in eight years – came just in time to save Admiral shareholders from bearing huge losses: $15–20 mil-lion in the first full fiscal year under Rockwell, whose president put the matter in a nutshell to *Business Week:* 'Had we foreseen [the stagflation] we would have delayed the purchase and got them at a lot better price.' Rockwell's loss, in other words, was Admiral's gain. For an entire decade, as another example, the Watney Mann breweries had increased British investors' wealth by no more than half in money terms. Then along came the financier Maxwell Joseph, infected with an inexplicable desire to own more and more beer, and the Watney equity soared by leaps and bounds in a few perfectly delightful weeks. Whether this is worth the bidder's while is another matter, to be discussed later (it wasn't worth Rockwell's or Joseph's), but the moral is plain – no bids are bad news for inves-tors at the *receiving* end.

The political ill-favour of mergers in the seventies, strongly aided by the decrepitude of the markets, thus fed the latter debility. The strong probability is that future markets will also lack the old arti-ficial merger stimulus, at least to the same degree. Directors have become more adroit at resisting boarders (like the United States company which, faced with unwanted advances from Litton Indus-tries, which included the furniture trade among its over-stuffed and over-spread assets, promptly bought a couple of furniture com-panies itself, so as to produce an anti-monopoly defence).

The rules of the authorities have also become increasingly in-hibited. Shareholders, moreover, mostly remain sunk in the usual everlasting and loyal apathy. And the big institutions, as share-holders, still perennially sit on the fence, getting off only to join the side of the Establishment (of which they themselves are founda-tion members, of course). Many of the former big spenders, further-more, must have lost their lust for corporate girls of easy virtue.

The spectacle of such an unmitigated admission of merger failure as Xerox closing its computer division, to which we have already referred, was no more heartrending than that of Singer trapped in an analogous quagmire by its inability to make its Friden business machines provide anything but pain. As for Rockwell, its twenty-three-merger binge helped to push up its debt to over a thousand million, while cash was draining out of the company at $30 million a month. Small wonder that Rockwell tried (unsuccessfully) to part Gulf Oil from $200 million in exchange for a fifth of the company: if your own buys beat you, seek a buyer yourself.

Rockwell's misfortune with Admiral might well have befallen the Peninsular & Oriental Steamship Company in Britain. Bovis, a once-conservative building firm with ideas above its station, wangled an offer on most expansive and expensive terms from the P & O, an organization on which the sun once set as infrequently as on the Army & Navy Stores. This was a prize example of the reverse takeover gambit. Provided only that the bid is pitched high enough, the smaller entity gets effective management control of the whole. It will not usually get full control of the combined equity, but this may be no bad thing. It means that the amount of stock around has not been excessively swollen by the swoop. Although the merger mania contributed mightily to the boom of the sixties in the short term, in the long run the amalgamations seriously undermined the strength of the market. This was because the purchaser who paid too much for the victim, having thus weakened the combined equity's underlying base of profits, simultaneously proceeded, as we have seen, to weaken the market in the stock by creating considerably more of his paper than ever existed before.

In so drastically altered a supply–demand relationship, only the most extraordinary feats, or incredible faith, can keep up the share price. Hence such famous non-performances and empty triumphs as those of the conglomerate emperors. To the victors the spoils, however. A management which comes out on top in the takeover stakes at least gains *carte blanche* to carve away at the acquired body. And dissection and resection are generally the only way in which to extract benefit for the shareholders. The longer these processes are delayed, the more likely it is that other intractable problems (partly those produced by the merger itself) will supervene. According to John Kitching's statistics, 80 per cent of hostile bids succeeded in meeting the bidder's management targets, and only 10 per cent failed. With agreed bids, only 51·4 per cent succeeded; a third flopped. Naturally, agreed bids outnumber hostile ones by 10 to 1 . . . .

For Bovis, the results of its attempt to reverse into P & O were no less humbling than the celebrated visit of Frederick II to Canossa. A faction on the shipping line's board, led by the wealthy and independent Lord Inchcape, violently opposed the plan to buy Bovis and its alleged management abilities for a price so exorbitant that it outraged even the more hobnailed City consciences. The attempt to buy Bovis was defeated, and it shortly transpired that the builders' brilliant management team had led the company into a banking venture so ill-founded that P & O's new regime (the pro-Bovis group having been expelled into outer darkness) was able to pick up the residue for a song. That incident may have marked the end of the reverse takeover ploy. Bovis, by being too greedy, just missed the last boat for Shanghai.

Thus many of the devious and various ways by which shareholders could be protected against the follies of their directors by a timely takeover have been sadly reduced. Judgement on the consequences is a matter of difficult balance, like that on Victorian painting, in which the good and great is frequently negated by the awful and trite. The best guide, as always, is the best interest of the individual shareholder. The purpose of holding an investment is to reach the day when somebody else will pay more for that possession than it cost. The removal of cash-rich predators, indiscriminately buying whatever they fancy, eliminates a potential purchasing force, and is thus greatly to be deplored, at least from this narrow viewpoint.

On that same criterion, however, the investor should never be in any doubt when the now less-frequent offer happens along. There is only one test: which alternative (accept or reject) will produce the largest amount of cash in hand? That amount is verifiable fact; anything else is pure speculation about an impure (i.e. uncertain) future. Yet you will still find self-appointed pundits (this happened in the aforementioned P & O bid for Bovis) supporting the deal even though, on their own confession, the price is wrong.

If the price is wrong, to the clear and correct mind, the deal cannot be right. After all, if an investor is offered shares – any shares – at a quarter above the going market price, he won't exactly jump at the bargain. If P & O was offering too high a price, the only people with a right to cheer were those to whom the gift was being offered – the Bovis shareholders.

All considerations of the national economic weal are totally beside the individual shareholder's point. He may share, but should nevertheless ignore, the amazing views of such as Professor G.C. Allen, who believes: '... the merger is part of the process by which efficient firms grow ... it may be regarded as a civilised alternative to the bankruptcy of the unsuccessful firms.' Not only is there no guarantee that the company which grows by merger is efficient, but takeovers of the Allen variety are in the minority. Most such deals are consummated between firms of roughly equal competence, one of which simply happens to be larger. Another learned academic, Dr Brian Hindley, holds that 'assets are typically more effectively operated after they have been removed from their acquisition management. Much of the evidence for this contention comes from the United States....' The doctor was right on only one point – that there is much evidence on the point from the United States. The Federal Trade Commission (FTC), for instance, spent three years studying nine conglomerates and it found no significant difference in the management or the performance of the 348 companies devoured by these corporate wolves in the period 1960–8. In theory (the one which revels in the name of 'synergy') some of these purchases were ideal demonstrations of the beneficial effects of mergers – when a big company buys into a concentrated industry by taking on one of its smaller units, and blending its muscle with the latter's market experience. Alas, more often than not, according to the FTC, the acquired company wound up with a *smaller* share of its markets than before the takeover geniuses moved in.

Two countervailing points can be made here. First, some of the conglomerators, Richard Nixons of commerce, never intended to practise what they preached and were merely purchasing companies for the sake of preserving a credible image: all the talk about revitalizing management and earnings was just that – all talk. Second, the FTC findings may say more about conglomerates than about mergers *per se*. But most takeovers are conglomerate to a greater or lesser degree; and in any event figures are so rarely published to show how well or ill the taken-over outfit has performed under its new aegis that no defender of the merger faith can have much of a statistical leg to stand on. The new subsidiary simply gets lost in the maze of corporate accounting.

When one devoted merger-grubber of the bull years sprang to his own defence a few years before his financial demise, the facts included an annual rise in exports of the victim concerned of 50 per cent annually, 'from an admittedly low base'. It must have been knee-high to a small grasshopper: after four years the outfit was selling only £892,000 worth of goods abroad. When he finally sold off the jewel, the purchasers' accountants came to the early and regretful conclusion that its profits – on which the claims of conglomerate management excellence were based – had been overstated by about half. Of such large and small self-deceits were the conglomerate stories partly made; and those deceived were more often to be found in the investment community than among the public whom it serviced.

Even in their purple patches conglomerates tended to sell below the average market multiples, entirely because of the neither-fish-nor-fowl phobia. No matter how rapidly the earnings grew (or appeared to grow), the investor insisted on buying conglomerates at a discount from the value of their parts. It follows that no bids are both good and bad news: bad news for the shareholder who might receive one, since a weak purchaser (that is, somebody who will pay too much for the shares) has been removed from the lists and not replaced; good news for stockholders in the potential purchaser, who are not going to be lumbered with the awful results of over-buying – like Maxwell Joseph, our beer-fancying British hotelier, who dropped £7 million on paper in 1973 alone as his merger mistakes came home to roost. The idea of aggrandizing his Grand Metropolitan Hotels was to enhance the value of the equity. (Throughout his career Joseph had shown scant interest in any other policy.) But the results, pouring milk into beer, putting bingo halls into hotels and so forth, were wholly lacking in stock-market attractions. Despite prose poems in the business press about the masterly methods of management employed, the damaged credibility could not be restored.

Working methods of any acquisitive management can be given the same treatment. They are nothing but *post hoc* rationalizations of ways of managing which work well as long as they work well, which means until (inevitably) they fail. The company executive who buys another company, anyway, is not actually managing at the moment of purchase, but investing. He is in exactly the same position as an ordinary investor, except that 1) he usually has to buy all the shares, thus increasing the risk factor; 2) he usually has to pay above the market price, which reduces the potential return: 3) his action must have an effect on the rest of his 'portfolio' – that is, a bad buy will pull down the valuation of the other assets in the company. At least the private investor's bad egg doesn't spread contagion.

The ability of companies to make their bids in paper was and is one defect in the capitalistic system that lay and lies within the possibility of correction. Its weakness resides in the additional power given to managements, who can sometimes proceed with paper deals without seeking the approval of shareholders, and who can do so while damaging the basic strength of the corporation. For those who welcome sturdy corporate independence, the extra power which paper bids give to the predator's elbow should be abhorrent. Unquestionably, the amount of acquisitions would drop sharply and permanently if acquirers could purchase only for cash.

The fact that a company can proceed with a cash bid out of its own resources is some small guarantee of its viability. Firms might still seek to raise cash to finance corporate buys; but in that event their plans would be scrutinized by the financial institutions which would have to provide the currency. But here, too, the true interests of the shareholder as investor cut across the artificial interests of the shareholder as taxpayer. Just as the capital gains tax makes investors reluctant to switch out of investments when the laws of timing and rules of common sense direct, so the same exaction makes investors opt for shares, on which no tax need be paid (at least yet awhile), rather than for cash, from which the taxable element of their profit has to be deducted.

Once again, the distortion of tax helps to explain the ugly face of capitalism. As the merger movement bogged down in the midseventies (although the forces of corporate aggrandizement were only sleeping), such considerations must have seemed of remote concern to the authorities appointed to control stock-markets and theoretically to protect investors. In practice, the possibility of a good bid which will bail the investor out of a bad situation is one form of protection which does not depend on the guardians of the people. The lessened chance of this happening is sad in that one respect, since the investor needs all the protection he can get.

But in any event this shield proved to be a thin defence against the excesses of the sixties and seventies – especially for shareholders who stayed on board the foundering vessels into which their original investments had disappeared. In the long run, in stock-markets as in life, the Lord defends those who defend themselves. Those who rely on the defences erected by governments, as the next chapter establishes, have a protector made of papier mâché.

21. Who watches the watch-dogs?

Sherlock Holmes, creator of the dog who didn't bark in the night, would have found eminently satisfying the trail of frauds and failures that helped to undermine investor confidence in the 1960s. In scale these crashes were collectively and sometimes individually as large as the historic scandals, like the financial and personal suicide of Ivar Kreuger, the Swedish match king, which paved the way for the First Great Crash.

Nearly all the lessons applied to the regulation of investment were derived from the events which led up to the tragedies of 1929. Yet in the sixties one of the most conspicuous lessons was ignored both by the investment industry and by the well-fed, non-barking watchdogs who were supposed to prevent 1929 recurring. That lesson was that a trail of frauds, confidence tricks, gross speculation, peculation and hocus-pocus points directly towards a general and irresistible financial breakdown.

The process is self-reinforcing. Each scandal undermines the nerve of the investing public on which the industry ultimately depends, and not just the nerve, but the financial muscle. The investors who dropped a bundle in Investors Overseas Services, or got caught in the downfall of Lewis Gilbert's enterprises, or bought any of the hot stocks which suddenly entered their own private icebox, simply had fewer funds to put back into the market, even if, for some masochistic reason, they still wanted to revisit the scene of their downfall. Even more important, the scandals were the outward and visible signs of the inner corruption that was eating away at the health and structure of markets. Yet none of the watchdogs flickered a muscle while all this evidence was unfolding before their eyes.

True, certain rules were laid down to ensure that you could not sell fool's gold under a label saying that the gold was authentic. But if people chose to buy fool's gold for a true gold price, and yet had possessed full and equal opportunity to know and act on the truth, then that was their foolish fault. Thus any keen Sherlock should have foreseen that the plethora of schemes for collective investment in property were bound to collapse, because they were based on the untenable proposition that property values would always advance, year in year out. The watchdogs, however, proved no wiser than the United States banks, which were left in the autumn of 1975 with $11,000 million in loans to real estate investment trusts, with which they also shared $15,000 million of non-interest-bearing loans on property. Much of this $26,000 million may never come home. One of the few near-certain laws of economic life is that all rises eventually reverse; but men must be brave as well as wise to voice the warnings of Cassandra while all the Trojans around are sure that they will thrash the Greeks.

The fools and their money were duly parted in the property ramp, as in many others. The property venturers had created their own illusory currency – constantly appreciating yet inflation-proof, both solid and liquid. In exactly the same way the securities industry manufactured another spurious store of wealth: our old friend, the growth stock, whose price bore no relation to current real values (so far as these could be determined), because future values (which could not be determined at all) were the only ones which counted.

The problem for the regulators, even if they had wanted to check the resulting abuses, would have been to identify the wrongdoing, or even the wrongdoers. The outward and visible offenders were the short-cut villains who always emerge at times when the public is being taken for a costly ride. The buck can never be fast enough for them. Since selling genuine earnings to the public at an inflated price seems too lengthy a process, the inventors of such schemes simply manufacture false profits. That criminal act can be identified and punished (too late in the day, which is another matter). *Deliberately* producing shoddy investment goods is a crime; but what about *selling* them?

In law there is no extra culpability when a broker sells a share whose false value turns out to be based on fraud and deceit; the blame is no more than that attached to promoting a stock on future earnings prospects which fail to materialize. The fatal flaw, however, is that the investment industry has a vested interest in believing the stories which it is told. Fast action in fast-climbing stocks produces fast profits, in the shape of commissions and dealing profits. But this chain reaction needs to be broken only once (as the fall in property values broke the chain of confidence in property funds) for the profitable game to come to an end.

A broker may very well advise clients that the market, either in general or for some particular stock, is too high for the present. But if he goes on to suggest that it will not or should not ever see that height again, the basic psychology of the market is under threat. And much of the investment world has been steeped in the psychology of boom up to and beyond its necks – small wonder, since the market men's fortunes depend on their faith.

The watchdogs are there to protect investors from criminals, at which they lacked great success in the sixties, when much criminality flourished under their very noses. They also have some responsibility for defending the weak from the strong (ensuring that minority shareholders get equal treatment, for instance), and even for protecting fools from their folly, to some limited extent. Thus curbs on stock-market credit, which were instrumental in preventing the Second Great Crash from mushrooming into a worldwide depression, helped to save the investor from the most unpleasant financial affliction of all – losing more than he had invested. To be partly wiped out is better than to be totally destroyed.

But the watchdogs barked and bit no more impressively in this sphere than in spotting wrongdoers early enough to prevent the innocent from being hurt. Lax administration of the rules laid down for financial solidity on Wall Street brought the New York Stock Exchange perilously close to collapse. Only strenuous and all-but-despairing efforts, akin to the shoring up of banks in the United States and Britain a few years later, stopped the insolvency of distinguished Wall Street names from proving that the dubious domino theory which dominated United States foreign policy at the time certainly worked in domestic economics. The over-trading and irresponsibility of the bankrupt brokers was of a piece with the misconduct of their fathers back in 1929.

The domestic domino theory was fully seized by the men in Nixon's White House. A country's economic health depends in part on a healthy stock-market, much to the annoyance of left-wing economists. The market value of a company's stock is a crucial constituent of its ability to borrow money and thus to invest. It also affects the level of personal wealth throughout the economy, or at least the perceived level of wealth, and thus affects willingness to spend.

A prolonged slump in the market produces falls in other barometers of confidence, with a general lowering effect on business activity akin to the baleful activity of hepatitis, and there is a more palpable gathering of gloom still as the investments held by companies as security start to collapse below the value of the loans (exactly what happened with the property disasters), so that both lender and borrower suddenly find their backs to the financial wall.

Thus Richard Nixon, like Herbert Hoover before him, felt bound to advise Americans to buy common stocks at a time when every consideration of economic self-interest demanded that they should retreat from the market in full flood – which they continued to do; the citizen has long since learnt to disregard the financial advice of politicians. The soft touch which the Nixon administration brought to the management of the Securities and Exchange Commission, its main watchdog, was another factor in the débâcle. This behaviour was wholly consistent with the president's general attitude to regulatory agencies and the welfare of businessmen, but in the climate of 1968–72 it was as dangerous as an unexploded bomb.

Even if the SEC had set out to return the markets of the sixties and after to sanity, the difficulties would have been insuperable; and the problems would have become still more stupendous the more the regulators had tried to regulate – simply because the weight of the workload was beyond the lifting powers of bureaucratic man. The SEC, in any event, has to administer detailed laws – so detailed that meeting its disclosure requirements involves an immense and (for the ordinary investor) impenetrable mass of verbiage.

Disclosure, like patriotism, is not enough. The United States sees time and again the ridiculous charade of the Empty Chalice: a company comes to market on a prospectus which declares honestly that the product isn't yet in production, the market for it may not exist, the technical difficulties (which are immense) have not been overcome, there is no management ability whatsoever, nor adequate finance, and if, by some miracle, the whole thing works, the directors will pour most of the gravy over their own meat. The SEC will duly allow this farrago to come to market; but forewarned is not forearmed, and the licensing of such offerings is indefensible.

The quality of disclosure, too, is as vital as its quantity – probably more so. Accountancy is a game of interpretation; the regulators cannot reasonably be expected to check through every set of accounts, fine print, thick language and all, as carefully as the auditors of the company. There would be neither time, nor, in most cases, necessity. Which is why the SEC could claim to be regulating a situation in which, say, National Student Marketing Corporation (NSMC) gaily included in its profits those of acquisitions made after the end of the financial year, NSMC, what's more, issued blatantly misleading statements, all of which served to boost the share price, without anybody's knuckles getting rapped (or better still, cracked) until (again) far too late in the day, when the company had inevitably collapsed, under the burden of its own weirdo ways. Malfeasance is brought to the authorities' notice by misadventure, and rarely by vigilance, since corporate life is too large and varied to invigilate. So the investor receives the attentions not of a physician or a surgeon, who might affect a cure, but of an undertaker and gravedigger.

In the City of London the bureaucratic failings of the SEC and its poor batting record against low curves have not gone unnoticed. Not because the City wants to produce a superior regulatory agency, shorn of the SEC's defects, but because, like the lawyers, doctors, unions, cricketers, politicians and other richly vested interests, it wants passionately to avoid any kind of official regulation at all. Britain, like the United States, boasts laws against financial frauds of various kinds; but these laws share the principal defect of the mills of God, in that they grind exceeding slow, while lacking the virtue of those mills, which also grind exceeding sure. At the end of years of investigation, the result may be a lengthy trial whose complexities leave the jurors gasping and from which the guilty financier may emerge with a modest fine, or at worst a short spell behind bars (more accurately, in an open prison). And there he may contemplate either his navel or the fortune in his wife's name which is awaiting his return.

The British investor has a whole kennel of watchdogs, including the civil servants of the Department of Trade, the cops of the Fraud Squad and the worthies of the Takeover Panel – a body hastily cobbled up by the City when it became clear, during the mighty merger wave, that those on the inside were surfing to great profits for themselves over the drowning, flailing bodies of the outsiders.

The watchdog operation could hardly be called combined. For instance, in a case of suspected chicanery the Department will appoint inspectors from the appropriate professions. Then, usually after a year or two of sifting documents and uncovering slimy tracks, a report can be published – but only if there is no prosecution. If the assassin of the people's wealth is to be prosecuted, the report is passed in secret over to another limb of the law, which must work through the whole tedious investigative process all over again. This is simply another of the charming antiquities and oddities of British life, like the beefeaters in the Tower or the maze at Hampton Court.

The idea that the City should regulate itself, free of the attentions of outsiders who may not share the same gentlemanly code, is another such survival. The flavour of that code can be tasted from the grim and grimy episode in which a former Lord Mayor of London, Sir Denys Lowson, was found to have made some £5 million of personal profit by selling assets to a public company under his control for far more than they had recently cost. With howls of fury echoing round his head, Sir Denys (whose death saved him from ultimate disgrace) announced that he would surrender the £5 million (even though in his opinion the deal was 'fair and reasonable'); he then described his own renunciation as 'in accordance with the best interests of the City of London'.

Making profits by illicitly exploiting an inside position is thus defensible; giving them up when you are found out conforms with the unwritten code. The Stock Exchange Council does administer a large number of written rules, and it possesses the ultimate deterrent of stripping a company of its stock-market quotation – a process from which, of course, the shareholders suffer most of all. But any similarities to the American SEC end with the initials. The Council consists of stockbrokers and jobbers, who would be inhuman if their main concerns did not include the welfare of brokers and jobbers.

An illustration of the essential psychology came in the battle to reform the United States Stock Exchange, admirably described in *The Go-Go Years* by John Brooks. Would-be reformers found themselves opposed at every turn by vested or purblind interests; the vested ones would probably have won had not the mess at Wall Street's second most important exchange burst into an outright scandal. Those who rely on insiders to police their own patches have the kind of temperament which fancies walks by night in Central Park.

The well-being of investors always comes into the equation, of course, since, leaving all matters of ethics aside, bilked investors are rotten customers. But the control of speculative excesses, or of excess speculation, while it is the business of both SECs, is almost impossible to exercise – so long as no breaches of the rules come to their august attentions.

In the twin money capitals of the West the main weight of regulation leads not to the protection of the investor, which is an important by-product, but to that of the securities industry. That was the historic origin of the SEC in the United States: without Roosevelt's reforms, the investment industry would not have been able to resume its rudely interrupted function, and the multi-millions made since by the heirs of the men who hissed FDR could never have been amassed. By giving the public confidence in the honesty of the markets and the soundness of the wares offered therein, the laws made the sale of those wares possible, even to a generation which remembered vividly the havoc wrought by the over-selling and under-protection of the past.

The recognizable abuses can be legislated against and punished, if not prevented. But there is a more generalized, more insidious, far more expensive abuse – that of allowing perversion of values to burgeon so long as it is not founded on outright criminality or on an egregious inflation of credit. There is no redress against this abuse, and certainly no prevention for it. Possibly no prevention exists. If some authority were to take its courage in both hands and declare that at a price–earnings ratio of 40 not only IBM but any stock is over-valued, would the investing public react with any more sense of self-protection than a smoker notified on each packet of the government's health warning?

The job of regulators is not to prevent investors paying too much for securities; nor could it be, given that the question of how much is too much is hypothetical *in excelsis*. The regulator merely tries to stop the investor being flagrantly cheated, not to prevent him from paying over the hypothetical odds. Any other policy would negate the *raison d'être* of regulation, which, as we saw, is to enable markets to flourish. But the twin objectives – acting only when criminality or deception is suspected and making no moves that might disrupt the ordinary business of the investment community – were among the good intentions with which the road to the stock-market hell of the early seventies was paved.

When, after the débâcle, the SEC became more active, the dilemma immediately reared an ugly head. The SEC felt that banks, when soliciting new funds, should include the bald and horrific facts about their eleven thousand millions of dud loans to the real estate investment trusts. The Federal Reserve Board, which was supposed to regulate the banks, objected strenuously to this demand, on the grounds that disclosure would undermine the public's increasingly fragile confidence in the banking system. The interests of the individual investor, who might subscribe to the bank issues, and surely had a right to know about the large, uncovered and irrecoverable debts, were, in the mind of the Fed, to be subjugated to the rights of the wider community, which didn't want its banks to cave in. In much the same way, any investor would like to be warned off buying a stock whose market price bears as much relation to its real value as the evidence of Haldeman and Erlichmann did to the Watergate tapes. But those self-same investors would deeply resent any move which pushed down the general level of stock prices, including those of equities stashed away in their own bottom drawers.

The concentration on wrongdoing and the avoidance of rocking the investment industry's boat thus leave the investor with scant protection – even against criminals. Since there has to be a fire before there is any smoke, the regulators don't move until the blaze is under way. Their action, once it becomes public, in any event destroys the value of the shares – assuming that the cops have acted while some value remains. More often than not, the horse has already bolted – and the stable door remains wide open for other escapes with other people's money.

Doctors are supposed to pass exams to prove that they know the difference between the vermiform appendix and the small colon; lawyers likewise are expected not to land their clients in bankruptcy by oversight. Both can (with great difficulty) be prosecuted for professional failure. But any fool can float a public company (and many do), and any other fool can pass the shares off at incredible prices to a credulous public – and nobody can be taken to legal task. Even auditors, professional men to the fingertips, have been able to claim immunity after passing the accounts of companies whose finances would not have deceived Little Orphan Annie. If the auditors stumble across the fact that the company has less than no hope of receiving any cash for something as simple as an alleged sale, then they will pursue the matter. If they don't spot the weakness, then the missing millions are not their affair, but that of the board. The directors in turn can plead the best of managerial intentions, or possibly the worst of managerial misjudgements: either one a possible source of stockholder suits, but neither of them a hanging matter.

The recent crop of actions against the most reputable firms of accountants in the United States, as well as against some fairly disreputable directors, may redress the balance. The auspicious name of Peat, Marwick and Mitchell, although the largest in the United States, had to submit to an SEC judgement which castigated its conduct in no less than five dreadful corporate messes: National Student Marketing, Talley Industries, Penn Central, Republic National Life Insurance and Sterling Homex. That formidable list alone should give pause to smaller firms, in much the same way as stockholder suits in cases like Memorex (whose directors had to settle for a fat sum of money) have tightened the attitude of outside directors to their responsibilities.

But if the burden on such directors becomes too onerous, people will refuse to serve on boards – the money isn't enough to compensate for the inconvenience of being sued, or of trying to avoid that fate. In any event, the law is an uncertain and slow-working ally for the private investor. The latter was failed lamentably in the seventies, and will doubtless be failed again, because the official protectors had no primary interest in safeguarding the financial security of those whose money, directly or indirectly, made the stock-market possible. The market, its defenders would say, is inherently speculative: those who gamble on stocks and shares, like those who bet on horses, mustn't be surprised if they lose from time to time – all the authorities can do is to prevent the runners from being doped or otherwise nobbled, and this is rarely achieved before the off.

But if stock-markets do play the crucial part in the economy that we have outlined, they matter far more than horse races, just as the savings of a lifetime are more important than a $10 or £5 bet. The men who run companies, promote securities and sell them to the public are not licensed in the sense of other professionals: they merely have licence. In the speculative orgy of the sixties, it proved to be like that of Ian Fleming's James Bond: a licence to kill.

22. I know something you don't know

Hypocrisy is inseparable from the trade of investment. All good men and true, together with not a few bad men and false – not to mention every watchdog among the authorities – deplore, despise and deprecate the practice of insider trading. Nothing is better calculated to put the common man off any market than the suspicion that others are using privileged positions and private information to batten off the lack of privilege and inner enlightenment of the average investor. No professional misconduct, short of outright theft of a customer's securities, is more likely to bring on permanent disapproval and blackballing by the Establishment than the inside crook. Yet hardly a professional breathes who has never used any variety of inside information for his own inclusive benefit. To expect anything else demands too much from the natural condition of economies, markets and mankind.

The issue is far less clear-cut than the average burglary. Certainly the director, manager, accountant or lawyer who uses to his profit secret information gathered in the course of his duties is a thief – just like the store manager who accepts a kick-back (or too gross a kick-back) from a supplier. When Texas Gulf Sulphur made its unlikely find of an Eldorado of silver and zinc at Timmins, Ontario, its executives might conceivably have been wise to keep the discovery private for the good of the company's business; but they were unquestionably sinful to add to their personal piles of shares while the news was still in their privy possession. Those robbed were the investors from whom the Texas cowboys bought their additional shares: had the Timmins lode been public knowledge, those investors would never have sold – at least not at the price at which they were robbed.

That ranked high among the scandals which, as we proposed in the previous chapter, should have alerted the powerful authorities of the United States to the fact that the hectic stock-markets of the sixties were seething with corruption that was itself symptomatic of the coming crash. The markets bubbled with inside information and inside activity. Chairmen customarily attempted to push up the price of their stock, even those without benefit of the usual large options or holdings. Public-relations departments were instructed to pump up the price with any hot air available. Executives with large stock options hovering tantalizingly over their financial futures were under constant pressure to deliver, privately or publicly, the good news that might turn their castles in Spain into yachts off Florida or St Tropez.

The professionals in the markets were, and are, eager customers for nuggets of good news. All professional investment is governed by the ceaseless search for information. The difference lies in what kind of information is sought. Type A knowledge, for example, is as innocent as a new-born company: knowledge which may or may not affect the market price, like the good word that current trading is exceptionally fine, or that second-quarter profits will be 27·6 per cent higher. One of the several necessary delusions under which the Securities and Exchange Commission operates is that it performs a valuable duty by insisting that type A news be shared at once with the United States public. The truth, nine times out of ten, is that no man knows which way the market will turn on such tidings.

If the price rises, the onlookers will wisely attribute the advance to the second-quarter forecast. If the price falls, the same onlookers will sagely remark that the market had been 'discounting' good second-quarter earnings for some time past: 'discounting' is one of the excuse-words which serve wrong-footed experts uncommonly well at all seasons. In a bad season, anyway, reports of higher profits, or a contract to supply all the chieftains in West Africa with gold beds, will probably make no headway against the prevailing tides. At times during the Second Great Crash even the announcement of an oil strike on Staten Island or Jersey would have left a great petroleum combine with stone-cold stocks.

Similarly, in good seasons all news is grist to the mill, because the pros are hungry for any excuse to make the mill grind faster. The individual investor is thus highly unlikely to be bilked by lack of access to type A information, and it is at best foolish to try to stop a director or his friends and family from riding a good year in type A manner. This doesn't mean that the latter's dealings should not be instantaneously and fully revealed, just in case. The cornerstone importance of a director's honesty in relation to the shareholder – his fiduciary responsibility – is so vital that nothing should be left to chance or delay.

However, as a point of sober fact, few fortunes are made on this type A route. Directors are notoriously bad judges of the value of their own companies' stock. British boards, you might think, have fastened on to this inadequacy of the directorial mind, judging by their often tiny holdings in their own concerns. It's quite typical (the example is a giant engineering group) to find a company whose directors hold between them only £100,000 worth of shares in a company valued in the hundreds of millions. In this case, moreover, half of that tiny quantity was held by a doughty octogenarian, who had pioneered the business. During the year in question, only one director dabbled in the shares: five hundred of them. To set these figures in proportion, the amount paid to the board that year in emoluments (i.e. total loot) was £259,000, or 5 times the total shareholdings of all the directors save one. And nobody should suppose that this was the result of collective shrewdness. It happened to be a marvellous year in which to buy the shares – they all but trebled in the period.

These company insiders, and many others, are unlikely to be in difficulty over type A information: even if it were a gift horse, they would look it in the mouth without hesitation. An American might argue that the British company director's innocence about financial matters is not shared by his American counterparts. This may be true – although some of the biggest names in American boardrooms did fall for a Ponzi fraud in the oil game (in which old subscribers are paid, if they insist, not out of the non-existent investment proceeds, but from the money coughed up by the next lot of suckers). Probably most executives are too overcome by the cares of managing to spare much time for their investments, which is possibly one of the reasons why the American executive so eagerly embraces the stock option, which does his investment thinking for him – and on the cheap.

Executives who are innocents in the way of the market are unlikely to let drip from their mouths honeyed words which are much use to the recipients. Urging all listeners to purchase their company's shares because of their sublime cheapness hardly adds up to inside information; and hardly ever amounts to good advice, for that matter. Perversely enough, the exceptions – where the shares truly are cheap, under-valued by the criteria of past and present alike – tend to stay exceptional. They are cheap for a reason – such as the belief by powerful investors that the presiding genius is a thief. He may never have thieved; or reformation may have made him no more dishonest than everybody else. But until the old Adam is erased from the image, no amount of inside information will shift the market status of the shares.

As a rough (very rough) rule of thumb, the stock with an amazing record whose share price and price–earnings ratio have *always* been earthbound is a much safer investment than the contrary situation, which occurs when the record continues to delight, but the stock-market rating, after years of flying high, suddenly but resolutely refuses to respond to the chairman's zest – and is thus promptly labelled a bargain.

Stock-market tipsters, however, tend to fall for the latter shares much more readily – just like most investors. They thus disobey the most important law of inside information: that its existence and possession matter only when action is taken on that inside knowledge. If a share misbehaves itself in an inexplicable manner, somebody else must be buying, or selling, on a significant scale – and perhaps, as in the case of Texas Gulf Sulphur, for a significant reason. If this is so, the proud possessors are almost certainly using type B information, the variety which will unquestionably affect the shares: like the news that some uninstructed multi-national is about to pay four times the going price for the stock. Those who profit from privileged or sure-fire type B information to plume their own nests are worthy of scorn, hatred and fear, no less than those (often the same people) who use their power to manipulate shares exclusively for their own benefit.

The manipulators deserve hatred because every penny of their profit has been garnered at the expense of weaker (i.e. less-favoured) and probably poorer brethren. But the fear is not for them: very few, if any, of history's sharp market crooks ever amounted to much, except in inflated reputation, even in the runaway days of Wall Street's robber barons, still less in the sixties and seventies. The fear is rather that their corruption will undermine the market; and markets, including stock exchanges, make the difference between a free and a controlled economy. The overwhelming case against the manipulators is precisely that they control or rig what is supposed to be free, and thereby they jeopardize its continued existence.

But the philosophy of free enterprise is remote from the realities of markets and from the practical difficulties of determining inside from outside, right from wrong. As the dust of the Second Crash collected round the clay feet of the fallen City idols, one of them, Jim Slater, came out with a cogent attack on practices which he felt should be outlawed. Since they included several which this particular expert had been widely supposed to deploy more skilfully than anybody else, it sounded less a case of poacher turning gamekeeper, than of the poacher showing the landlord how to fix the defeated traps. Some Slater deals, for instance, involved bids by one company under his control for another in which his firm also deployed a master stake; and Slater investment funds, not to mention little trusts controlled by the master and his men, might hold interests in either or both.

The tricky act of divorcing the investment from the banking sides, and keeping the latter's information from seeping into the former's consciousness, has long been a speciality of the London merchant banks. A client might fall to earth in a welter of shareholders' blood : the bank which advised and succoured the company might miraculously be found to have rid its trust, in the nick of time, of once substantial holdings of the afflicted shares; and outsiders were then begged to believe that the investment managers had moved entirely on the promptings of their inner wisdom, without even consulting the banking colleagues who were close to the company's crumbling affairs. According to the authorized version in one such case, the bankers were unaware of the full impending calamity; their comrades, on the other hand, had picked up the scent of disease with nothing but twitching nostrils. Thus both sides of the bank had perfectly clean hands to wash.

Those who find that story believable are possessed of truly touching faith. Not that belief or disbelief are of any account in the context. Nobody, by the lights of the City of London, had misbehaved. By the lights of Wall Street, or at least of the Securities and Exchange Commission, the incident would have attracted attention and possibly action. The SEC's eagle eye alights even on some small, if significant corners of alleged inside malpractice. For instance the SEC claimed that two Metro-Goldwyn-Mayer financial decisions had been motivated by the desire to help one Kirk Kerkorian in paying off his bank loans. MGM's helpfulness, of course, would not have been discouraged by the fact that Kerkorian is vice-chairman and principal shareholder.

The SEC has also latterly been taking a jaundiced view of brokerage houses and banks which it suspects of acting on adverse information before the general public has had a chance of doing likewise. Favoured clients with large future funds to invest are the first people an investment house would want to tip off when one of its herds starts producing sour milk. Yet a nod, a wink or an eloquent silence can achieve the same result as a leak – and for every deliberate indiscretion that the SEC suspects, or can prove, a thousand others go unnoticed and unpoliced. Besides, who needs to be surreptitious when open deals can yield so much juice? The Wall Street house with a large holding in company ABC, whose partners arrange a merger with company ITT, benefits both from its fat finder's fee and from the aggrandizement of its holding. Thus when the Bowater paper combine bid for the Ralli commodity trading business, paying a nice price at the end of a bull market, the aforementioned James Slater could hardly lose. His financial empire owned 12 per cent of Ralli, which was controlled by the most earnest of the Slater disciples, and also 15 per cent of Bowater. The niceness of the price was thus a matter of much personal import to Slater.

The Ralli price had carried equal personal meaning before. As Oriental Carpet Manufacturers, the name under which Slater spotted its charms, the shares entered the spring of 1969 at a price of £2·125. By August they were £9, before resurfacing in new form in November at £15. A small Slater investment company, travelling along this road, saw thirty-five thousand shares which cost £224,000 transformed into £700,000 in a handful of months – which gives some idea of the wealth creation that had previously occurred inside the Ralli web.

The merits of the Bowater deal itself were hard to disentangle or even to discern from an industrial standpoint. Any resemblance between Ralli's commodity trading and Bowater's making of paper is strictly coincidental; and the logic of their combination was hardly demonstrated by subsequent events, when the commodity side (and the Slater disciple) went down as the paper business went up on one of its rare joy rides. The best that valiant defenders of the deal could do was a statement like this: 'The main logic of merging two such different groups seems to centre on their being to some extent complementary in their overseas operations.' This turned out to mean that they both operated in North America, Australasia and Europe. Without doubt, had the pair operated in *different* parts of the world, that would have been advanced as an equally glorious justification – widening the geographical spread of both at a stroke. The truth is that the marriage was made not in some industrial heaven but in the logic of investment necessity.

There was no other way of taking out the Ralli insiders (led by Slater) while the stock-market going was reasonably good. Given the complex corporate interrelationships, however, the Slater camp must have performed prodigies of secrecy and self-denial as Slater's right hand (Bowater) was egged on by his two-handed self to bid for his left hand (Ralli). It seemed, however, that Bowater was uneasy at having any one shareholder, even so disinterested a man as Slater (right hand), holding too many shares in the company. So Slater, alone among the Ralli shareholders, was bought off with cash, as opposed to paper, pocketing a round £11 million for the package and his pains. All told, it was fortunate that the left-hand was perfectly happy with the terms proffered by the company in which the right hand was interested. The schizophrenic results if the two hands of bankers who are on the inside of deals ever fell out would write a new chapter in the annals of psychiatry.

The only reliable defence of the outsider in these conditions would be total prohibition on those managing public companies from owning any equity in either their own firm or any other with which it had business dealings. The ban isn't without precedent: executives are not supposed, for example, to own undeclared interests in firms which trade with their own – otherwise the temptation to negotiate especially large and gratifying contracts with themselves might become irresistible. Such a connection has long been suspected, but never proved, to explain the consistently awful performance of one Anglo-American trading group. It was certainly at the root of the rumpus which toppled a Chrysler boss, Tex Colbert. But capitalism is built by capitalists. You could hardly separate the capitalist from his capital without destroying the system, any more than, without changing their function altogether, you could prevent investment banks from taking stakes in companies in which they are or might be interested.

The law can intervene only like the cop on the beat: when there is an indication of sin. Otherwise the main guarantee of good inside behaviour from insiders, under the existing dispensation, is their own integrity. When any financial market reaches the point where the only limit to gain is the extent of the insider's own greed, however, eventual disaster is written on the wall. In the good old days, the theory was that elder statesmen of the utmost propriety would protect the greedy man from his own greed, and thus safeguard the interests of the outsiders. But such greybeards were probably always less common than the theory maintained; nor were all Solons above garnering a little inside loot themselves.

In the bad (or worse) new days, the cult of performance has removed the last barrier to naked avarice. After all, if the object of the company is to maximize its financial horse-power, any device that guns up the engine can only serve the cult, enriching the insider most assuredly, but incidentally benefiting the other shareholders as well. The blotch on this picture of mutual, if somewhat one-sided, profit was that riches grown by artificial means are bound to wither before the chill breath of reality.

Paper fortunes made by promoters evaporated in mere weeks when the cold wind blew. After all, if company A sold its stake in company B to company C, which A also controlled, for a huge profit, where precisely had the additional wealth been created? Since the answer was nowhere, some of the people had been fooled all of the time. But they positively wanted to be fooled: the nature of the deception was, for a time, to increase their own paper wealth. The affection of investors for men who make them rich is so intense that it will even survive a series of body blows to the wallet.

A group of directors, acting just like the grand old greybeards of legend, challenged the board of Lonrho, the African trading octopus headed by one Tiny Rowland. The dissidents objected to various aspects of the way Lonrho carried on, both on the dark continent and at home. The objectionable features included deals which involved the attacked insiders in a personal capacity (including nifty use of the Cayman Islands tax haven). But it rapidly became apparent that Rowland's money-making skills impressed the shareholders far more than the fervour for business ethics of his critics, even though, after multiplying 15 times in two years' progress from low to high, the shares had at one point fallen as low as one-sixth of the peak.

It was the proper, senior, non-executive, outside directors of Lonrho who lived to rue the day, while Rowland and his inside cohorts went on (as it happened, to fresh surges of profit) as if no accusations had ever been levelled at their heads. Their chairman, the Churchill son-in-law Lord Duncan Sandys, also continued in place, with his reputation apparently undamaged by the fiscal addiction to the Cayman Islands which had helped to spur his own Conservative Party's leader, Edward Heath, to fulminate against 'the unacceptable face of capitalism'.

The unacceptable faith which outsiders repose in those inside cannot be fully explained by pecuniary interest. Lonrho is merely one of many cases which demonstrate that stock-market fans can remain faithful through fire and water. Perhaps the loyalty expresses psychological necessity. The act of confiding money to a company is an act of dedication. The faith becomes transferred, like the sexual affections of the analysand to the analyst, to the human personifications of the investment. To Samuel Mitchell, whose addiction to Xerox we reviewed earlier, the share had become more than an investment of money: it was an investment of *persona*.

If the Freudian argument holds any water, the analogy can be taken a stage further. The profit-producing inside genius becomes a father figure to the investor. He has thrust on to another person the responsibility of caring for his money. Having accomplished the transference, the last thing he wants is to admit that the chosen figure had failed him – whether by not feathering the stockholders' nests, or by placing far too much plumage in his own. Lord Thomson, the Canadian newspaper and broadcasting proprietor, used to tell employees: 'You make a buck for me, and I'll make a buck for you.' Corporate outsiders say to those inside: 'You make a buck for me and I don't care if you make ten for yourself.'

The attitude opens the way, not only to arrant sentimentality, but to exploitation. An investment is simply a deposit of money that should stay where the investor has placed it only for so long as no better home comes to his attention. The investor owes nothing to the managements of companies, especially if they have failed him, and above all if their failure consists of using their inside position for personal gain. The managers are paid to manage; what happens to their personal fortunes above and beyond their salaries should be subject to the same rules and limitations as those that apply to the outsider's treasure.

The investor has no option but to accept the fact that, ninety-nine times out of a hundred, he is on the outside looking in; that those on the inside looking out, except in cases of fraud, are in a far better position to protect their interests; and that only in rare instances (for example when a powerful and wealthy shareholder happens to dislike what's going on) will the outsider get any effective support from any source save heaven. The only safe course is to invest solely on results, not on reputation, and to behave in general like the celebrated detective of fiction who, asked whom he suspected, looked darkly round the room and whispered to the inquirer: 'Everybody.'

Part VIII. The management mish-mash

23. What price glory?

The shares which made the headlines and the money, for longer or shorter spans of time in the sixties, had one general characteristic: the purchasers, for however brief an encounter, held in high regard the qualities of the management of the companies concerned. This respect might be not only awarded, but even enhanced if the management, to the naked eye, consisted of only one man. Genius in management, like genius in art, but for less good reason, is commonly held to be at its best when undiluted by the presence of others. Those who backed a Ross Perot in computer services, a Charles Bluhdorn in conglomeration, a Bernie Cornfeld in mutual funds did so without knowing or caring about the quality of the minions. It was enough that a maestro was on the podium: he could be trusted to hire a good orchestra, or at least to make it play lucrative symphonies.

In a sense, those who took the maestro's eye view were reverting to the days and attitudes before management came into fashion. Between the wars, business was thought of in terms of men rather than of management. Only after the Second World War did the pioneering work in organization and methods blossom into the modern school (and the many schools) of management.

As the level of organizational expertise rose in the postwar years, as the numbers of men trained in management theory grew and as the output of that theory increased, so the idea gradually gained currency that management was like a company's resources of technology – an identifiable asset which could be added to, compared to the equivalent stores of other companies or assessed as part of the firm's basic strength. The problem is that although a firm's technology can be identified easily enough by the number of its patents, the quality and uniqueness of its products, its pace of innovation and so on, management consists almost entirely of men. They cannot be inspected or judged as easily as a set of blueprints. True, the men have methods – like, say, the famous decentralized organization of General Motors. But the methods are inseparable from the men who use them, and in any event nobody knows how to separate the contribution of methodology from the other strengths of a company : like the sales network bequeathed by corporate ancestors, or the technological strength which, even if inherited in an age of galloping progress, can last out two or three generations of top management.

Still, the statement that a GM, or a Shell, or a Du Pont, or a Boeing has superior management is safe and obvious enough. The heavy job of holding these complex operations together down the years demands the development of high organizational skills; and the pressure for high skills, together with the grandeur of the corporation and of its jobs, attracts the best quality of organization men – recruits to whom the giant corporation can afford to pay the highest rewards. But investors are not attracted by this proposition – probably with justice. The solid extra management qualities of the giant are offset, often outweighed, by the solidifying effects of bureaucracy and the other constipations of large scale. Only the investor seeking safety will turn to the big blue-chip, although his sole security is that the business won't go bankrupt, and will certainly rise (but also fall) with the economic cycle. The investor wanting to sample the joys of dynamic management turns elsewhere.

He isn't seeking quality of management in itself: he is seeking the *results* of 'good' management. From this formulation, it follows naturally that managers are judged solely by their results. Up to a point, this is entirely just. Results are what managers are paid to achieve, and no manager can claim prowess unless it is reflected in performance. But the linkage breaks at the point where results are identified with managerial brilliance. The analogy is with two men throwing unloaded dice. A gambler backing one of the throwers wants his man to come up with the winning number more times, but he wouldn't conclude that the winner is actually more physically skilled at throwing dice. The success of managements similarly may have little to do with innate skills: luck and timing play as large a part as brilliance, and science a smaller role than hunch.

Since giant corporations, by virtue or vice of their very size, could not produce the results which the gamblers were seeking, the latter turned to the second, third and fourth ranks; and wherever they found performance, the performance seekers also located managerial brilliance. In some cases this error did actual harm, where a man or a group possessed of mediocre ability fell in love with a false image and proceeded to ruin a perfectly respectable business with their subsequent excesses: for example, the sound paper business of Boise Cascade was turned into one of the dizziest and most disastrous seekers after conglomerate glory.

But the main result was to accentuate both the positive and the negative. The myth of management expertise pushed the price of the shares higher still in the phase of ascendancy; then, with the discovery of gross failures in financial control, or fatal product obsolescence, or some other unsuspected ailment, the devaluation in the down phase was all the sharper for the exaggeration in the days of glory.

The rise and fall of management heroes was also a constant feature of the fifties, following the tidal movements of business itself. But the sixties produced a brilliant refinement of the illogic which identified excellence of results with wonders of management. By then the science of management had been reinforced, not just by each year's output of business school graduates, many of whom swelled the ranks of consultants whose stock-in-trade was scientific management, but also by the public-relations effort on behalf of great national programmes in aerospace.

The technology of landing men on the moon was breathtaking, and outsiders assumed that equally stunning scientific applications of management underlay the technological achievement. Just as everybody wrongly believed that the miracles of space hardware would be readily transferred into civilian product lines, with incalculable benefits, so many assumed, equally wrongly, that new scientific management skills developed in organizations like the National Aeronautics and Space Administration could be applied with equal impact to civilian firms. The theory bobbed up in the argument of defence contractors that their specific skills in military programmes were not limitations, but golden opportunities. The theory also played a more subtle role in the emergence of companies whose main offering was simply management. Their promoters said, not just in effect but specifically, that since outstanding performance stemmed from superb management, a company manned entirely by scientifically trained and superbly competent managers was bound to perform superbly, to land men on the corporate moon, even though mission control had not made up its mind in which business or businesses the performance would be achieved.

Their business wasn't business – it was management. And the object of management was not to manufacture goods, or to market them, or to provide services: it was to produce earnings per share, and to multiply them so rapidly that the share price would quite inevitably perform with the exact precision of the first flight to the moon. Not only that, but because the company was oriented entirely to management and earnings growth, the forward motion could be expected to be perpetual.

The super-managers were not attached to any one business or market, and would know when and how to switch when prospects dimmed. If troubles arose in any part of the diversified empire, they constituted a ready-made consultancy team, able to arrive as rapidly as any fire brigade to put out a conflagration. Every article of this faith was a lie – notably the assumption that management can be separated from specific markets and businesses, the idea that educated skills can be universally applied, the notion that a permanent corporation can be built on shifting sands. But the most dangerous error, because it ramified beyond the conglomerates into the ranks of traditional business, was the identification of management with financial results – specifically earnings per share.

The collapse of the conglomerates was itself a powerful cause rather than an effect of the Second Great Crash: the uncovering of their big lie antedated the worst of the stock-market collapse. But the impact on managers in traditional businesses of the new theory of management had more pervasive effects. First, pride alone inspired them to prove (if they could) that they were just as skilled at managing as the sweetest young thing in conglomerates. Second, they accepted the criteria which the latter had laid down: they agreed that maximizing capital gains for the stockholder was the true task of management. Third, they adopted the methods of the con-glomerators – the search was on for diversification, for high-growth industries, for financially oriented central direction.

The disease infected staid, solid old Middle West companies like Honeywell, which reversed Horace Greeley's celebrated advice and went east – grafting on to itself a horrendously expensive computer operation which transformed the whole nature of the corporation, without contributing much in most years save an unsustainable elevation of the price–earnings ratio into the upper 40s. At Honeywell the objective of the corporation became something which its founder, a single-minded salesman who used to sit in a buggy at the end of the road supervising the troops as they peddled his heating controls, would not remotely have understood: a 15 per cent rise in earnings per share, year in and year out. If there was a rationale in this objective, it was that a 15 per cent growth company would surely always command a substantial price–earnings ratio, which would with equal certainty produce a handsome share price and capital appreciation. Its irrationality lies in the fact that, while management has many identifiable functions, none of them (outside the specialized area of the corporate finances) has any direct, immediate connection with this newer-fangled financial goal. Given that, as we know, the connection between earnings performance and the stock price, while direct, is wholly indeterminate, there is no way in which the earnings-conscious management can guarantee the results on which it sets its collective heart.

A strong or good management can achieve a variety of concrete objectives. It can avoid or eliminate no-hope, loss-making situations; on the other hand it will develop to the maximum attainable potential the sound businesses in which the company is engaged; it avoids investments (diversifications or otherwise) that overstretch its resources of money and management; it stays alert to changes in its markets that demand changes in products and practices; it looks for opportunities within its competence that will return large and early amounts on shareholders' funds; it ensures that its subordinates and replacements are of the necessary calibre; it keeps the company's products and processes up to date – and so on, right down a long list of visible and attainable objectives. Other things being equal, all or any of these attainments will very probably have the effect of improving the company's earnings. The exceptions to this rule, however, are of extreme importance – for instance, when a company is forced to bunch heavy investment into one year, so that earnings necessarily take a beating. At crucial moments like this the pursuit of earnings as the prime objective of the company ceases to make sense, and may impose dangerous nonsense, like the various formulae which company after company adopted to keep current expenditure on research and development out of the accounts.

Investors, even if they noticed such devices, probably didn't care. After all, if the object was to elevate earnings, how could any means that achieved that end, even a stroke of pure accountancy, be any-thing but divine? Similarly, shutting down a loss-maker, if it demanded a large write-off, might seem infinitely less appealing than simply allowing the losses to continue and hoping that they could be stemmed, or (by some miracle) turned into profits. Time and again the imperative of a fixed target for earnings growth was translated into an unrealistic figure for divisions which were in the above leaky boat and also for others that in contrast were well-found vessels.

Within the corporation, too, the attainable object took second place to the unattainable, and managements down the line were lumbered with targets which they either could not meet or (worse still) could meet only by forms of cheating. In some conglomerate operations a new form of business cycle became apparent. The new man arriving for the normal three-year stint as chief divisional ex-ecutive would find a mess – a sharply declining profit trend, which largely resulted from inadequate investment in the previous reign. In his first year the new man remedied the deficiencies and took the losses in profit on his predecessor's departed chin. The second year showed the inevitable sharp upturn, earning the incumbent praise and pay all round. But progress could be maintained in the third year only if investment and other supporting expenditure were cut back, which meant, of course, that after the new man had been promoted, or had moved out of the conglomerate altogether, to take a striking new job, his successor found himself in exactly the same mess in his turn.

Another damaging process was classically illustrated by a cele-brated case in which a profit forecast, instrumental in averting an unwelcome raid on the company, was missed by a grotesque margin. The company was organized into divisions, each with its own subsi-diaries – this now standard form of organization is the most perva-sive contribution of the new postwar school of management. When the forecast was drawn up each subsidiary boss added 20 per cent to his original budgeted profit. The division added all the forecasts together and, not to be outdone, added its 20 per cent on top. And the central management added 20 per cent on top of that. This geo-metrical progression guaranteed total disaster – by the time the original one-fifth boost had been subjected to this treatment, the group had transmogrified it into a 72·8 per cent target.

The efforts to make the manifold contributions of a welter of divisions and sub-divisions, not to mention their individual managers, add up to a given earnings target of 15 per cent or whatever often had much the same asinine character. Moreover, there was an inherent absurdity in the insistence on a particular time span – and a short one of twelve months at that. If an investor is making a short-term bet, then it might make sense from his viewpoint to crowd all possible profits into (and defer all possible expenditures out of) the year immediately ahead. But most investors, especially the big institutions, have much longer time horizons: in 1965 an insurance company might have been predominantly interested in the outcome in 1985, when its policy-holders would cash in their chips. Sacrificing the long run for the short is maniacal seen from this angle, since by the nature of things the process must come to an end: the deferred expenditures will catch up with the overstated profits, and the result is a Penn Central or a Rolls-Royce.

The real manager, as opposed to the counterfeit variety, has no option but to manage for the long term. A good company (the kind in which most investors would prefer to place their money) is a long-running attraction, which means that management decisions taken in any one year must be weighed against the long-term as well as the short-run interests of the corporation. In any event, many of the projects essential to a company's development take a long time to mature: longer than the three years of a conglomerate job-changer, at any rate. Earnings matter to the real manager, partly as a measure of his real attainments, partly because they finance his future corporate growth. As ends in themselves, however, the financial targets are meaningless.

Another trap lay waiting for the manager seduced by the new blandishments. The emphasis of modern management, as practised by the conglomerates and their imitators, lay in the future, which the old-style manager, of course, also had to consider. But if the company was going to be valued solely on its future growth, the tendency was to forget to some extent about its present performance. At one and the same time managers were cooking the books to show the highest possible earnings figure for the period just past, while ignoring the evidence which showed that in the current period (or over a long string of current periods) their performance, measured in absolute rather than relative terms, was inferior.

An emphasis on future growth rates, in any event, meant that present levels of performance were no longer relevant. Suppose that

two identical companies with stockholders' equity of £100 million
start off from the same base date, the one earning £10 million and
the other £20 million, but the first growing by 15 per cent annually
and the second by 10 per cent. Even if those relative growth rates
are guaranteed to remain constant, which cannot be promised by
God or man, after ten years the first company would be generating
£40·5 million of profits and the latter £51·8 million. Thus at all
points in their decade of progress, the second firm would have been
markedly more efficient. The first firm would have been able to congratulate itself solely on moving from relatively hopeless to comparatively moderate.

Possibly the greatest error and the most hard-lined management
trap of all lay in the concept of glory itself. Business is a splendid
occupation, a worthy way of spending a career, and the foundation
of the modern economy, east and west of the formerly Iron Curtain.
But like all occupations, from sport to politics, literature to public
administration, it throws up few genuine heroes. Other occupations,
however, seldom carry within them the means of their own apotheosis: sportsmen, at least initially, are turned into gods by their fans
and their successes, not by the efforts of public-relations departments – and especially not by PR operations paid for by the fans.
By convoluted logic, the business managers who employed these
trumpeters, hired with shareholders' funds, to sound the virtues of
their bosses even persuaded themselves that it was really for the
good of the shareholders. After all, if the publicity pushed up the
share price, wasn't that what the holders wanted?

Real management is an inglorious activity, compounded of equal
parts of caution and dash, of unremitting attention to detail as well
as ability to stand back and survey the panorama, of awareness of
the public reaction to the company's deeds and of indifference to
transient manifestations of that reaction – like, for main instance,
the price–earnings ratio of the equity. Once the man puts the transient manifestation first and foremost, he is doomed: each and every
action, from an otiose purchase of another company to an over-
optimistic forecast about a new business venture, can be justified
by the putative beneficial effect which it will have on the company's
standing in the stock-market.

But the path of cause and effect in the market follows no known
route. Nor is the short-term boost ever translated into the long-
term gain. Managers who chased the share price were pursuing a

chimera; and investors who chased managements dedicated to financial growth were equally hot in pursuit of a will-o'-the-wisp. Good management is something which you recognize only when you've got it, and which may never be reflected – if you are lucky – in a supreme price–earnings ratio.

24. The cult of earnings

Although earnings per share had so little to do with management, their cult was embraced most fervently by two distinct groups of managers, yet for one and the same reason. Executives in the larger corporations in the United States, and the founder-managers of new, thrusting companies in both Britain and the United States, were the most fanatical devotees. This wasn't because of a common conviction that the new growth cult was the be-all and end-all of business activity, although the seductions of fashion did play a part. Far more persuasive was the seduction of money. So long as the cult held sway, managers who lived by the cult, for the cult and of the cult would reap maximum personal rewards.

The mechanism operated in the United States mainly through the stock option or through the founder's shareholding in the case of the entrepreneurial companies. Whether or not it was good for stockholders, workers or the company itself to maximize earnings per share, it was unquestionably good for those with a vested interest in the share price: good, that is, for as long as investors were prepared to pay fanciful premiums for rapid growth in the magical numeral. The fortunes made by stock option fat-cats were large enough to match even a founder-manager's takings: as late as 1974, million-dollar options were being taken up in giant United States corporations.

Even in the awful conditions of that year, four executives in United States companies reporting one-year option gains cashed in to the extent of $500,000 of pre-tax personal profits. The year before, according to McKinsey figures, five salted million-dollar option gains away in their personal gold mines. True, the number exercising options had fallen by 1974 – down a third on 1973 and 55 per cent on 1972, leaving a mere 165 executives with their fingers in the gravy. Shareholders were expected to acquiesce joyfully in such convenient arrangements (and many did) on the old routine of sauce for gander equals sauce for goose. The more the stock price soared, the more the options were worth. But since the shareholders' worth was expanding in step, who cared? The lack of a direct relationship between the reward to the manager and the results of the company bothered nobody, especially those who were pocketing the rewards. Since we know that there was no direct link, either, between the movement of share prices and the movement of the earnings per share figure, we also know that a perfect circle of nonsense was created. Within the circle many managers waxed fat (and stayed fat, if they remembered to sell their option shares before the crash), while shareholders were set up for the big letdown.

Many hundreds of executives shared the disillusion, however – not because they were caught with devalued paper fortunes (although many were), but because they altogether missed their chance to seize the fortunes. As share prices descended to the nadir, the value of stock options swiftly evaporated. This was deeply unwelcome in the executive suite, whose inhabitants promptly awarded themselves 'stock appreciation rights'. These allowed their happy owners to reap a rich harvest from any rise in the companies' shares while sparing them from the inconvenience (not to mention the risk) of having to purchase the things.

What must have stung those landed with worthless options of an older, less sophisticated and more painful variety was that their devaluation often occurred regardless of the results of the company. Many large United States corporations went on raising reported profits throughout the Second Great Crash, yet their shares suffered revisions scarcely less drastic than those of companies all but annihilated in the economic vice. Whatever the impact on the suffering executives, however, it's doubtful whether any up-and-coming contenders for the executive suite and its manifold joys were at all deterred by the experience of the unfortunates, mostly because no better engine than the option for the painless creation of personal fortunes has ever been devised, or is likely to be invented.

That is one of the main arguments against the cult of earnings. The stock option provided managers with a built-in personal incentive to boost the earnings per share figure by any means within their power. The stockholder of the sixties thus became the victim of the same process as had so smoothly defrauded his forefathers almost a century back, when the villains were robber barons intent on forcing up the price of their stock preparatory to offloading the inflated currency on the gullible public.

The advent of professional management in the territories once ruled by the likes of J.P. Morgan and Jay Gould was supposed to have much the same effect as the replacement of corrupt hereditary monarchs by elected democrats. In both cases, however, the public was sorely deceived. Corruption has many forms, and you don't actually have to own a company, or inherit political power, to abuse your position.

In simple cases of fraud, in simpler days gone by, the technique was to promise a dividend which the company could in no way pay. When it defaulted, the investors were left holding the baby. But this technique, even had it not been outlawed, would have had relatively little utility in an age when tax considerations put shareholders off their dividend feed. When growth companies were eagerly sought after, despite paying out only a minute fraction of their earnings, the cash dividend had plainly disappeared from the equation. Some measure, yardstick or talisman had to take its place, and that something could only be the figure for earnings per share.

The magic number was slow in arriving on the British scene. The investors of days before 1964 had to exist under an antiquated system which mixed up personal income tax and company taxation. It fell to the Labour government elected in that year to give the final push to the divorce of share prices from cash returns, to the almost infinite joy of a generation of share promoters, some of them only recently born. The motive of the socialists was to stimulate the plough-back of funds into investment: the old system did not discriminate between profits paid out in dividends and profits retained in the company. Under corporation tax, money retained carried a lower impost than money handed over to the shareholders. Thus the company could in theory invest the shareholder's money, even at the same rate of return, more effectively than the shareholder himself – because the personal income tax didn't have to be deducted before making the investment.

Even before this change, which gave the earnings cult a mighty shove forward, the British had been partial to something called the earnings yield. This is simply the reciprocal of the price-earnings ratio. That is, if earnings per share are 20 and the price of the shares is 100, the earnings yield is 20 per cent, and the price-earnings ratio is 5; 5 times 20 equals 100 – and thus the reciprocal relationship is demonstrated.

But the earnings yield, unlike the price–earnings ratio, can be related directly to the dividend. Thus, if the above company was paying out 10 per cent per share in dividend, the City of London at that time would say that it had a 10 per cent dividend yield, twice covered (which, of course, equals 20 per cent). A twice-covered dividend is obviously much more attactive than one with single cover, but only because it is that much more unlikely to be cut.

In this way, the earnings yield keeps in touch with the reality of dividend payments. But the price–earnings ratio, even though it is the reciprocal of the yield, is expressed in a different numerical form: a percentage and a multiple do not relate as readily in the normal non-mathematical mind as two percentages. Moreover, the earnings yield is not dynamic, quite the reverse. A red-hot stock, earning 20 per cent a share and priced at 800, has an earnings yield of 2·5 per cent, which sounds terribly small (as, indeed, it is). But that same stock has a price–earnings ratio of 40, which sounds fantastically high (as, indeed, it is). But anybody would prefer a fantastically high figure to a terribly small one: the ratio is simply a far more alluring method of stating the same mathematical fact.

Thus London ended up on the same bandwaggon as New York. The emphasis on earnings per share introduced a wholly new element into the game. Growth had always been the game's name, since, as we know, shareholders believed that higher profits year by year would be translated more or less automatically into higher share prices. But the overall profits figure can't be readily translated into terms which apply to the individual shareholder – in the same way as a dividend payment can, for example. Divide the net earnings between each share, however, and you derive a figure which looks much the same as a dividend payment – only the company doesn't actually have to pay over the money. Moreover, it's a figure with much more elasticity than a profits total.

The classic equation is that of the £10 million company with a million shares in issue and a 20 times multiple which buys another £10 million, million-share firm with only a 10 times multiple. The profits thus double, but the earnings per share of the first company will rise by a third. That might seem a poor exchange, until the implications are considered.

The two companies before merger had a million shares and

£10 million of profits apiece. Therefore putting them together, at first glance, should in no way improve the lot of the shareholders concerned. The amount of earnings available for distribution as dividend, or as anything else, hasn't increased by one red cent. Looked at from this angle, the conjuring up of a one-third rise in earnings per share is a feat worthy of any magician who ever sawed a woman in half. The trick is worked by in effect withdrawing half a million shares from circulation and from the corporate sums. The highly valued company exchanges the above number of shares for twice as many of the underdog's. Exactly the same effect could be achieved if a quarter of the top company's shareholders were persuaded to tear up their stock and forget all about it. The amount of earnings will not be changed as a result, but the number of pieces of paper to which those profits are attached will be sharply reduced. Since the earnings per share figure is achieved by dividing net profits by the shares in issue, there must be a rise – and in this case a real one, since a quarter of the investors no longer have any entitlement to the loot.

But does the same truth apply in the merger case? Suppose that both firms paid out £5 million in dividends, retaining the remainder for necessary investment in the business. After the merger, the same investment is required: so £10 million is available to be distributed among 1·5 million shares, instead of among a couple of million as before. But it's not as simple as that. The investors in the taken-over company will have to accept a sharp drop in income if they go along with the above arrangement. They have only their half-million shares now; and their one-third share of £10 million, or £3·3 million, is £1·7 million less than they were entitled to before. In fact they would never agree to a merger on those terms. But to match their previous pay-out, the combined company would need to pay £15 million in dividends – which means either investing £5 million less or borrowing the money from some other source, paying interest on the loan and incurring lower profits as a result.

So the woman hasn't really been sawn in half. The realities must assert themselves sooner or later, and the apparent sharp improvement in the well-being of a company which has improved earnings per share by cutting the number of shares in the sum is like all conjurer's tricks: once you know how the trick is worked, the mystery and the entertainment value disappear.

Not that the earnings per share figure is useless to the straight and good manager. Any deal or financing arrangement that reduces the figure is immediately suspect and needs to be carefully scrutinized to ensure that pigs are not being bought in pokes. But this control is essentially negative, a financial discipline applied to managerial plans and ambitions. It's a very different matter from making the enhancement of that figure the sum of those devices and desires.

The number of shares can be altered in several ways other than mergers: the neatest trick, available in the United States but barred under British law, is to repurchase the company's stock in the market for cash. Between 1968 and 1973 United States corporations splashed out many millions on buying back their own stock (a total whose proportions can be gauged by noting that it was equivalent to *half* of all new funds raised by non-financial corporations). As shares slid and staggered downwards in the Second Great Crash this stratagem had become increasingly attractive as a means of trying to stem the tide. Once again, no results in real terms followed the move. But the retired shares no longer ranked for dividends, or for allocations of earnings, and the directors had thus accomplished the trick of raising the magic figure without lifting a finger. It was scant consolation for an investor who had bought at a multiple of 20 and was nursing a fall of three-quarters in his capital to be presented with this mathematical gift. What the boards concerned were doing was to make the best of an exceedingly bad job.

Many companies lacked the cash, even if they had the will, to use this device. As the market slump was followed, in the usual pattern, by a genuine business recession, the squeeze on companies' cash flow intensified all over the world. Good managements had always kept close control of cash as an instinctive part of their housekeeping and supervisory roles. But stagflation, the combination of low or no growth with double-digit price increases, turned the normally desirable into the acutely necessary.

Almost overnight, profit ceased to be the name of the game: the game's new name was cash. No firm ever went bust through earning insufficient profit. But nearly every bankruptcy is the result of a critical shortage of liquidity. It's a distinction that managements of large companies tended to forget until the recession of the 1970s brought it painfully to their notice.

The most remarkable impact came in the arcane world of corporate accounting. Since cash is an indispensable control of managerial excellence, as we noted earlier, excellent managers would presumably do everything in their power to keep money within the company – for instance, by paying as little tax as possible as late as possible. But the presumption ignores the influence of the earnings cult and its devotees. Managements were pulled in two opposite directions. On one side, sound business principles tugged them towards minimizing profits and maximizing cash retentions. On the other end of the rope, the lure of the stock-market (and of their own stock options) lugged them towards over-stating profits and reducing cash retentions by the amount of additional tax which then had to be handed over to the government.

In the United States this beneficence was entirely optional in one unique respect. The Internal Revenue Service, while not generally given to generosity, allows United States companies to opt for FIFO or LIFO when accounting for stock. We have seen that these heavenly twins, respectively first-in-first-out and last-in-first-out, have profoundly different effects on company finances, and the effects become more profound the more rapidly inflation advances. A company in love with FIFO assumes that the stocks used in making the latest product to leave its assembly lines were the earliest purchases left in the warehouse. If the prices of its raw materials and components have risen since the earliest purchase, it follows that the resulting profit will be the highest which it could report (not *make*, mark you, merely report). On the other or LIFO hand, if the company assumes that the latest purchases are the first consumed, the profit will be reduced by the amount of the higher price of the stock. A company using a hundred units of stock in a year, starting with a hundred purchased for a dollar each (= $100); buying a hundred more for $2 apiece during the year (= $200); and selling its output of a hundred units for $300, can show a profit, after incurring other costs, of $100 or nothing, depending on which accounting method it uses.

Now if a company has made $100 of profit, you would expect to find the money somewhere about the house. But in the case above, the company has shelled out $300 in the year and received only $300 back. The sole improvement in its circumstances is that instead of $100 in stock, it now has $200. But the profit locked up within that stock can't be realized until the stock is sold as product – and, even then, only at a price a good deal higher than $3 apiece.

Actually the situation is a good deal worse, because the $100 of supposed profit will attract corporation tax, which means that the firm has to find $50 of real cash (which it hasn't generated, remember) in order to keep the tax wolves from the door. All elementary stuff: yet, as we saw in chapter 5, it wasn't the simpletons of United States business who fooled themselves with FIFO, nor even the whip-smart boys who were intent on lashing the share prices of their conglomerates into a lather, but most of the larger corporations in the United States.

The truth was that in earlier years all red-blooded United States businessmen preferred to show the biggest possible profit to encourage the stock-market; in recent circumstances, when the market wouldn't have been moved by the Second Coming, these same corporations have preferred conserving their cash to paying higher taxes. In many cases (following the usual procedure) managers were deceiving themselves as much as the shareholders. Like the latter, boards of directors thought that the illusory earnings which they were reporting truly existed. The chairman of Arthur Andersen, one of the biggest international accountancy firms, put it as follows to *Business Week*: 'The high-flying era of the 1960s was in many cases a misallocation of capital. It appeared to a public not fully informed that certain companies were growth opportunities. But then the sales started to slow up and you started to have other costs. It turned out that these weren't really economic profits at all.' Note the fine remoteness of the language: 'It appeared to a public not fully informed' is one of those passive locutions which suggests that some impersonal force has been responsible both for creating the appearance and for the lack of full information. In fact the responsibility for informing (or not informing) lay as much with the western world's accountants as with anybody else.

Throughout the high-flying era, however, the auditing firms showed remarkable readiness to patch up rickety aircraft and send them sputtering back into the high skies. Accounting conventions have so great a degree of elasticity that two sets of auditors operating on different assumptions could quite legitimately come up with utterly different sets of earnings from the same data on costs and sales – in fact even the definition of a sale is a matter of opinion and disagreement.

Thus even the statement of total earnings could not be understood by the public unless it was also fully informed on the conventions which had been applied. Even if all the relevant information had been supplied in the footnotes, the subtlety of a financial Jesuit was often required to apply the necessary correction to the published accounts and come up with an alternative number. Since most members of the public (like most members of the New York Stock Exchange, as it happens) lacked either the time or the talent for the exercise, they were bound to fall back on the hope that what was good enough for Arthur Andersen, or Price Waterhouse, or Touche Ross was good enough for them.

Now if the earnings figure is elastic, and the total of shares in issue can also be manipulated, it follows that the arithmetical product of dividing the one by the other is a number of singularly low reliability. Certainly, investors cannot rely on that product to demonstrate either that the real value of the business has increased, or that its ability to pay a higher dividend has been enhanced, or even that its financial future is secure. If the earnings per share plummet, true, that is a bad omen. But in many cases the augury comes too late: the oracle pronounces *after* the damage had been done.

The reason is elementary. Over-statement of earnings is concealed by rising sales. The company is in effect borrowing from next year's profits, which can be maintained so long as the true earnings are advancing year by year. But when the true profits dip, the reported figures must bear the brunt of the earlier borrowings from profits as well as the losses from the present calamities.

Yet this was the flimsy foundation on which the stock-market boom of the sixties rested. The earnings per share figure was hypothetical; the ratio which linked that number to the price of the stock in the market was evanescent; and yet managers, as the previous chapter noted, fixed their targets in terms of percentage growth in that figure as if by doing so they were fulfilling their duty to both the shareholders and themselves.

If earnings per share meant anything, it was as a measure of the company's ability to pay the cash dividends that shareholders preferred to shun. Yet the figure measured nothing of the sort. To quote again from *Business Week*, this time from James W. McSwiney, chairman of a conglomerate, Mead Corporation, 'Financial accounting tends to emphasize reported earnings. The name of the game [there's that phrase again], however, is cash on hand and the future availability of cash.' Mead, in fact, could be taken as a paradigm of the high-flying years: a sober and conservative paper company that embraced diversification and modern management ideas as its strategy for taking its place among the ranks of those few firms that would enter the New Jerusalem. Mead played the big company game (to be examined in the next chapter) to the hilt. It even invented a system of matrixes, known as RONA (Return On Net Assets), to govern its crucial investment decisions. And yet in 1974 the total return to Mead's investors, in dividends and the price movement of the shares, came to an annual decline over a decade of 1·01 per cent. This ranked Mead at 304th among the 500 top companies listed by *Fortune*, from which it may be correctly deduced that around half of the above companies, even without allowing for inflation, had yielded a nil return to investors over a full decade.

Yet Mead, for one, had raised earnings per share by a noble 12·4 per cent compound over the same period. Not only was the pursuit of earnings per share growth illusory, in that it meant nothing and proved less. It was open to a worse condemnation still: to use McSwiney's phrase yet again, it wasn't even the name of the game.

25. It's only money

Virtue is usually made of necessity. Big companies, all the way from Mead to General Motors, attract most of the attention in the investment world, despite their conspicuous dullness, less because of their looming power on the economic scene, national and international, than because, if the stock-market is considered as a casino, large companies supply the overwhelming majority of the chips. If the game is to be one for many players, or, to use the pompous title, a property-owning democracy, all of us – and not just the fund-managing professionals – have no option but to play with big company chips. They are the only ones in large enough supply to go round. Indeed the ratio between the Goliaths and the Davids is among the more awesome discrepancies in world finance.

The market capitalization of a London-based multi-national like Shell was £2000 million in the autumn of 1975 – and that accounted for only 40 per cent of the Anglo-Dutch group's total majestic assets. Over in Wall Street, US Steel, by no means either gee or whiz, cashed in at the same time at $500 million more. Between these Everests of commerce lies many a mighty peak: to buy International Nickel would have cost £1500 million; Kaiser Aluminium £385·6 million; Rank Organization £281 million. Against these, the middling companies of the Anglo-Saxon world hardly weigh much. Out of the two hundred largest public companies in Britain in June 1975, only forty-three had market capitalizations of more than £100 million. If the investor's interest was confined to the fastest-growing or most profitable companies, moreover (and why not?), few apples of his eye would have weighed in above £30 million.

Of course saying that it would cost £2000 million to buy Shell is a manner of speaking, a grand euphemism. London newspapers are fond of reporting that so many millions have been wiped off the value of a company's shares because of some natural calamity (like forgetting to count the inventory, or the celebrated fracas at the Rank Organization, when the chairman and chief executive had a difference of opinion over policy and personal matters). But the loss is purely on paper, which is just as true of the market capitalization: it is a paper calculation. The market can value only what is actually on the market. Even in a loosely held company, only a small proportion of the shares will be available or potentially available at any time, and a major chunk of the equity may be tied up as securely as a Christmas parcel.

This isn't necessarily because some founding family is clasping the shares to its bosom for ever more. A large, inert body of shareholders always exists: institutions and individuals who for some reason, or no reason, regard their holdings as precious heirlooms, never to be disturbed. The motivation is the same as that which generates abysmal loyalty to delinquent boards of directors: self-identification coupled with ignorance. The most remarkable demonstration of the latter attribute came in the troubled Britain of 1975.

After the British Leyland car giant had collapsed into the arms of the government, more money had to be funnelled into the sickened-unto-death corporation by its new overlords. This was accomplished by an issue of new shares, which naturally had to be offered to those individuals who, since they had rejected the government's far from princely offer of 10p per share, still held part of the equity. Since the new shares were priced at 200p, however, only a certifiable lunatic, or a socialist minister, would take them up, and so the shareholders were advised again and again. Yet a goodly number positively insisted on shovelling good money after bad – paying their 200p for shares which they could then buy in the market for 80p.

In a market where such misguided minds can survive, the attachment of holders to hollow shares is no surprise. But the free proportion of big company equities is certainly greater than in the case of the middling-to-small variety, where the chances of proportionately large holdings being stuck firmly with families and friends must be greater. Moreover the presence of institutions, who are somewhat less likely to take permanent, unreasoning shines to a stock, is much more marked among the big battalions. From the supply and demand point of view, therefore, the shareholder should be on their side: especially since mammon, if not God, is on that side as well – the received view at all times in the second half of the twentieth century has been that the large corporations, however un-dynamic in stock-market performance, will inherit the economic earth.

The rationale is encapsulated in the ideas of economies of scale. Over time the race has gone, in market after market, to the competitors who can spread their costs over the largest and longest product runs; or, at the retail end, to those who can buy and distribute in the greatest quantities. Not only are there scale economies in production and distribution, but management, if theory means anything, should reap a similar benefit. One brilliant man handling £100 million of sales should earn at least 10 times the profit of an equally clever executive with only £10 million of turnover to exploit. And the extra financial muscle bulging in the first fellow's biceps, in terms of both cash flow and borrowing power, will turn an edge into an overwhelming and irreversible advantage.

But theory means only as much as practice will allow. Many industries may well have a minimum size below which the diseconomies are so great that competition becomes impossible. But it doesn't follow, even in theory, if theory is re-examined, that economies of scale are subject to no ceiling at all.

In management, this phenomenon is well established and well understood. Above a certain size – some say two hundred, some five hundred, some a thousand – factory employment passes beyond the ability of one ace to exercise effective control and direction. No matter how excellent he may be, the task has expanded beyond his span. The larger the company gets, the more layers of management have to be inserted between top and bottom, which means often enough that the ace at the summit, far from reaping economies of management scale for his own talents, isn't engaged in any activity that could truly be called managing.

But if the economies of mass management are a chimera, few people, even today, have queried those of mass production, although in one of the world's most conspicuous markets – motorcars – the middling, not to say relatively piddling, firms like Peugeot, BMW and Volvo have consistently confounded the giants like General Motors, Ford, Volkswagen and Fiat, whose million-car runs should have carried all before them – in theory. In fact a paper delivered in 1972 by two Shell International Chemical experts at a conference in Bratislava not only queries the benefits of massive scale, it demolishes them. The experts argued that every giant chemical maker in the world (and few such firms are not gigantic) built plants well above the optimum size (partly because they ignored costs and considerations that would have spoilt the pro-leviathan sums). Since all the giants were building these 'monuments to megalomania' simultaneously, they also guaranteed a condition of over-supply that savaged their prices and profits beyond short-term repair. Of course they stayed in business. But this saving grace of the great company is its underlying weakness: the *diseconomy* of scale in the matter of wealth. The diseconomies of scale are many and varied. In ethylene plants (the particular baby of the Bratislavites) they include disproportionately high commissioning and ancillary plant costs, over-production of unwanted 'co-products', higher penalties for sub-capacity working. But the wealth diseconomy is especially pernicious because it enables companies to absorb horrendous difficulties like the above, and almost to pretend that they have never happened.

From the manager's angle, that is a consoling ability. But for the caring investor, the cushioning of mistakes, the making of losses and the sterile commitment of capital add up to a running disaster. The price of the great company's absorption powers is that the return on capital, the source of all goodness, remains stuck in the nether regions.

Merely consider the case of Du Pont. Sales in 1974 came to $6910 million, or $18·9 million for every working and weekend day. Even after all costs, interest and taxes had been lopped off, the company had $910·4 million left in net profits and so-called depreciation, or $2·5 million a day. If the company's comptrollers would contrive to delay payment of expenses ('costs of goods sold and other operating charges') for a day after receipt of income, its directors would have $13·9 million more to play with round the world. A week's delay adds up to no less than $97·3 million on the 1974 figures.

Nor are Du Pont's figures especially gigantic. Royal Dutch-Shell's British half (with its 40 per cent of sales) sold as much in pounds in 1974 as Du Pont did in dollars. For a company of Shell's size, losing £8·6 million in three years in partnership with the United States Armour giant in a forlorn effort to gain £20 million of fertilizer sales is a breeze. Even dropping £85 million, with equal futility, in nuclear energy (another Shell misfortune) isn't enough to spoil the boardroom luncheons.

The cash-flow factor means that there is no practical limit to the grandiose nature of the plans which directors of large companies can form. Most such dignitaries will throw up their hands in horror at this juncture: to them life is a constant procession of schemes for which the capital can't be found, of having to appropriate limited funds between clamouring claimants – especially in the tight money conditions which accompanied the great fight against inflation and which threaten to last into the eighties. But the horrified ones over-look two points: in the first place, minor expenditures, even up into the millions, proceed without let or hindrance; and in the second place, the capital shortage arises partly because grandiose new plants have been piled upon the relative failure of equally superb monu-ments to past megalomania. Thus it's not surprising that Lockheed is strapped for cash for new projects as a result of the entirely predict-able, and predicted, drain on its resources generated by the blood-sucking Tristar airliner. Yet even though the Tristar was beyond Lockheed's financial powers, it was still able to proceed – foolishly, no doubt, but as inevitably as death or taxes, just as Chrysler was able to go on supporting its money-losing British subsidiary while its own equity capital was being eaten up.

A high return on capital not only generates all goodness, as we noted above, but is the source of all future capital – self-generated or borrowed from outside. The besetting illusions of big boards in-clude the idea that money borrowed doesn't come from the company itself. Their self-deceptive thought is that the money meanders into some wondrous asset, where it rests in perpetuity. So long as the investment generates an after-depreciation return which is higher than the interest paid on the borrowed money, and is sufficient to repay the capital, the company must win. They forget the catch that the asset must be replaced for far more than the depreciation money; and often equally negligently overlook the inconvenient fact when the investment actually returns less than the interest cost. A twenty-year borrowing at 10 per cent, in any event, requires the generation of cash equal to 300 per cent of the sum borrowed merely to take care of the interest and capital on the loan. Since the capital repayment has to be made post-tax, that means a total return of 20 per cent a year, and very few large companies have ever managed that much for more than one glorious summer out of five.

But low returns on the capital they have already invested never stop managements of the mighty corporations from investing still more, be it in mammoth plants worthy of Bratislava-type scorn or

mergers which, time after time, will go the way of much corporate
flesh: into relative failure. This is more likely with big company
mergers than with those further down the pecking order – another
paradox.

In that evanescent theory, again, the large company should have
the resources of men and money, plus the know-how, to make its
mergers work. In practice, big company mergers take as long to succeed as elephants to gestate, except that, in the latter case, something
always comes out of the process. Big company buys come unstuck
in part because they are mostly friendly, agreed affairs: giants don't
like to be seen committing rape and, as we noted previously,
resented and resisted mergers far out-score those concluded in an
atmosphere of sweetness and light.

From mergers to marketing, however, money is only as much of
an objective as the entrenched management cares to make it. At least
investment spending is subject to all manner of controls, often
culminating in mandatory board approval for all expenditure above
a certain low limit. For some arcane reason, money invested is considered more holy than money spent on current account. Thus at
the very moment when a board is gravely deliberating whether to
spend £250,000 on an extension to one of its plants, some unsuper-
vised fellow may well be committing the company to an over-spend
of £2·5 million on a current item like materials. No doubt the board
of Rowntree-Mackintosh, which was looking somewhere else while
one of its senior men took a plunge in cocoa (that unluckiest of commodities) that eventually cost the shareholders £32 million, scrutinized every penny of the money invested in its chocolate and
sweets machinery.

When they do approve investments or other spending that turns
out to be woefully ill-advised, managers are only sometimes guilty of
simple error or profligacy. In most cases, the spring of their motivation lies in the survival of the corporation. It was the sight of its
defence business going out of the window that inspired the management of Lockheed to seek civil salvation – and financial damnation –
in the Tristar. It was the knowledge that one day mounting competition and market saturation would reduce the profitability of traditional lines that led so many managements, from RCA to Xerox, into
the hopefully rich, actually ruinous, world of computers. Many
studies have come to the same finding: that the perpetuation of the
company, far more than any pecuniary motive, is what serves as

the foundation of the managerial life and the true corporate philosophy of most major groups.

But perpetuation is of singularly low interest to the investor. He wants the company to survive only to the extent that he can cash in his chips whenever he wants: he doesn't want to be stuck with a 10p burnt offering, like those unfortunate owners of British Leyland. From his point of view, the managerial idea of survival is no use – because survival is so easily contrived. So long as the management can maintain an adequate cash flow (which in any company of vast turnover is a simple trick for people of remotely competent stature) the corporation can survive even with inadequate profitability.

The shareholders might be better served if the business were trimmed down to its profitable elements, or sold off completely. Some textbook examples of the conflict of interests came with the proposed nationalization of the British steel industry. Of all businesses to escape from, steel has been high on the exit list for most of the postwar period. Yet the two largest engineering conglomerates which owned steel works, Guest Keen & Nettlefold and Tube Investments, hotly resisted this disinvestment. Naturally the fell deed at once raised their return on capital to a degree which no effort of management could have achieved, in steel or anything else.

The evidence shows, moreover, that shareholders in trust-busted enterprises, like the former components of the Standard Oil Trust, fared much more lavishly after break-up than they did before, or could have expected to do if John D. Rockefeller's robber barony had remained intact. And it's hard to believe, for another example, that an integrated I.G. Farben chemical empire could have outperformed the three component parts into which it was split by the unintentional kindness of the Allies.

The picture is fully supported by our reports on the dismal showing of big companies in the annual ten-year league tables published by *Fortune* and *Management Today* on their respective sides of the Atlantic. While the point is true that smaller firms dominate the lists in part because ten years ago they were of insignificant size, that is another way of expressing the equal truth that the diseconomies of scale apply to growth potential as well. Nor can the mathematical advantages of beginning from near zero be easily distinguished from the inborn managerial assets which go with tininess.

If money is tight, it tends to be tightly used. This general rule has many exceptions, like one little company of my acquaintance which was worrying its head off over a ten-year prospect while its cash was disappearing at a ten-month gallop; or Venesta, the good plywood firm which splintered itself by diversifying (no less than two of its stabs being separate disasters in the reprographic field) until it was earning only a third of its one-time all-plywood profits.

The smaller company has one other attraction for the share selector: at least the management's track record, if any, is visible. Nobody can even take a stab at judging the management calibre of the General Motors board. Even if (and the proposition is dubious) the chairman and the president do run the company, their stay is so short, and knowledge about their work beforehand so scanty, that the question isn't worth attempting. Who, after all, will reach for his chequebook on being informed that one Richard G. Gerstenberg, aged sixty-three, of whom he has heard nothing either good or bad, has been elected to the GM chair? In the occasional years when a leviathan turns in bumper earnings, they cannot be attributed to any one man or any group of men; the reigning group, anyway, is by the laws of averages and the business cycle likely to have presided over at least one year of doom. And even when the track record is discernible, there is no guarantee that the past provides any guide to the future. Heroes of business and their corporate vehicles are, like man himself, born only to die.

Take as one case in a thousand exemplars the story of Playboy Enterprises, Inc. On the strength of a marvellous record, Playboy went public in 1971, with the populace snapping up a quarter of the shares for $23·50. Nobody suspected that the phenomenal ability of Hugh M. Hefner, he of the round bed and bunny jet, in magazine publishing was coupled with a striking inability in every other field, including the running of clubs and hotels. Had Hefner proceeded with his plan to become private by buying back the shares, which had dropped to $3, the deal would have rubbed in the new robbery. A man who sells goods for $23.50, and buys them back, say, for $5, has made a profit of $18.50 from the transaction.

If the investing public can go wrong judging a Hefner, whose works and ways are out in the comparative open, it hasn't a hope when it comes to one of the amorphous neo-conglomerate managements which dominate the shareholding lists of the world. Nor can the investor now repose much faith in the traditional strengths of size. The Bratislava concept has begun to permeate the consciousness of big company managers: in an age when small steel plants can be highly profitable, and large ones return minuscule yields, the penetration of management minds by the virtues of smallness is proceeding apace. This is especially true in this era when, truly or falsely, shortage of capital has begun to loom among the largest single preoccupations on the economic scene. If the economists' calculations are correct, industry will need almost three times as much capital in the 1975–84 decade as in the previous ten years; and there is not the faintest sign of where such mighty sums can be found.

Probably, the capital starvation of large companies, like the recurrent reports of the death of western civilization, is greatly exaggerated. But from many angles the big company seems a less safe refuge for investment money than in the past. This raises an almost insoluble paradox. If the smallest companies include the best buys, yet there are not enough to go round, what is the investor, institutional or private, to do with his money? Was the ridiculous run-up in the price of alleged growth stocks in the sixties in part the reflection of too much money retreating from AT&T or ICI and plunging into too small a supply of the lesser-sized alternatives?

The situation could perhaps be resolved if the big companies were to revert to the old gilt-edged, blue-chip status of which AT&T was once the prime example. Such an investment would be cash-rich: its managers would concentrate on paying bigger and bigger dividends in perfect safety year after year; they would distribute capital surpluses back to the shareholders; and growth in earnings per share would be as meaningless to their managements as the Koran. Above all, they would watch the spending of the shareholders' money with unremitting attention. To many big company managements, seven-digit sums have become only money. But to the investor, it's only money – his or her money – that counts.

Part IX. The old order cracketh

26. The tax monster

The post-mortem on the disaster of 1929 readily identified the main cause: a piling-up of credit that grew with the obscene acceleration of some giant mushroom. Forty years on, money excess on an indecent scale was again the explanation. But the source of the excess was different. In the twenties private finance, then largely unregulated by government, had dug its own grave. In the sixties public finance, in an era when private money was under stricter public regulation than ever before, took on the role of irresponsibility. The profligacy of governments not only constituted the origin of the boom and bust, but answers a more intriguing question still: where the money that disappeared in thousands of millions from the pockets of private investors went. Most headed straight back to the governments whence it came.

The stock-market was not the only area struck by boom. From commodities to Old Masters, the surplus money unleashed by the governments of the West necessarily sought a limited supply of goods. The resulting inflation fed upon itself. The more prices rose, the more people attempted to protect themselves, or to improve their fortunes, by investing in those durable or seemingly durable assets which were rising most rapidly in price. The shenanigans of the stock exchange, the fraudulent claims of the offshore promoters, the sudden passions for oil drilling, Scotch whisky stocks or first-growth clarets – all these played supporting roles in a larger drama in which the main plot was the upward surge in public spending.

In sheer volume, the public boom vastly outstripped all the others. In the United Kingdom, which possibly led in heroic extravagance, given that it had less to spend, what the British Treasury defined as public spending rose from 43 per cent of the gross national product in 1965 to 60 odd per cent in 1975. Within a GNP total of £72,000 million, that represented the outpouring of no less than £12,250 million above what, ten years before, would have been the accepted level of the public sector.

The phenomenon was repeated right across the West. Over the decade to 1975, the United States government's spending, including transfer payments like social security, rose by 9 per cent a year – more than double the private economy's pace of expansion. In six key countries of the West, governments raised spending by 51 per cent in four years – much of it wasted, some of it well spent, but all in response to preconceived or supposed demands from the citizenry for goods and services which allegedly only the public sector could provide. Nor was it only central governments which swelled the public sector's appetite. Local governments chipped in strongly on their own account. New York City can be taken as a microcosm of the macrocosmic catastrophe. Year after year the amount which the City's elected leaders wanted to spend exceeded the tax revenues which the taxpaying public was willing to provide. The gap was filled by borrowings, or by pretences that the spending didn't exist, until the City, unable to raise its revenues by enough to cover the mounting interest payments on its accumulated debt, faced that monstrous 1975–6 deficit of $641 million.

Between 1956 and 1974 the numbers of state and local government employees in the United States rose from just over 5 million to around 11·5 million; at that point the bureaucratic army represented nearly 15 per cent of total non-agricultural employment, compared to under 10 per cent eighteen years before. Most other governments, local and national, were only slightly more willing than New York's to raise enough revenue to cover their spending or, conversely, to cut their spending to fit their revenue. In the period 1968–72 spending in the OECD countries outran economic growth by eight percentage points. That may sound minute, but applied to the billions upon billions of national income it produced shocking results: in 1972, when the OECD nations reported a combined rise in output of $351,000 million, inflation accounted for $225,000 million of the rise.

It was mainly through government over-spending, that, as we saw in chapter 8, the world money supply ($92,700 million in 1970) virtually doubled by 1973. Almost all the increases took place in holdings of currency. By May 1975 the International Monetary Fund was reporting that the total was $228,700 million, a rise of 147 per cent in only five years. Even that grossly understated the true rate of inflation, since the large gold element in world reserves was valued at $42·20, when a realistic figure would have been well over double.

The rulers of the West thus showed themselves to be no wiser than the monarchs of sixteenth-century Spain, who destroyed their economies in a flood of gold and silver mined from the new world. There was a basic contrast, however. The Spanish monarchs knew not what they did. Their OECD descendants, chasing too few goods with too much money no less recklessly, believed they knew what they were doing – and deemed it eminently respectable. As usual, they were hearkening to the teaching of an earlier generation, in this case that of John Maynard Keynes. The great economist had proved that in times of deficiency of demand, the government, by either spending more or taxing less, or both, could fill the 'deflationary gap'. Thus budget deficits, which earlier generations had equated with adultery and blasphemy, became virtues.

But Keynes specified that deficits were to be used at time of recession. After the war governments eagerly boosted spending in relation to income in lean economic years, but they showed remarkable reluctance to reverse engines in fat years. Anyway, they tended to embark on ambitious programmes that, even had they not shown a marked tendency to exceed original estimates, would have committed thousands of millions of public revenues for years in advance.

The apotheosis of this maltreatment of Keynes came with the work of President Kennedy's economic advisers, led by Walter Heller. It was the economic equivalent of the Bay of Pigs. Heller designed a camouflage called 'the full employment surplus'. The theory, which in hindsight has far less logic than Sam Goldwyn's 'include me out', was that, so long as the federal budget *would* have been in surplus *if* the economy had been operating at full employment, it didn't matter how large a deficit was incurred at a time of less than full employment. The argument was roughly the same as that of a bankrupt who affirms that, if only his income hadn't dropped, he wouldn't have gone broke. The Heller school was postulating that, so long as the total level of demand in the economy was below the potential level of supply, the government could spend as much money as it liked.

An enormous number of questions were begged – what, for instance, is full employment? Are there no limits to the amount which the citizens can owe themselves as both beneficiaries and holders of the national debt? Is the external payments deficit, which auto-matically accompanies the internal budget shortfall, of equally small account? (Actually, the Keynesian economists of those days didn't fully appreciate the link between the two deficits, even though the great Keynes had clearly established the equation.) But the main begged question was this: if the government couldn't expand its spending in relation to its revenues without enlarging the money supply (and it evidently couldn't), and if the supply of goods and services in the economy was either declining or not expanding fast enough (and by definition that was happening), then how could in-flation be avoided? It couldn't: but the problem was ignored because the monetary economists, and monetary theory, were almost as unfashionable as the flat earthers.

One reason for that, in turn, was that permanent restraint on the growth of the money supply, as advocated by the voice crying in the wilderness of Chicago's Professor Milton Friedman, would have imposed permanent restraint on the growth of public spending. Governments have only three sources of funds worth mentioning: taxes, borrowing and inflation. Friedmanite policies would certainly have restricted the amount of borrowing (which either adds to the money supply or subtracts from the money available to finance the private sector). The policies should also have kept inflation at very low levels (and probably would have).

Inflation is only a variation on the first two sources of public funds. This principle operates in two ways. The State, when it issues loans, borrows the taxpayer's money in bank notes of one denomina-tion and repays the debt in notes of much lower value, thus turning a profit on the deal – at the taxpayers' expense. At the same time, under a so-called progressive tax system, the State reaps a hefty (unearned) reward simply because taxpayers who are earning exactly the same amount in terms of purchasing power are pushed into higher tax brackets, and are thus forced to hand over a larger percentage of an identical real income.

In most countries in the West, people earning twice as much in-come pay more than double the tax. If, say, £650 is tax-free, and tax then starts at 35 per cent (the British situation), the £1500-a-year man pays £289 in tax: the £3000 man must fork out £814. Yet the £3000 man of 1975 had real earnings worth no more than a £1200 fellow back in 1964. The former was painfully worse off than the latter after tax.

What was poison for the geese, however, was caviare for the State. Without having to lift a finger, raise a tax or pass a law, the politicians were enabled by inflation to lay their hands on more and more of the people's wealth. In fairness, few, if any, politicians realized that this was the name of their game. The process is described by a euphemism equal to Walter Heller's 'full employment surplus'. Robbing the taxpayer of his money by failing to adjust for inflation is referred to as 'the buoyancy of the revenue' or 'fiscal drag'. Nor did public finance gain much benefit from these windfalls: inflation pushed up the government's costs like anybody else's, which meant that the budget deficit tended to rise rather than fall, which meant still more borrowing, which meant still more expansion of the money supply, which meant still more inflation. Thus the vicious circle was perpetuated.

The damage, moreover, wasn't confined to people's incomes. The same inflationary forces have not only reduced people's real wealth, but capital taxes levied by all governments have similarly taken a bigger and bigger bite from smaller and smaller real sums. Progressive scales of inheritance tax, like progressive rates of income tax, snare progressively less wealthy fortunes, again without any benefit of legislation, or any opportunity for the fleeced to protest or defend themselves. Worse still, governments have even been levying taxes on capital gains that have never actually materialized. An investor who bought his stock in 1965 and saw it treble by 1970 might then have suffered a halving of its value by 1975: it then stood at 150 against the original 100 price of the stock. If the investor sold out, in disgust and disappointment, or from sheer necessity, 30 per cent of the difference would have been taxed as profit in Britain – even though 100 in 1965 would have needed to reach 250 in January 1975 merely to keep pace with the declining value of money.

The same fiscal rot that has decomposed investors' money via notional gains has also affected investors on the income side. Corporate taxes are based on profits which became increasingly notional as time and inflation went on. In a year of 12 per cent inflation a company, even if it used the Last-In-First-Out method of stock valuation, needed to raise profits by more than 12 per cent to cover the rising cost of replacing its assets. If it recorded a 12 per cent rise, the tax bill would mount only in step – because the corporation tax, at least, isn't progressive. But in reality the company might not have been making any surplus at all.

If nevertheless it paid out a higher dividend, the recipients, since they were embroiled in a progressive tax system, paid the penalty. A 12 per cent dividend hike was no real increase. But the tax on that static dividend might well be a higher proportion of the sum paid. These injustices, moreover, have been piled on top of a system of double taxation that for years, and now especially in the United States, has penalized savings placed in equities more than any other form of savings.

The average United States company pays 35 per cent of its profits in tax. Any money placed in its equity is more than likely to be post-tax money: that is, to get $100 to put in the stock, a man in the 35 per cent tax bracket has had to earn nearly $154. His share of the earnings, say, is $20; $7 levied in tax leaves the poor chap with $13. If all of that is paid him in dividends, another $4.55 gets snatched. Out of $174 the Internal Revenue Service has collected $65.55, taxing the yield on the man's savings ($11.55 out of $20) at a far higher rate ($57\frac{3}{4}$ per cent against 35 per cent) than his earnings. The system might have been designed to discourage the ancient economic virtues of saving and thrift, even in a non-inflationary period. But with surging inflation this combination of rising tax brackets and taxes on non-existent profits deprived the investor of his income – and then set him up as a sitting duck for capital taxes on his non-existent or over-stated gains. With government also vicariously demanding more and more of the available savings to finance its deficits, the result was to raise serious doubts over industry's ability to finance itself.

As it is, United States business was forced by inadequate real profits to borrow $1·60 for each $1 of internal cash in 1974 – against only 60 cents of borrowing per internal $1 a decade before. The tax monster not only drained blood from industry, thus contributing to the sluggish recovery from the Great Inflation and the Second Great Crash. Its clawmarks and bites also tore gaping social wounds which demanded desperate healing attempts. Deficit spending and over-expansion of the money supply pushed up basic prices beyond people's threshold of tolerance. So prices were held down by controls, and the holes in profits were filled by subsidies. But a subsidy is, of course, a tax. It means that revenue has to be diverted from somewhere else, and replaced either by a new tax or by borrowing (which is delayed tax) or by inflation (which is a concealed tax). Efforts to appease the monster only increase its gargantuan appetite.

In the sixties, under the influence of John Kenneth Galbraith's *The Affluent Society*, westerners had largely swallowed the thesis of public squalor and private affluence. If public spending on schools fell behind the need, while that on washing machines soared, plainly the order of priorities had to be reversed. The argument led inexorably to the easy conclusion that public spending was essentially good, and that anxiety about its total was misplaced – because most public money went back into the private economy in wages or payments for goods and services, or in direct payments to the neediest members of society. Quite apart from the logical difficulties – the more the State bought, the less there would be for citizens to buy with the money the State returned to them – the idea ignored the tremendous leakage in the transfer system.

If the State uses resources only a degree more wastefully than the private sector, the whole economy is impoverished by increased transfers from the latter to the former. And there is plenty of evidence that the State is more profligate, as would be expected from any operation which faces no competition of any kind. Ignoring the giant albino elephants in aerospace and so on, the figures indicate that government is less careful about its spending and less likely to resist pressures to spend more. Thus in 1955–73 federal civilian employees in the United States pushed up their earnings by 5·9 per cent a year. State and local government was a little further behind, with 5·6 per cent. The figures compared with a 4·7 per cent rise for all private industry; and cumulatively they meant that in the decade federal employees had received pay rises worth half as much again as those of workers in the private sector.

The tax monster took in more and more money, misspent more and more of it and returned less to the saving classes than to the lower income groups. (Even so, the impact of regressive taxes, such as customs duties, tobacco imposts and sales levies, plus the abrupt transition in the tax system from nil income tax to taxpaying at rates of up to 35 per cent, meant that many poor people paid as much proportionately in tax as the rich.) But the more the monster forces the saving classes to spend or makes it more difficult for its members to save, the more it eats away at the seed-corn of future growth and of future tax revenues.

In recession, government revenue is reduced, but the demand for public services is actually boosted – with emergency or stand-by measures to deal with unemployment and bankruptcies added to the unchanged requirements of education, defence, security and the rest. To take the New York City case as an example, a large-scale miniature of the destructive progress, the city tries to cover its huge spending out of revenue, but the high taxation combines with other factors to drive business and individuals out of the metropolitan area, thus reducing the revenue base, thus forcing the city either to borrow or to tax still more.

In much the same way, high spending at the level of the central State, unless the latter is forced by some automatic discipline to resist fiscal temptation, leads on to high taxation, which in turn weakens the revenue base. The fall in the profitability of large companies in the West in the sixties went on too long to be considered merely cyclical – and it led directly to the excess of debt and shortage of capital in private companies which marked the beginning of the seventies.

On the conventional measures of profit, which undoubtedly overstated true resources, the median profitability of *Fortune*'s five hundred largest United States firms slid from 11·8 per cent in 1965 to 9·1 per cent in 1972. The rise in the next two years largely reflected the record inflation which undermined corporate finances still more insidiously. It wasn't so much the direct loss of real tax revenue which mattered in this context as the indirect effects on investment, economic growth and employment (although the direct effects in the United States, which gets 12 per cent of its revenue from corporations as opposed to 5 per cent in Germany and 8 per cent in Britain, are not to be sneezed at).

The tendency for taxes to rise as a proportion of national income, combined with the impact of inflation on both taxability and resources of all kinds, is to erode personal wealth. The erosion is subtle and gradual – perhaps not even noticed. People in the United States still regard $100,000 a year as the level of making it big, just as people in Britain would settle on £10,000; the target figures have not changed in years, even where their true value has halved in little more than a decade. Expectations and worth are equally devalued, while the government, the theoretical guardian of money, actually aids and abets its destruction. The effect is exactly the same as if government bonds were issued on the condition that they would be repaid, at a time of stable money, at a discount from the original purchase price, and that the interest would bear successively higher tax charges. Nobody, of course, would buy such bonds save at the point of a pistol. Yet that is precisely what was offered – and purchased, because no better security seemed to exist.

The effect of the government's semi-rubber cheques was that of all bad money. As Gresham's Law of 1558 states, bad money drives out good. The low reward for savings deposited in the traditional resting places of conservative money forced investors to look elsewhere. If a real return of 3 per cent, with the capital preserved in total safety, had been available on blue-chip stocks, how many of the masses would have been tempted by equities which offered lower yields and put the capital's safety gravely in doubt?

The insecurity of government stocks, which was the product of government-induced inflation, gave the con-men their opening. They could and did hawk their wares as safer than gilt-edged, which looked none too difficult in the light of a stock like Britain's War Loan, originally issued at £100, and settling in 1975 at every bit of £20 at the low point.

Yet United States Treasury bills in the decade 1964–74 – about as stodgy an investment as can be imagined – actually did outperform Wall Street by a small but decisive margin. Legg Mason's Washington Service in August 1975 reported that $100 placed in the bills at the end of 1964 would have grown to $175·31 by May 1975 – or a rotten $104·34 in uninflated dollars. But $100 invested in the stocks composing Standard & Poor's five hundred, even with dividends reinvested, would have got no further than $152·80 – a loss of $9·05 in real terms. Only in four years out of ten, moreover, did the cumulative gain on the five hundred come out ahead of the Treasury bill.

To arrive at the same, or rather a worse, end, investors had been forced to pass from peaks to valleys, from exaggerated joy to dreadful despair. In part, this was merely a reflection of the business cycle. But the economic and fiscal policies of government, instead of evening out the peaks and troughs, exaggerated the swings by undermining their monetary basis. The tax monster, in cutting its wide swathe through the finances of the West, had raised a final paradox: the equity investment which had been so dramatically encouraged by the monster's inflationary excesses could now be saved only if somehow the monster could be persuaded to cease and desist.

27. A new kind of scandal

Frauds come in diverse shapes and sizes, but they have one characteristic in common. The fraudulent operator persuades the people
to part with real wealth in exchange for objects, or apparent objects,
which are either worth much less than the price paid, or worth nothing at all. The law rightly takes a poor view of this activity, and
exacts punishment with its full bumbling majesty and rigour whenever it can prove that the operator knew that his bill of goods was
false, and that the public was accordingly falsely advised. Even if this
task proves too difficult, the villain has usually contravened some
regulation or other (difficult enough to avoid even in legitimate business) and can be nailed for that offence. The punishment may not
fit the crime any more than Al Capone's imprisonment for income-
tax evasion was suitable treatment for multiple homicide, but at least
justice is not completely mocked.

The sale of securities to the populace has always been a rich field
for fraud. Selling tourists fake Parker pens (a major support of the
economy of Rome for many years) or offering foreign visitors the
chance to make easy money on some local variant of the three-card
trick (a popular game in London for some summers past) is of the
same essence. But compared to security frauds they lack quantity
and safety – forgeries and confidence tricks have to be enacted before
the eyes of the public, who may include a representative of the forces
of law and order.

All securities, however, are mere pieces of paper – a description
that applies to shares in American Telephone & Telegraph as accurately as to a title to non-existent land in the Bahamas. And it takes
a particularly sharp-eyed member of the fuzz to distinguish between
dishonest and genuine embossed certificates. Even true certificates
may be false: in modern times felons like Lewis M. Gilbert, for instance, raised badly needed wind by issuing securities which were
not backed by the assets to which they were legally entitled. So

long as the supporters of a Gilbert believed the shares had full worth, and hung on to the paper, no harm could befall them. But any efforts to dispose of the watered stock inevitably undermine the financial basis of the whole corporation. The principle is the same as that of the man who sells the same house twice to two different people. The scheme is inviolable so long as one of the victims never seeks to claim his property.

Many other approaches have been taken to the ungentle art of parting the victim from his monetary wealth, ranging from the mis-appropriation of insurance premiums to the creation of assets out of thinnest air. But these operations share with watering the stock the difficulty that they involve criminal acts and, when detected, will be punished by the criminal law. Most of the historic scandals have fallen into this category. The Swedish match king Ivar Kreuger sold the same bonds again and again; the salad-oil swindler Tino de Angelis borrowed money on the security of salad oil that wasn't there; the French financier Stavisky did his borrowing on the strength of forged pawnbroking tickets. Like Lewis M. Gilbert, they either ended up in gaol, or avoided that fate by the bullet (Kreuger's and Stavisky's end) or by exile (Brazil is still playing host to several refugees from the Securities and Exchange Commission).

The sixties and seventies saw several collapses that were a match for the celebrated crashes between the wars. The fall of Bernie Cornfeld's Investors Overseas Services, like its previous global spread, was the equal of the Kreuger destruction. The crumbling of the Sindona banking empire could be spoken of in the same breath as the Stavisky *affaire* (without quite so many political over-tones). These were only two of the top-ranking investor disasters of the epoch. The off-shore property funds, the Pennsylvania Central Railroad, the dozen or more exploded conglomerates in the United States, the secondary bank fiascos in Britain, the break-up of C. Arnholt Smith's financial empire in California, the Equity Funding insurance ramp – scandal followed scandal, but it by no means followed that scandal was met with judicial retribution.

By 1975 the only punishment meted out to Bernie Cornfeld in the aftermath of the 1968 collapse of IOS was a prolonged spell in a Swiss gaol before and without trial. That apart, neither he nor any of his minions paid any personal penalty for carryings-on which had cost the investing public of the world millions. The IOS practitioners had lawyers and legal devices to ensure that at all times they kept to the right side of the law, however narrow the margin of legal safety. And the lax or non-existent regulation of offshore trusts by onshore governments greatly aided the process of keeping within legitimate bounds. But the false goods sold by IOS were intrinsically safe in the legal sense: the fund's founders sold what they *said* they were selling. The lies lay mostly in their promises, rather than in their properties.

If the charges which IOS levied for its management services were excessive, and if the money paid over to the Cornfeld treasury earned large dollops of cash for Cornfeld & co. before being invested, at least the charges were relatively open and at least the money was invested where IOS said it would be. The buyer had the chance to beware. If he chose to be pressured into paying Cornfeld fees, that was his problem. After all, some people prefer paying delicatessen prices to shopping in supermarkets; and on their own heads be it.

Admittedly, the situation changed when IOS began investing in its own in-house funds instead of other people's. But these investments, too, however ill-advised, were at least made; and the egregious errors of the Cornfeld managers in buying beaten-up no-hope growth stars and unregistered securities of doubtful status were committed by other investment managers by the score. Even when the IOS instigators cashed in their own chips by selling shares in the management company, the operation was no different in principle from other offers-for-sale of go-go outfits at the peak of their prosperity and fame. Only a charitable ninny sells out below the crest of the wave. He who sells at the top of the market, indeed, very often ranks as a prince of commerce by that token alone.

What were the IOS crimes, after all? When floating the company, the promoters had, it later appeared, over-stated the profits. But they operated in an era when auditors were expected to lend a hand in boosting the figure on the bottom line, which in turn could elevate the crucial number of earnings per share. The accountants who let pass, at Sterling Homex, sales which consisted only of letters of intent to buy houses on sites as yet unnegotiated were merely taking too far practices which had long been enshrined in business. Where sums owing, even for goods not yet ordered, let alone delivered, were considered reasonably secure, those amounts could legitimately be counted as profit. Where exceptional items, like the disposal of assets, could be taken either into the profit or into the reserves, taking the earnings route always had respectable precedents.

As for selling securities to the public on the basis of forecasts which later proved to be hopelessly optimistic, that too was a common event of the epoch. The essence of forecasts is that they may be wrong. The future is not a fact, but a supposition, and in the great majority of cases where promoters failed to meet their promises, the failure was genuine. They themselves truly believed that the sensational momentum of their past growth would continue. Very few had any thought of getting out while the going was good, and some even sold shares with reluctance because of their ardent faith in the golden times just ahead. One of Britain's fringe bank promoters, in the last flush of his sucess, was only typical in explaining his preference for buying other companies (by the yard) for cash, on the grounds that his shares were worth more than pound notes. It wasn't long before they were worth less than sheets of Kleenex.

True, that same man, while extolling the virtues of his shares to the skies, and hopefully beyond, was perpetrating crass errors of management – gratuitous boobs which did as much as global inflation, the Arab oil *démarche* and other assorted acts of God and mammon to devalue his shares. The go-go years, which gained part of their psychological impetus from the belief that management had been turned into an exact and productive science, saw concentrated demonstrations of ancient mismanagement processes, often by the same eager students who most trumpeted forth the claims of the modern manager.

As noted earlier, the bankers borrowed short and lent long, as if to prove the continuing validity of an ancient recipe for disaster. The manufacturers built up overheads beyond any hope of recovery through trading operations whose potential they grossly exaggerated. Both financiers and manufacturers – whom the smart money boys called thing-makers – displayed an unnerving penchant for paying too much for other companies, and then managing them into the ground when, inevitably, the expected earnings failed to flow.

Still worse, these self-confessed geniuses often lived by control systems of total inadequacy – at whose shrines they invited others to worship. IOS was continually begging journalists to fly out to Vevey to admire, not just the Cornfeld bevy of beautiful girls, but the perfection of the management systems – even though one consultant, unable to find any evidence of system at all, had returned to California after telling the IOS moguls of his lack of discovery. The mob persisted in its self-deception until the fall of the house duly confirmed the consultant's findings. Money was gushing out of the company, under nobody's control, and without anybody taking care or thought to see that the next year's, month's, week's or day's bills could be paid : even the basic simplicities of financial control were not honoured.

Some of the architects of the jerry-built empires of this period may have known full well what they were doing. The over-statement of profits, the cooking of books in the tastiest sauce available, the false (but legally impeccable) prospectuses, the mismanagement which diverted cash to known and unknown destinations: all these could fit as easily into a cunning, deliberate plot to defraud as into a picture of incompetence magnified by greed.

In history, as in everyday life, however, it doesn't follow that because the conspiracy theory fits the facts, a conspiracy exists. In many cases the criminal and near-criminal deceivers of the period blundered into their deceits. Thus the authors of the Equity Funding insurance scandal did not start out in business with the intention of reinsuring phoney policies made out on the lives of phoney people. The device was introduced later, when other ways of maintaining the company's handsome investment profile were flagging. In truth, however, the Equity behaviour before the frauds was cut from the same cloth. The excesses grew out of the pursuit of supernormal growth in earnings per share, which was itself the supreme excess. It drove these operators across the line which separates honest dishonesty from the dishonest kind : from being uncatchable to being caught. The line between innocent ignorance on the one side and knowing fraud on the other is difficult to draw, and this difficulty is the main reason why a new kind of scandal, the disappearance of millions in savings with no hope of redress or civilized revenge, has come to loom larger than the huge organized frauds of earlier generations. The scandalous task is made easier, moreover, because society in the shape of the State cares little about the milking of the citizenry – so long as no legally defined crime has been committed in the process.

The British government, for example, was so unconcerned about the plight of the shareholders in Burmah Oil, brought low by a

combination of massive borrowing, plunging tanker rates and misguided diversification, that, acting through the Bank of England,
it relieved the equity owners of their company's major asset: its
holdings of a quarter of the mighty British Petroleum. The sale was
a forced one, the condition of assistance to prevent the company
from collapsing completely. Within a few months the shares wrested
from the shareholders, willy-nilly, were worth some £260 million
more than the government had paid.

If the State can deal in high-level larceny, practitioners lower
down the scale can be, if not excused, explained when they use the
same principle of *caveat emptor* to unlock Aladdin's cave. The rewards can be far higher than those of common-or-garden larceny.
A thief seldom finds a couple of million lying about, as in the Great
Train Robbery or the Brinks' raid. But the market capitalizations
of public companies are so large even in bad times that the sale of
a quarter of an inflated equity can yield a sum beyond the dreams
of any bankrobber.

Far better, in other words, to ruin a bank than to rob one. Back
in the spring of 1975 the Levitz furniture business, with a stock
which had investors falling out of bed all the time, was valued in
the market at $388 million. A man who holds even a small chunk
of a business like that (and the Levitz family's chunks were large
and juicy) can make himself a million overnight if one morsel of
well-cooked news sends up the price of the stock.

The point of weakness, as in all frauds, is that at which the populace parts with its money. The equity purchaser has no guarantee
that any of the numbers on which he might base his judgement of
the purchase are what they purport to be. The dividend may not
in reality be coming out of cash earnings; the earnings may not be
the surplus actually generated from the sales made in the current
year; the sales reported for the current year may not have been completed; the costs deducted from those sales may not be the costs,
the whole costs and nothing but the costs; there may be liabilities
looming ahead of which nothing has been reported, possibly even
suspected. The purchaser has no real means of knowing whether
the managers of the company are crooks or honest beavers, idle or
intelligent, always on the premises or mostly in Florida or the South
of France.

In most cases the shares will cause no more injury than that inflicted by the market as a whole. But the inherent deficiences of

the deal open a barn door so the dishonest can exploit the exposed position of the purchaser. Their tool is the price–earnings multiple. So long as a pound of earnings can be changed into £5, or £10, or £20, or (to return to the bad old days of the sixties) £100, the company promoter has a licence to print money. Since the money is spurious, however, the time must come when its true value reasserts itself, and the shareholders are left holding an empty bag. But the crooks and the self-deceivers could never accomplish their new kinds of scandal without the enthusiastic co-operation of others who may not even be cut in on the deal. This doesn't mean only the stockbrokers and other retailers of shares. It means the big institutions and the professions; the banks and investment funds which finance and invest in the scandalous companies; the auditors who manage to find a thousand reasons why they can allow certain advantageous but highly arguable methods of accountancy to be applied; the lawyers who help to devise deals which have the effect of benefiting the directors at the expense of the shareholders; the academics and consultants who feed the vanity and the appetites of the unbridled expansionist with inflated, false concepts; even the media which insist on creating heroes in a business and management world where Olympian figures are even rarer, and feet of clay more common, than in the arts.

Every action breeds an equal and opposite reaction, given a chance. As the pieces of the Second Great Crash were being picked up, the accountancy profession in particular started to repair the damage its members had done, sometimes inadvertently, but often with results as devastating as if they had actually intended to weaken the trust of investors in the system.

Quite apart from their belated discovery that inflation over-states company profits, the accountants came out with a number of other tightened rules. After long years of investor abuse they finally decided that it was wrong to capitalize research and development, instead of charging the spending against current income. For all those years, the argument had been faithfully trotted out, like some old poodle being taken for a walk, that the R & D was a source of future profit, just like a new piece of plant, and that its capitalization was no different in kind from that of fixed investment in machinery. But in 1974 the American Institute of Certified Public Accountants took a closer look at the tired old dog, and came up with an extraordinary conclusion. 'Evidence of a direct causal relationship between current research and development expenditures and subsequent future benefits generally has not been found,' said the accountants. 'Even an indirect cause and effect relationship can seldom be demonstrated.' That being so, what were the accountants of the United States (and those of Britain, for that matter) up to when they allowed company after company to proceed on exactly the opposite assumption, declaring current profits when in many cases none existed? Shouldn't they have made the inquiries which resulted in the 1974 verdict long before—before, in fact, putting their names to earnings statements which they now confessed to have been misleading? And wasn't it somebody else's responsibility to nudge, prod or smack the accountants into doing their duty?

Here bad old *caveat emptor* rears its grizzled head again. Companies which did treat their R & D as a contribution from the great hereafter were compelled by law or their auditors or both to inform shareholders of the practice. If the investors failed to read the notes, or having read them, to take any notice, that was their problem. Forewarned might not be forearmed—in which case, tough luck. This convenient formula glossed over the fact that an overwhelming majority of the saving population is not, financially speaking, in the literacy class of the accountant. Even the meaning of 'capitalizing R & D', let alone its significance, would escape many people completely. *Caveat emptor* in these circumstances makes about as much sense as printing 'Poison—Not To Be Taken' on liniment distributed exclusively to homes for the blind.

The door which is swung open by *caveat emptor* is no different from that through which lesser con-men force their entrance. Take the three-card trick. Anybody of reasonable acuteness knows that fly-looking gentry do not circulate round the streets of London giving away £5 notes to complete strangers who can do a simple card trick. Yet the crowds gather round, begging to be robbed—and in the stock-markets of the sixties the crowds were similarly crammed in by exploitative promoters. In any human arena, however, it's a great mistake to underestimate the ultimate shrewdness of man. Indeed all circular cons (in which succeeding investors pay their predecessors, and the con-man takes his slice from the top) eventually founder when the supply of gullible investors runs out. The new kinds of scandal which emerged in the world's stock-markets run the same risk. The Pennsylvania Central Railroad; the W. T. Grant store chain; Burmah Oil; Rolls-Royce—these were not inventions of fly-by-night promoters, but apparently solid, gilt-edged companies into which an investor might stash his money, and sleep safely o' nights.

Their setbacks, ranging from complete collapse to loss of confidence, removed thousands of millions in buying power from the investors in the West. Between 1972 and 1974 some £32,000 million of equity values disappeared in London alone: something like £640 per man, woman and child in the population. The bulk of this was accounted for by the general fall in share prices. But a significant proportion arose from situations where earnings here one day were gone tomorrow, where net assets suddenly became inadequate to cover more than prior creditors, and where, after the first come were first served, nothing was left for the equity-holders.

Maybe the number of public companies has simply become too large for effective policing. Maybe the variables in double-entry book-keeping are simply too many for any hard-and-fast rules capable of covering all eventualities to be drawn up. Maybe the equity-buying classes are too unimportant politically to be worth the attention of the rest of the community. Maybe so, but the fact remains that the pieces of paper being exchanged do represent the real industrial wealth of the community.

The shareholder, in that sense, is a representative of society as a whole. If he is cheated, then so is the community. The loss of that £32,000 million directly and indirectly affected every citizen of the United Kindom. Which makes it a matter of some urgency that new measures of control be devised to meet the new kind of scandal. It is, however, a matter of great certainty that no action will be taken until another financial catastrophe brings home to the people and the politicians just how substantial, and how crucial, small pieces of paper can be.

28. A crisis for capitalism

In the year of calamity 1974 it was fashionable, especially among the enemies of the economic order, to argue that capitalism was on its last legs. The destruction by its own contradictions predicted by Karl Marx had duly come to pass. The immediate agents of destruction were as far removed from socialism as the oil plutocrats and autocrats of the Persian Gulf – but communism, like God, may choose to work through unlikely agents. In any event the quadrupling of oil prices by the best-organized, most powerful and most open cartel in history was clearly more the symptom than the cause of the crisis in capitalism. The two factors that generated the cartel's new power were the worldwide inflation (in which some other commodity prices actually rose faster than oil) and the Arab–Israeli conflict, which a left-wing theoretician could readily present as one of the last colonialist wars. The demolition of savings by inflation, the steep rise in unemployment, the instability of governments, the bank failures, the crash of the stock-markets: all these bore out the theory of a system on the edge of ruin.

The Second Great Crash had in fact been predicted by the most acute historian of the First, John Kenneth Galbraith. The warning message in his book *The Great Crash*, to the effect that what had happened once could very well happen again didn't seem to be based on any stronger predictive grounds than observation of human nature and the evidence that speculative excesses could surge into riotous life as easily under the new order as the old. This economic Cassandra's wisdom appeared essentially no different from the repeated noises off-stage of a pessimistic market seer like Elliot Janeway.

Prophets of gloom had a glorious time in the Second Great Crash, although their vindication merely reflected the uninspiring truth that if you predict disaster often enough, you must one day be proved right. Galbraith, however, was in a class by himself, as he demon-

strated in 1975 by saying correctly that his predicted Second Crash
had not only come, but gone. The crisis of capitalism, in so far as
it was a crisis in the stock-markets, is over.

By late 1975 it was also clear that the inflationary forces, far from
becoming self-perpetuating, were in retreat before the defending
forces: monetary restraint, slackening demand and inflation itself.
Like a virus creating antibodies, inflation is paradoxically an engine
of deflation. The rises in price choke off demand. As demand falls,
surpluses of goods emerge. In the desperate effort to dispose of the
surplus, producers and distributors cut prices, voluntarily or under
duress.

The process can be clearly seen in free, unrigged markets. Despite
the oil cartel, oil prices came under formidable pressure as con-
sumers cut back in the wake of the price rises. The pressure burst
through in tanker rates, which were not protected by the cartel, and
slumped so acutely that new super-tankers went straight from the
building yards into mothballs. Copper was another illustration:
from £1400 a ton at its peak to under £500 in a matter of months.
Falls in the prices of New York co-operative apartments, London
office blocks, fine wines, cut-price durables; all were symptoms of
the same automatic correction.

The Second Great Crash was a straightforward correction in the
greatest market of them all: that in the ownership of industry in
the West. What came down fell for much the same reason as the
price of copper did. Speculation had piled on the back of genuine
increases in demand to drive prices up beyond the point of reality:
in other words, past the level where people were prepared to buy
more of the commodity, be it copper or shares in IBM. When
demand disappears, any supply automatically becomes excessive,
and the collapse of prices becomes inevitable.

That is the beauty of markets, and their ultimate justification.
They allow basic economic forces to work, to restore balance where
disequilibrium has appeared. In this sense a stock-market in
which IBM sells on a multiple of 15 (in mid-1975) is far healthier
than one (in mid-1970) where the relevant figure is 34, although
the victim/investor may feel no happier about the treatment than
an amputee at losing a gangrened limb.

The situation would be far from healthy, indeed downright sick,
if the Second Great Crash had become self-feeding, like the first.
No chain reaction developed – partly because the base of borrowed

money was much smaller than in the 1929 boom and bust; partly because the financial institutions were not hopelessly dependent on equities; partly because the gaping rents which were nevertheless torn in the financial structure were hastily sewn up by the financial authorities; partly because the automatic regulators of the Welfare State prevented the recessions around the West from gathering destructive pace.

The drop in the United States gross national product came to only 10 per cent, and for every man or woman in the country out of work, nine were gainfully employed. Moreover, the human sufferings of the recession, while real and painful, bore no comparison with the horrors of the Depression, mainly because of the cushions provided by the years of past affluence, and by the tax-paid benefits of the Welfare State. Thus twelve months after the prophets of doom had reached their apogee, with the fainter-hearted citizens stocking up bomb-proof hideways with food, weapons and gold coins, the crisis had lost its burning intensity – even though the problem of combining full employment with expansion and stable money now seemed to be beyond the scope of Keynesian or even neo-Keynesian economics. The crisis was, however, the work of the disciples of Keynes – not in following the great man's teachings, but in abusing them. Apart from a few years at the end of the Eisenhower era (which seems more and more a haven of unearthly peace as those years recede further into history), governments paid far more attention to growth than to preserving the value of the currency. Nobody observed that countries which have in contrast put stable money first, like Switzerland and West Germany, suffer not at all from comparison with other economies on criteria such as growth and full employment.

Reasonable stability of prices is a potent force for economic expansion: in a non-inflationary situation, people happily invest more at lower prices (i.e. interest rates) and still become genuinely richer simply with the passage of time, because the marvels of compound interest are not overtaken by the evils of declining money values. Deficit financing, over-stimulation of the economy in the upward phases of the cycle, balance of payments transgressions – all these were insults to the memory and teaching of Keynes.

But if mistakes of economic management set the scene for the great showdown, profound changes in the business system were also responsible for the direction taken by events. The sweeping nature of the changes has not gone unnoticed, even if their significance is misunderstood. The significance, however, was widely interpreted cance is misunderstood. Trends such as the growing scale of the multi-nationals, the decline of the shareholder as the professional manager rose, the tendency towards amalgamations in many markets and across markets, the rising influence of the institutions on corporate ownership – these trends have been inescapably obvious for a long time. The significance, however, was widely interpreted in political terms: it was the nationalistic reaction to the spread of the multi-nationals, far more than the economic counter-attack of the unions, that made life uncomfortable for the overlords of world business. But developments in the markets and management circles of the West are more important in a general context: the weakening of the foundations on which capitalism in the industrialized non-communist world has been built and rests.

The underlying shift is that from owner-management to manager-management. With rare exceptions, the multiplication of the multi-nationals has been an expression of managerial rather than proprietorial drive. The main result of the divorce between ownership and control has been to create a management machine with access to far more money than the Rothschild family mustered at its zenith, but whose objectives are necessarily fuzzy. The managers' personal ambitions – high present living standards and a comfortable future retirement – bear no necessary relationship to the progress of the corporation. Whether a company girdles the globe or confines itself to the ample territory of the United States is a matter of total choice; no categorical imperative drives the corporation abroad. The motives which led the Rothschilds to fan out over Europe were highly personal and highly profitable; they have no true reflection in the manager-managed company.

The special nature of the problem can be seen more clearly if we contemplate the many remaining wholly owned companies. Where the proprietor is the sole shareholder, no philosophical difficulties arise. The owner is as free as any old Rothschild to develop the business as he chooses. If that means, for instance, inability to pay dividends for a couple of years, because of a heavy capital investment programme, then only he, as shareholder, will suffer loss of income. The motivation of the company is what he and he alone chooses to make it, simply because he personally subsumes two sections of the tripartite nature of the firm (owner, manager and employee). And unless he can persuade the employees to co-operate in his ambitions, those plans are highly unlikely to be realized, in this life or the next.

The survival of successful private firms into the era of progressive, or repressive, taxation and of big-company domination is not merely an interesting curiosity, a modern anachronism. The continued existence of groups like the Littlewood's betting and retailing empire, with its old-fashioned insistence on paying its bills within seven days, or of the Johnson's Wax family satrapy, with its worldwide reputation, not only testifies to the power of uncomplicated motives, but also reasserts a simple fact of business life. For a private firm to survive in acceptable splendour, the prime condition is high profitability. As they have no equity to mobilize, the proprietors cannot insouciantly merge, or expand the capital base. That in turn limits their ability to run into debt. Because they cannot offer glossy substitutes like stock options, they are thrown back on employing corporate servants who respond well to good jobs and high salaries. None of this exempts the private company from the weaknesses of organizations large and small. But it imposes essential elements of discipline.

It is no part of the theory of joint stock companies that financial discipline should be relaxed, although since the history of their genus began, these vehicles have always been used by unscrupulous men as a way of bilking the unwary. The diffusion of ownership, however admirable from other respects, such as weakening the power of wealthy oligarchs and enabling prodigies of financing, in enterprises ranging from railroads to North Sea oil, has the disadvantage of forcing the masses to share in corporate failure. If the private company over-spends, or under-invests, or disguises losses as profits, only the proprietor, his employees and the creditors suffer. But the shareholders in public companies not only have the sins of non-proprietorial managers visited on their heads; unlike creditors, they are helpless.

Society has recognized and accepted the equal helplessness of the depositor in a bank. The crimes of mismanagement which undermined an institution like the Franklin National were little different in nature from the managerial misdemeanours of a Penn Central. Yet the resources of the State and the banking industry were hastily mobilized to ensure that nobody with money in the bank lost a dime. Those who had in effect placed their funds in the care of the railway directors (many of whom happened to be bankers) were left to sink or swim, just like the unfortunates whose funds were locked up in IOS mutual funds or the property rackets. Investment in the ownership of industry, it seems, is a speculative affair, in which *caveat emptor* applies. The shareholder has all the risks of the proprietor, but in practical terms none of his power.

Sadly for the shareholders, the managers, who do possess nearly all the power of the proprietor, have decided to emulate him, or at least his fortune. A respectable theme-song of big business is the necessity to make young managers think of their pieces of the corporation as 'a business like their own'. The attitude ignores the crucial difference between proprietorship and the professional: the latter has a fiduciary responsibility to the shareholders which is, or should be, as paramount as the obligation of a bank to its depositors. Yet no sanctions compel the manager to execute his duty; no defences worth speaking of protect the shareholder against managers who neglect their fiduciary role. The little old lady in Dubuque, or, to take a less sentimental case, the general practitioner in Wimbledon, have the investment of their savings in industry treated with little respect.

A British government demonstrated the prevailing faith when the Rolls-Royce company was allowed to go bankrupt, having been egged into a disastrous engine contract by ministers and civil servants, who wholly ignored the abundant evidence of the company's financial and managerial failings. The shareholders might have been left with nothing. As it was, they collected their money last in the queue, after the bankers, the secured creditors, the loan stock holders and so on.

The justification of this maltreatment in the old days was that the equity-holder, unlike the lender of fixed-interest money, was entitled to a share of the profits. The risk of being wiped out was the price the equity-holder paid for his privilege. But where is the privilege in modern times? For decades, dividend pay-outs have compared unfavourably with interest yields: undistributed, ploughed-back profits, ostensibly belonging to the equity-holders, have often yielded negligible or wholly inadequate returns in the hands of the company.

The equity-holder, in return for taking all of the risks, has received short rations in the way of reward, a deprivation faithfully reflected by the collapse in stock-market values, a collapse which in its vicious-circular turn made the equity investor's plight still

worse. Not surprisingly, distinguished accountants are beginning
to challenge the whole concept of 'free' (that is cost-less) equity capital. A company needs £50 million, say. If it raises the money by
a new issue of shares, no charge is made against profits, and those
who provide the money have no security. If the same sum is raised
via a debenture, the interest (unlike the dividend on the shares) is
charged against profits, and the borrowing will be fully secured
against some of the company's assets. Nor is it any use pointing
out (correctly, in legal fact) that all the assets belong to the equity-
holders: owners of last resort (as in Rolls-Royce, as in Penn Central)
get their hands on the goods only when all other claims have been
met.

In justice, equity capital should receive at least the same return
as the going rate available on alternative investments, and these dividends, like interest, should rank as a prior charge against income.
If this interest were tax-deductible, like any interest cost, the profit
reported by many corporations would wither away. Instead
the prevailing idiocy allows companies to report huge returns on
shareholder's equity or 'invested capital', when in reality only
microscopic proportions of that return are made available to the
shareholder.

Britain's giant ICI textile group, for example, had a 16·2 per cent
return on invested capital of £1 567 million in 1974–5. But the total
payment to shareholders came to £54·1 million, or 3·5 per cent on
the capital. The company's loans of £763·4 million – half as much –
required £64·1 million of servicing, or 8·4 per cent. A United States
company like ITT, for another instance, reported an 11·2 per cent
return on stockholders' equity in 1974. But the total payment on
that capital ($4 134 million) was $206 million, or 5 per cent. With
$3611 million of debt, the interest and other financial charges paid
came to $368 million. Thus although the shareholders take great
risks, and the fixed-interest lenders virtually none, the former
receive the *lower*, not the higher yield.

If the alleged identity of interest between directors, managers and
investors truly existed, such questions would at least be confronted
by the corporations of the West. But directors and managers, who
are effectively the same people, have no interest in losing the supply
of uncharged capital which the shareholders provide, whether they
like it or not.

Suppose that a company has £10 million available after tax and interest. If it pays out £5 million in dividends and keeps the rest, that provides, when money earns 10 per cent, £500,000 in pre-tax profits without any directorial effort whatsoever. If all the £10 million were paid out to the shareholders, and the £5 million then had to be replaced from another source at 10 per cent plus – there would be a £500,000-plus charge *against* profits. The preference of the corporate establishment for ploughing back is thus totally explicable.

In the above case the unenlightened investor might prefer his company to be half a million up rather than down. But the half a million, of course, comes out of his own pocket; and there is no guarantee, because of the fragile link between the market and the company results, that the investor will receive any reward, here or in heaven, for putting the profits above his pocket.

What is true at the level of higher financial strategy applies as strongly at the lower level of managerial money. The shareholder–manager conflict emerges clearly if a grossly over-generous stock-option scheme is put up for approval. So most schemes are not gross, because boards of directors wish to avoid opposition from stock-holders: most of the latter, again, fail to realize that profits from the most decent of option schemes must also come out of their own heavily raided pockets.

The profitable option, at the moment of issue, is worth more than the option-holder paid, which is another way of saying that it is worth more than the shareholder is receiving at the time of selling part of his equity interest. This unequal deal is based on the convenient theory that managers and investors have an equal interest in seeing the share price rise.

On the upside, the theory works – although inadequately, since there is no good reason why the manager should benefit more, and with far less risk, than the investor, as he does under an option scheme. But on the downside the theory collapses: the manager under the most popular schemes simply loses potential profit, while the investor loses real capital. The option merely enshrines the conventional nonsense of the go-go years, which was to persuade (very easily) managers to pay attention to the short-term behaviour of the stock-market rather than to the long-term interests of the investor.

For all the concrete abuse he suffered – from neglect, appropriation of his savings and castration of his powers – the shareholder became steadily more unpopular as the sixties turned into the seventies. In Labour-governed Britain in particular he was portrayed as the modern equivalent of Solomon's lilies of the field, which toiled not, neither did they spin. None of the critics could explain, nor did they even bother to inquire, why a man, woman or institution putting unsecured funds into the equity of a company was in any way less worthy than the bank which extended the same firm a secured loan that could be called in at short notice. Putting money into industry was respectable, in other words, so long as it involved only indirect ownership of the assets, as opposed to a direct property right in some of those assets.

The maltreatment of dividend income on both sides of the Atlantic might have been planned by some malevolent Marxist. In Britain from 1963 to 1974 dividends dropped from 4 per cent of all personal income to 2 per cent. Over the decade to 1973 dividends fell by a fifth in real terms, while every other kind of income went up. On Wall Street the ratio of dividends to earnings of the Dow stocks fell from over 70 per cent in 1961 to 38 per cent – its lowest level ever – in 1974. In other words, where 70 cents of the profit dollar had gone to stockholders, only 38 cents reached them thirteen years later.

Yet it was deemed right and proper for dividend payments to be frozen (a tactic adopted by Richard M. Nixon in one of his highly variegated phases of economic policy) at a time when interest payments on loans by the same companies, possibly made to the same recipients as were being denied higher dividends, were being allowed to achieve the highest levels on postwar record. Plainly, ownership is the essence of the attacker's position. The odium once directed at a Henry Ford, who personally reigned over the life and work of hundreds of thousands of men and women, has been transferred to innocents whose only sin is to purchase the titles to ownership by which the industrial dynasties of the past were broken down and converted into the manager-managed corporations of the present.

The ownership is a fiction, in the sense that the individual shareholder's ability to influence the managers is infinitesimal; in any event, he seldom chooses or wishes to try to influence them. To be maltreated by the State for wielding a fictitious power adds insult to injury: it is not compatible with the capitalist system as it is supposed to exist. If companies are to be managed for the benefit of the managers, and if the shareholder is to be pushed further down the queue by the modern upsurge of worker representation, then capitalism on the postwar model is genuinely dead, although in a sense different from that used by the mongers of doom. Unfortunately nothing in sight can replace the corpse – except either the appalling prospect of a State-run and owned economy, or the disciplines that would be imposed by an authentic shareholding democracy. Such a system, imposing high fiduciary and performance standards on the managerial élite, would remove for ever some of the febrile excesses that made the Second Great Crash, for far less economic cause, as traumatic in its impact on savings as the First.

Some of the remedies are obvious – tax reforms that will treat dividend payments on equal terms with interest and end the present discouragement of pay-outs; accountancy reforms that will bar the deceitful game of maximizing reported earnings; legal reforms that will redress the balance of power between manager and investor by removing the defects, such as stock options and the cosy dependence of auditors on management, that currently distort the relationship; regulatory reforms that will make the seller, not the buyer, beware. While obvious, the needed reforms are politically and sometimes technically tough. Nor will they be adopted or effective so long as the fate of the investing classes (even though that means nearly everybody) is treated as immaterial.

As it is, the shareholder, harmless and all but helpless, suffered his biggest battering for forty years. Yet he is still supposed to supply the underpinning for most of the economic system of the West. In the corporate liquidity crisis which accompanied the Crash, the Victorian virtues of fiscal prudence and payment on the nail suddenly expelled tarnished modern ideas of financial cunning and manufactured indebtedness; and today, too, the last remaining large private groups suddenly seem to be oases of stability in a turbulent world. Their investors at least have not seen fortunes blown up like hot air balloons, only to burst into flames.

The brightest ray of light is the possibility that individuals will remember their burns, so that another inflation of stock prices, with the inevitable subsequent deflation, may not recur, for that reason alone. In that event the ownership of industry will pass still more rapidly into the hands of institutions, with serious, possibly alarming consequences for the concentration of economic power. But if the lessons have not been learnt, and the naked investor tries again to reach Utopian financial salvation through the stock-market, the Second Great Crash will not merely be a recrudescence of the First. It will prove to be a trailer for the Third – and the Third might be Last.